THE ECONOMICS OF NATURAL
RESOURCE DEPLETION

The Economics of Natural Resource Depletion

edited by
D. W. PEARCE

*Director of the Public Sector Economic
Research Centre, University of Leicester*

assisted by
J. ROSE

*Director, Institute of Environmental Sciences
and Principal, Blackburn College of Technology
and Design*

A HALSTED PRESS BOOK

JOHN WILEY & SONS
New York

First published in the United Kingdom 1975 by
The Macmillan Press Ltd

Published in the U.S.A. by
Halsted Press, a Division of
John Wiley & Sons, Inc.
New York

Printed in Great Britain

Library of Congress Cataloging in Publication Data

Main entry under title:

The Economics of natural resource depletion.

"A Halsted Press book."
Slightly modified versions of papers given at a
conference held at the Royal Institution, London,
Jan. 16, 1974; organized by the U.K. Environmental
Economics Study Group and the Institute of Environmental
Sciences.
  1. Natural resources—Congresses. I. Pearce, David
William. II. Rose, James, M.Sc. III. U.K. Environ-
mental Economics Study Group. IV. Institute of
Environmental Sciences.
HC55.E36   1975   333.7   75-9752
ISBN 0 470-67510-1

CONTENTS

6 *Contents*

PREFACE AND ACKNOWLEDGEMENTS

With the exception of one essay by Professor Ivor Pearce, the papers in this book are slightly modified versions of ones given at a conference on the economics of natural resource depletion which took place at the Royal Institution, London, on 16 January 1974. The conference was organised jointly by the U.K. Environmental Economics Study Group, an organisation sponsored and financed by the Social Science Research Council, and the Institute of Environmental Sciences, a private research and study organisation. The Environmental Economics Study Group was responsible for the commissioning of the papers that appear in this volume. In addition some of the comments made by conference delegates during discussion time have been included, in edited form, in short sections, following the individual contributions. Two formal 'replies' were also read at the conference and these too are included.

Surprisingly, very few economists in the United Kingdom are actively engaged in the study of natural resource problems. It is to be hoped that this volume will encourage others to investigate this much under-researched area. More important, however, it is to be hoped that the contributions will appeal for their intrinsic value and for the issues they raise. There can be no single 'economic' view of the natural resource problem. The essays in this volume indicate some of the ways in which some economists approach the task.

An immense debt of gratitude is owed to Mrs Jenni Burrow and to Miss Angela Bartoli of the University of Southampton, whose organisational wizardry ensured that the conference took place at all. And to the remaining host of helpers a special word of thanks is due.

D.W.P.

J.R.

1 EDITORIAL INTRODUCTION

While it may seem churlish for an editor to dispute a title of his own choosing, there is no such thing as *the* economic approach to natural resource depletion. Apart from being naturally disputatious, perhaps a characteristic of any professional discipline, economists do disagree about the 'proper' way to look at resource depletion problems. For example, there are widely divergent viewpoints about the optimal rate of depletion, centring on the extent to which the standard neo-classical approach based on the maximisation of some present value of future flows of consumers' surplus adequately allows for future generations' well-being. Similarly, attitudes to the varied estimates of resource availability frequently depend on the same issue, and on (a) the subjective attitude of the economist in question to selecting policy options from a matrix of highly uncertain outcomes, and (b) the extent to which the observer places faith in the workings of a mixed price system to secure some smooth pattern of individual resource substitutability over time. As far as (a) is concerned, for example, an optimistic attitude might be based on extrapolation of past experience of 'muddling through' and on personal beliefs about the future existence of technologies that are not currently feasible. With respect to (b) there are positivist disputes about the actual functioning of the price mechanism, particularly in natural resource markets which exhibit many unusual features, and about the extent to which substitutability between individual resources is really at issue in a context where the total set of resources in a particular category is threatened with shortage.

On these grounds alone there is room for substantial divergence of opinion. In addition, however, it is worth remembering that there can be no such thing as a *rational* policy prescription based on looking at the *resource* side of the issue alone. For the essence of the 'materials balance' view of the economic process[1] is that resources taken from the environment must eventually reappear as residuals of equal weight – though of transformed nature – to be discharged back into the environment. While residuals disposal is not synonymous with pollution the two are clearly functionally related, albeit in a complex fashion. Hence the application of some intertemporal welfare-maximisation model to a resource-depletion problem must automatically be suspect if the consequent residuals-disposal problem is not integrated in the specification of the model.

It seems legitimate to bear these cautions in mind when taking an over-all view of the contributions to this volume. By and large the general impact of the papers is one of 'optimism' if by that is meant that the authors tend to select from the uncertainty matrix policy options which imply that there is no crisis in resource use, let alone the prospect of an apocalyptic demise of the entire social system through resource exhaustion. Indeed, four of the main papers that deal with exhaustible resources – by Robinson, Surrey and Page, Heal, and Kay and Mirrlees – are critical, sometimes severely so, of the major work that to date has tended to draw ominous conclusions from resource depletion, namely, *The Limits to Growth*.[2] How far these critiques succed is for the reader to judge.

But whether or not the reader is in agreement with the standpoints taken in these essays, they have to be taken seriously as having a rigour of their own. Many of the criticisms they make of the 'conservationist' or 'environmentalist' case are telling, and they must serve to sharpen the debate between economists and non-economists on such issues as the desirability of economic growth, the proper conceptual approach to resource depletion, to pollution, and so on. Indeed, it is to be hoped that they will remove from the debate the almost tragic element of schoolboy debating that has characterised some of the argument to date. Examples of economists' gross ignorance of environmental science and ecology are not difficult to find, nor, for that matter, are examples of environmentalists' ignorance of even the basic elements of the 'standard' economic approach. But this is quite different to saying that all sensible people must agree with some of the conclusions reached in the essays in this volume. What matters is constructive communication between economist and non-economist.

1. Energy resources

Professor Robinson fulfils a number of objectives in his wide-ranging paper on energy resources.

First, Robinson is highly critical of what he regards as an essential feature of the 'materials balance' approach to environment problems: the fixity of the natural resource base. He very correctly points out that resource availability is a 'dynamic' concept, since the state of technology determines what is, and what is not, to count as a resource at any point in time. Messrs Surrey and Page stress the same point when they say that '. . . it remains generally true that no systematic effort has been made to find every deposit which might be economically recoverable in the unknown and probably different economic, technical and political circumstances of the distant future. The technological changes that may occur so as to extend the current concept of measured resource availability are changes in what we might call 'discovery technology' (making hydrogen produced from the electrolysis of water a resource, which at the moment it is not, for example); 'exploration technology' (making it possible, say, to mine the mantle of the earth, and ocean beds); 'recovery technology' (reducing the waste in energy terms as a resource is taken from the environment and transformed into usable energy or usable materials); and 'use technology' (a change in the type of nuclear reactor, say). Given changes in these factors, it becomes virtually impossible to estimate the *physical* limits to energy resources. By clear deduction, then, arguments such as that of *The Limits to Growth*, which are based on the concept of known or estimated physical limits, must be incorrect.

Such an argument has force; but some qualifications are in order. It is not, strictly, any part of the 'materials balance' view of the economic–environment process to assume fixity of the resource base. Even if it were, the assumption of fixity for the purposes of materials-balance models is a sound one since only solar energy and other 'natural' sources (wind and water) are in any meaningful sense limitless. The essence of the materials-balance view is the resource use–pollution linkage. While Robinson stresses the pollution problems it isn't always clear from his paper that the two problems – resource use and pollution generation – are definitionally connected. Furthermore, as Common points out in his reply, technological change is not an exogenous free good. On the resource side it is not at all difficult to show that the energy costs of securing further increments in non-renewable resources will increase. Reliance on technological change to extend the horizons for high-consumption resource use frequently suffers the same defect – the non-acknowledgement of the residuals-disposal problem that must be associated with such change. Professor Robinson is to be applauded for stressing this point, but it should be added that the residuals-disposal problem could be so serious as to set an effective limit to the adoption of new technology. Perhaps the most recent alarming warning in this respect has been sounded in the United States against reliance on nuclear energy because of the incalculable effects of minute releases of plutonium. It has been argued that a single plutonium particle – one micron in diameter – can induce lung cancer. Neither known or foreseeable nuclear technologies can prevent emissions of this minute size, and the half-life of plutonium 239, for example, is some 24,000 years. The hazards for this generation would seem to warrant cautious procedure – the hazards for many generations could be of horrific proportions.

In short, it is right to remind those who glibly quote reserve figures that technology, and relative price levels, determine what is and what is not, available. None the less, the 'technological gradient' argument can only be used to imply optimism if (*a*) the technological change is genuinely foreseeable, and (*b*) is not itself subject to an increasing pollution hazard gradient. Decision-making can only take place within the realms of the foreseeable: there is something more than Panglossian about arguments which appear reassuring – and hence imply something satisfactory about current usage rates – on the basis of technologies that are not known, or if dimly perceived, are not tested. Another valuable feature of Professor Robinson's essay is his careful delineation of the technological future in this respect.

Messrs Surrey and Page lend support to some of Professor Robinson's views on energy resources. They are more direct in their attack on *The Limits to Growth* (*a*) for being in error on fact and approach; (*b*) for diverting attention away from the 'real' issues; and (*c*) for implying policies which, if applied to underdeveloped economies, would leave them with their vast populations of underfed and starving. These reminders are salutary, although if *The Limits to Growth* were correct in arguing that physical limits set a limit to growth on a global scale, failure to acknowledge which results in global collapse, then it would have been decidedly odd for its authors to have argued that, despite this, growth should continue for the benefit of less-developed economies. In other words, *who* benefits from growth is not the issue if global collapse is a reality. The real issue must be whether collapse is likely or not, and if not, as some of the contributors to this volume clearly believe, then how those resources that are available are to be distributed geographically *now*, and, as Common points out repeatedly, how they are to be distributed over time. One can remain quite neutral on the growth issue and ask the question whether growth, as the world has experienced it to date, has benefited the poor *relative* to the rich.

The same issue of uncertainty also arises in Surrey and Page's paper. They are of the view that 'there is simply no way of accurately assessing world reserves of so-called "non-renewable" resources, nor of anticipating what materials will constitute usable resources in the distant future'. But again, if this is so, it is right to ask how decision-makers should behave under uncertainty. If we do not know the future, we do not know the future. Asserting that the future is uncertain hardly provides support for an optimistic view of high-level resource use, for the pay-off could be that there are no resources in the future. On the other hand, a lower use rate now can lead to a re-appraisal as new information on resources becomes available.

Surrey and Page conclude with a very sound demand that research into critical materials be encouraged on a far greater scale than is currently the case. The record in the United States is impressive in this respect, major studies having been implemented and produced within the last few years.[3] The record in the United Kingdom is poor by comparison.

Some delegates' reactions are recorded as Chapter 5.

2. Renewable resources

The emphasis of *The Limits to Growth* was on what the authors believed to be the physical limits to continuing increases in global G.N.P. But the tendency when thinking in these terms is to concentrate on non-renewable resources. Renewable resources such as timber and fish are, however, equally important if time lags in the reproduction system prevent supply meeting demand, or if the renewable resource is over-exploited. Butlin's paper concentrates on the latter issue by taking a comprehensive and critical look at recent contributions to fisheries economics. As is now standard theory, over-fishing is identified with the exploitation of a common property resource such that the externalities associated with reaping the resource harvest are not internalised. Current resource yields are then too high for sustainable reproduction to preserve future supplies.

The obvious complexity of renewable resource economics arises from the necessity of integrating biological inputs into any economic model which attempts a solution of the optimal rate of exploitation. Butlin divides his discussion into four main sections: (*a*) an analysis of dynamic models designed to incorporate biological growth functions; (*b*) an analysis of the types of externality that exploiting common property fisheries involves; (*c*) an outline of the limited amount of work that has been carried out into uncertainty in the fishing industry; and (*d*) a discussion of the implications of certain political constraints on policies designed to control the catch rate. He ends with an overview and assessment of the recent developments.

Butlin holds in high regard the work of those capital theorists who have turned their attention to fisheries problems, particularly where this work has analysed disequilibrium situations and biological interactions between species. Particularly interesting is the conclusion that continuous fishing at pre-set levels is unlikely to characterise an optimal fishing policy, but that 'periodic' exploitation with rest periods is likely to achieve higher yields.

Butlin concludes with an appraisal of the implications of recent work for fisheries management policies, and with a list of 'problem areas' that economists could more than usefully study in greater depth. He suggests that the application of spatial equilibrium models familiar in regional analysis could be usefully applied to the serious and immediate issue of coastal appropriation of fisheries, and he indicates some likely outcomes on the basis of some first-approach thoughts. He draws attention to the difficulties of actually measuring inputs in the fishery, to the need to experiment with less general forms of stock–growth functions when looking at dynamic aspects of the fishery, and to the need for more work on the management of fisheries which contain multiple species with all the consequent problems of special interaction, joint product catches, and so on.

Lastly, Butlin asks a pertinent question when he queries exactly what the opportunity cost of fisheries inputs are in a context where search is a precondition of catching anything. These are important issues that clearly require extensive further research at a time when over-fishing threatens many of the world's fisheries.

3. Optimal depletion rates

The papers by Heal, and Kay and Mirrlees provoked the greatest amount of discussion at the conference. In part the discussion was a reaction, sometimes angry, to the concluding suggestion by Kay and Mirrlees that current depletion rates may well be too low. That such a suggestion should have provoked some alarm is perhaps a good reflection of the extent to which the conservationist ethic has already pervaded the thinking of many professional people.

Kay and Mirrlees were in fact initially invited to report to the conference on their work, sponsored by the Social Science Research Council, on 'global modelling'. They declined to speak on that subject alone, and the reasons for this are readily seen when one considers the first part of their paper, which is a virulent attack on the work of Forrester and of the Meadows team. Essentially, Kay and Mirrlees take the resource sector of *World III* – the slightly modified model of *The Limits to Growth* – and show that it can be specified as a fairly familiar Harrod growth model, albeit with errors that even those simple growth models did not have. They then show that the 'doomsday' conclusion of *The Limits to Growth* can be obtained by elementary mathematical manipulation of that model: the initially impressive edifice of the computer is not required. In criticising the actual specification of the model, Kay and Mirrlees argue that almost any result can be secured from such simplistic approaches. The serious question they raise is whether models of this kind ever can say anything meaningful about distant events. They argue that '. . . in the case of exhaustible resources . . . forecasting models whose time horizon extends beyond a decade or so are worthless'.

Again, however, it is necessary to ask how plans should be formulated in the face of uncertainty about the future. Some of Kay and Mirrlees's optimism is based on assumptions about the size of reserves of various resources, assumptions which may well be false. The issue then reduces once more to one of deciding how to decide in the face of resource limits, bearing in mind the crucial fact that, whereas reproducible capital *is* reproducible, exhaustible resources, once used, are recoverable only to the extent that recycling is feasible.

The middle section of the Kay–Mirrlees paper provides some indication of what the authors regard as a useful approach to resource problems: the identification of the 'destination' of specified resources in terms of final product. The prospects for the application of refined input–output analysis to these problems is clearly immense, and the policy implications are also interesting since piecemeal policies designed to improve substitution possibilities, recycling, etc., become more import-ant than wholesale and indiscriminate 'zero-growth' arguments. Further, the approach can assist in the identification of critical areas where resource shortages will have the greatest effects.

The last part of the Kay–Mirrlees paper provides a general summary of arguments for and against the supposition that resources are being depleted too rapidly. This too is the subject of Heal's paper, although Heal addresses himself to the specific issue of the effect of market imperfections on resource depletion. In both papers the 'norm' is taken to be the rate of depletion that would occur in a perfectly competitive world. This rate is then taken to be Pareto-optimal in line with the standard theorems of welfare economics. We have again to remember that there is nothing sacred about the Paretian approach, but it seems as well to evaluate the Heal and Kay–Mirrlees contri-butions on this standard.

The economic optimisation problem is usually stated in the form[4]

$$\max V = \int_0^T (P_t - C_t) e^{-rt}$$

where P is the price of the finished product (say a metal), C is the cost of processing and extracting the resource, r is the rate of interest (strictly, the marginal rate of time preference) and T is the finite time horizon. V is then the present value of the flow $P - C$, which is the price of the resource *in situ* (the 'profit', 'rent', 'net rent' or 'royalty' – terminology is, regret-tably, non-standard in the literature). If V is maximised, we obtain the requirement

$$(P_{t_j} - C_{t_j}) e^{-rt_j} = (P_{t_i} - C_{t_i}) e^{-rt_i}$$

i.e. that the present value of the royalty must be equal in each period $(t = i, t = j)$. If this equality does not hold it will pay the resource owner to shift resource production between periods. We also observe that

$$(P_t - C_t)\mathrm{e}^{-rt} = P_0 - C_0$$

so that, if we let $C_t = C_0$ for convenience, we obtain:

$$R_t = P_t - C_t = R_0 . \mathrm{e}^{rt}$$

The royalty must rise at the rate r, the rate of interest.

Perfectly competitive conditions, it is supposed, will secure this condition and will have the incidental effect of maximising consumer utility. The approach adopted by Heal and Kay and Mirrlees is then to ask what kinds of market imperfections exist, and what these imperfections imply for the actual rate of depletion compared to the optimal rate. In both papers the comparisons between actual and optimal rates are qualitative so that an over-all conclusion as to whether depletion is 'too slow' or 'too fast' is inevitably a matter of mixing guess-work with some empirical estimate of the scale of the imperfections.

The essential reason advanced in both papers for supposing that depletion rates are too low is the existence of monopoly. Certainly, resource owners have become increasingly monopolistic over time, the most notable example now being the oil cartel OPEC, but, with cartels and oligopolies being formed in rock phosphate, bauxite and copper, the trend is a general one. Since monopolists are thought to restrict output by comparison with the perfectly competitive model outlined above, it follows that observed rates of exploitation are less than Pareto-optimal on this ground. Heal provides an interesting analysis of the actual phasing-in of monopoly power in the oil market, showing that the change in the real price of oil at the end of the 1960s reflected an awareness by oil producers of their newly-found powers. In addition, Middle-East producers no longer required the foreign exchange, or rather no longer desired it, in such large quantity because of its low real value in the face of inflation. Interesting, too, is Heal's suggestion that publications such as *The Limits to Growth* may have contributed directly to this awareness of monopoly power.

Heal concentrates most of his attention on the absence of forward and insurance markets in natural resources. In essence, the view that perfectly competitive markets will optimise the rate of resource usage over some selected time horizon requires that there must be perfectly functioning futures markets for resources, and that eventualities such as the failure of predicted technologies (future nuclear technologies might well fit this category) can be insured against. Heal first shows that because of the absence of forward markets future prices are expected prices and failure to predict correctly can bring about cyclical movements in prices, a possible direct explanation of fluctuations which are common in resource markets. The extent of accurate prediction is difficult to gauge. Kay and Mirrlees suggest that where current consumption is but a small proportion of the total resource stock, prediction is likely to be fairly accurate and they further suggest that these cases are more common than is generally supposed. In general, however, it would appear that the absence of futures markets will imply inefficiency in resource depletion (although Heal entertains the possibility that efficiency will result 'by chance'), but that it is difficult to say which sign to attach to this deviation from the optimum.

Uninsurability presents further problems. Heal carefully analyses the circumstances under which risk-aversion will cause deviations from the optimum rate. In general, risk-aversion will imply over-fast depletion rates, but the solution could be efficient if (a) there is some mix of risk-neutral and risk-averting individuals, and (b) the distribution of utilities through time is such as to produce corner solutions. Kay and Mirrlees also point to the fact that an individual resource exploiter will over-exploit a resource because the risks are, in fact, 'pooled' across many consumers whose individual attitudes to their own negligible risks will, collectively, amount to lower rates of depletion than that countenanced by the individual exploiter. On balance then, it would appear that risk aversion will lead to over-rapid rates of depletion.

Perhaps the most notable form of risk in the current political scene is the risk of expropriation by the country in which the resource is located. This has been a pattern in the Middle East and in some South American countries. If such take-overs are feared, and it would be extremely unrealistic to suppose that they do not figure largely in the decision-making of resource exploiters, then there must be an added tendency to over-rapid depletion.

The issue of future generations is discussed briefly by Kay and Mirrlees. They correctly point out that low depletion rates now leave larger natural resource stocks for the future, but also lower capital stock. The issue is complicated by the fact that natural resources can be directly consumed and used for the production of capital goods. The conference audience did not share the Kay–Mirrlees view that, on balance, future generations were well taken care of by the price mechanism. No doubt this reflects justifiable scepticism about whether the price mechanism really works this well, and also reflects differing judgements about the rate of interest which, as Kay and Mirrlees themselves point out, could be too high (and hence the rate of exploitation will be too fast, as inspection of the previous equations shows) because of Pigovian myopia. But, as Kay and Mirrlees argue, lowering the interest rate means lowering it for *all* investment: if interest rates are too high for the benefit of future generations' resource stocks (we consume now in preference to the future), they are also too high for all investment. Lowering them implies raising the growth rate. The problem here is that in order to lower interest rates to slow resource depletion the conservationist will need to introduce an asymmetry in the rate structure, a low rate to secure conservation, and a higher rate for capital investment. This, on the face of it, would distort the mechanism for optimally allocating money capital between holding resources and producing real capital. But it is none the less a possiblity that has been entertained seriously in the literature, and would repay closer study.[5]

In the paper by Pearce, the simple model which forms the basis of most writing on optimal depletion rates is used to demonstrate that the free market will not, in fact, distribute the consumption of natural resources optimally through time. Pearce argues that the existence of an interest rate leads to a consumption pattern which is independent of consumption and producing externalities, such that the market will generate *too rapid* a rate of consumption. In short, social and private rates of discount must diverge. Kay and Mirrlees observe this divergence as a limitation on the applicability of their own model. Pearce is more assertive in arguing that the divergence in rates is both intrinsic to the economic system and that it will lead to over-rapid depletion rates. In the process of this argument, Pearce ridicules more than the aspect of the use of discount rates, including the notion that the diminishing marginal utility of consumption combined with assumed exponential growth rates in real income 'justifies' positive discount rates. Instead, Pearce is prepared to accommodate the conservationist's ideal case for near-negligible resource usage on the basis (*a*) that the application of discounting analysis, as in Heal and Kay and Mirrlees, is more than misleading, and (*b*) a principle of intergenerational justice to the effect that we 'owe it to future generations not to take out what we cannot put back'. If such a view seems heretical to orthodox economists, one can only ask that Pearce's paper be read carefully.

Are resources being used too fast, too slowly, or at exactly the right rate? To venture a personal opinion, I doubt if Kay and Mirrlees are right when they conclude that 'in the currently topical case of oil, the arguments that the world is using too little rather than too much seem irresistible'.

In part my doubts rest on the validity of the assumptions underlying the optimisation model used – doubts which are well documented in Simmons's formal comment, and in Pearce's paper. More than this, however, they rest on the fact that the formal connection between resource use and residuals disposal is absent in the optimisation model. The social costs of residuals disposal might be taken as further reason to suppose that market resource prices are too low, although in the context of the Kay–Mirrlees model, social costs, being 'pervasive' to the economic system, presumably have little impact on the relative price of natural resources. But there is a category of social cost ignored in most discussions – the costs of increasing the risk of non-survival through altering ecosystem stability. It is significant that the precise mechanics of 'collapse' in *Limits to Growth* are not at all clear, even if one took world modelling seriously, whereas some ecologists have for some time expounded models of potential collapse based simply on the dynamics of pollution and its effect on ecosystem stability. These effects are, of course, uncertain. But all this means is that we have, once again, to consider what the optimal strategy is in the face of such uncertainty.

2 THE DEPLETION OF ENERGY RESOURCES*

COLIN ROBINSON

1. Introduction

For a year or more there has been open discussion of a 'world energy crisis' and, though not everyone would accept the term 'crisis' and we all have our own ideas on which are the most critical elements, it is obvious that the world faces some awkward energy problems. One of these was forced on our attention in the Autumn of 1973 when some of the Middle-East oil producers reduced their output below planned levels, causing world-wide oil shortages. Such a period is never the best time to examine long-term supply prospects because attention tends to become so concentrated on the pressing issues that an objective view of the longer term is hard to formulate. One of the commonest failings of long-term forecasters, in the energy field as elsewhere, is to give excessive weight to the immediate past. When the newspapers and television are packed with instant comment on Arab supply restrictions it is only too easy to project into the long-term future the experiences of the last few weeks.

This paper will attempt to stand back from existing shortages to examine in particular that aspect of world energy which is in the title – resource depletion. However, the various facets of the 'world energy problem' are interrelated and one cannot discuss global energy supplies entirely in isolation from the two other principal issues – pollution from energy, and the power of the

* This paper draws on a study carried out at the University of Surrey by Miss E. M. Crook and the author, some of the results of which are summarised in C. Robinson and E. M. Crook, 'Is There a World Energy Crisis?', *National Westminster Bank Review* (May 1973).

oil-producing countries to raise prices and curtail supplies. To begin with, we review very briefly the history of fears about energy shortage, then consider world energy supply, concluding with some shorter comments on other energy problems.

2. History and background

Concern about the rate of depletion of energy resources is by no means new. There were fears of an energy shortage in Britain after the last war which were revived in the mid-1950s (for example, in the O.E.E.C. Hartley Report[1]) and a close study of economic and social history would probably reveal many earlier examples of similar fears. This is not the occasion for an historical survey but it is worth mentioning in passing one previous example which bears a certain similarity to that recently published catalogue of fears about resource exhaustion, *The Limits of Growth*.[2] William Jevons's *The Coal Question*,[3] written in 1865, harks back to some of the pessimism of Ricardo and Malthus in pointing to the dangers of rising coal consumption in Britain as economic growth proceeds. Jevons was concerned about exponential growth and physical constraints on that growth; he argued that there is a 'natural law of social growth' which is geometric and to which 'exterior nature presents a certain absolute and inexorable limit'. The similarity to *The Limits to Growth* is, however, only superficial because Jevons was no believer in physical exhaustion. He anticipated a rise in the price of British coal, as mines had to be sunk deeper, which would destroy Britain's competitive advantage in world markets for manufactured goods – not that one day there would be no coal. Indeed, Jevons dismisses the 'erroneous notions' of those who believe 'that some day our coal seams will be found emptied to the bottom and swept clean like a coal cellar'.

Though one can look back and see earlier predictions of energy famine, there are some striking differences between the views now being expressed and those we can find in the past. An obvious change is that we are now in a period in which a relatively small group of oil-producing countries has control of most of world oil exports and is prepared to use that control for both economic and political ends. This is a far more powerful cartel than has previously existed in oil, if only because it is composed of governments, not of private companies whose behaviour is at least subject to national government anti-trust regulations.

The second difference, which is probably of greater long-term significance, is that present concern about fuel shortages is only one aspect of the much more general anxieties which have emerged since the mid-1960s about man's impact on the natural environment. In particular, many people have fears that continued economic growth will so increase both inputs of materials from the environment and outputs of waste to the environments as to lead to global disaster. These twin concerns about depletion and pollution are most neatly summarised by a simple materials balance diagram[4] (Figure 2.1) which shows that the processes economists usually describe as 'production' and 'consumption' are more accurately described as transformation, since what goes into the world 'productive' system comes from the environment and the waste products of the

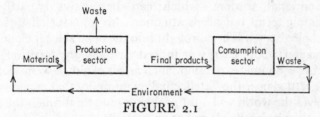

FIGURE 2.1

producing and consuming sectors flow back to the environment. Frequently, people jump to the conclusion that this view of the system implies that economic growth is bad since, other things being equal, the faster is growth the more rapidly are materials depleted and the greater is the output of wastes. Of course, this does not *necessarily* follow because it may be possible to reduce both material input per unit of output and waste discharges to the atmosphere per unit of output: for example, recycling has both of these effects. However, those who have pointed to the interrelationships between the natural environment and man's economic activities have performed a service by bringing to the attention of economists something about which we have been rather forgetful: the natural environment cannot forever be treated as a free good or it will suffer the usual fate of over-utilisation.

Thus energy is only one aspect of the problem of possible conflicts between environmental preservation and the production of more goods and services. Nevertheless, it is a particularly vital aspect since ample supplies of non-polluting energy would seem to be a pre-condition for many of the measures which would help us to control other forms of environmental degradation. As befits such an important issue, the debate about energy has assumed an intensity once reserved for theological disputations, and a sharp cleavage of opinion has appeared between the growth men and the no-growth men, the latter including both those who object to growth for environmental reasons and those who do not like the kind of materialistic society they feel is bred by the pursuit of physical possessions. One manifestation of this division is the extreme swing there has been in middle-class opinion in the industrialised world from a belief in the virtues of economic growth to the apocalyptic views now heard so frequently.[5] Though this is not the occasion to pursue the reasons for this remarkable shift in the conventional wisdom – which can be analysed partly in economic terms but needs attention also from sociologists and psychologists – it is best brought into the open since it clouds all discussions about energy or indeed virtually any question concerning economic expansion. Such an air of gloom seems now to have settled over the 'intellectual' community that anyone who believes the world will most probably muddle through the next fifty years is usually classed as an optimist.

3. Depletion of energy resources

We come now to the question of energy depletion, under which heading we shall deal separately with supply and demand variables. It is worth a reminder at the beginning that this is a *forecasting* problem; that is, it concerns an uncertain future about which we can make only probabilistic statements. It is not a matter on which one can make definite pronouncements, whether they be that catastrophe is imminent or that catastrophe is impossible because someone will always come up with the appropriate 'technological fix'.[6] We need to give some thought to what those technological fixes might be and to the chances that they will come to pass.

(i) *World energy supplies*
The world has both a stock of resources of 'energy' (fossil fuels, uranium, etc.) and an income of energy (principally

from the sun). This paper deals mainly with the energy stock, but in section (5) below there is a brief discussion of energy income which may well turn out to be man's major source in the long term.

The assessment of future energy supplies is difficult. The economist, who would like a schedule indicating the supplies which would be forthcoming at various energy price levels, finds himself confronted by a mass of geological evidence about the energy stock, which is not usually based on specified assumptions about future costs, prices and recovery technology. The case of energy is a good illustration of one of the dangers of the more simplified versions of the materials balance approach, which on the face of it assumes a fixed stock of materials which can be supplied by the environment. There may be a sense in which there is an upper limit on the very long-run supply capacity of the environment, but it is doubtful whether the idea of a fixed and known stock of energy resources has much meaning. There are two reasons for this.

The first is that the size of the world's resources of energy is a function of the state of technology of converting matter into useful energy. We cannot carry out a geological survey of the earth which will tell us all the resources which we and future generations will call 'energy'. If one looks back over human history, it becomes obvious that the constitution of the earth's energy stock, as perceived by man, has been continually changing. In primitive times energy resources were the food which man could eat and thus convert into muscular energy. However, primitive man was saved from an energy shortage by technological and managerial progress which brought the invention of fire (that is, the world's trees became sources of energy though they had not been so regarded before) and the organisation of animals to provide their muscular energy for man. More technological progress brought the use of wind and water power and the utilisation of coal for raising steam. In the very recent past (relative to the time-span we have been considering) we have gained access to oil and electricity produced from nuclear fission. It has been estimated that in the course of this development, *per capita* consumption of energy has risen from about 2000 kilo calories per day in very primitive times to around 230,000 kilo calories per day in the United States today.[7]

History therefore indicates that man's development has been closely associated with the substitution of one form of energy for another, and it also reveals that at virtually any time there could have been fears of a future energy shortage merely because of the difficulty of seeing what the next energy form would be. In other words, the world's stock of energy must be seen as a dynamic not a static concept – what is not useful energy today may be useful energy tomorrow. Consequently, it is misleading to use models which assume that we are living off a fixed capital stock the size of which we know. This is not to say that we can sit back and assume that new energy forms will always appear when they are needed, but it does mean that we need to think where we stand in the long time-scale of the development of energy resources. So far man has been saved from exhausting the world's resources by the use of his ingenuity: perhaps a more basic question than whether we shall run out of 'energy' resources is whether we shall run out of ingenuity.

Second, even if one considers only the stock of resources at present believed to constitute 'energy' – essentially, coal, oil, natural gas and uranium, supplemented by relatively small amounts of hydro-electricity (see Table 2.1) – the meaning of 'world energy resources' is by no means so straightforward as might be imagined. In the past man's ability to find and recover what he believed to be energy has been constantly improving so that both the total quantity of resources known to be in place and the proportion recoverable have been rising. To measure the world's resources of presently-usable energy forms one needs to know, in addition to what is in place:

(*a*) The proportion of resources which is *accessible*. For example, until very recently it would not have been possible to extract oil and natural gas from under the North Sea and other difficult offshore areas because the technology was not developed. About one-fifth of world oil output now comes from offshore areas and it has been estimated that this proportion will rise to 30–40 per cent by 1980.[8]

(*b*) The *recovery rate* for accessible reserves. The best illustration here is again oil for which the recovery rate averages only about 30 per cent of oil in place over the world as a whole. The recovery rate is clearly a function of recovery technology, which will determine costs, and of energy prices.

(*c*) The extent to which it will become possible to exploit various '*unconventional*' *sources* of fossil fuels, which, though accessible, has been unprofitable to utilise in the past because the costs of exploitation were high relative to the prevailing level of energy prices. The best known examples here are the deposits of shale (such as the Green River Formation in Colorado) and the tar sands (for example, the Athabasca tar sands in Alberta and the Orinoco tar sands in Venezuela) in various parts of the world, which contain large amounts of oil but which have not been tapped except on a very small scale.

TABLE 2.1   World Energy Consumption

	Million metric tons coal equivalent *1925*	*% of total*	*Million metric tons coal equivalent* *1970*	*% of total*
Coal	1230	83	2419	36
Oil	197	13	2850	42
Natural Gas	48	3	1418	21
Hydro and Nuclear	10	1	157	2
Total	1485	100	6844	100

Sources: J. Darmstadter, *Energy in the World Economy* (Resources for the Future Inc. 1971), table 4. *U.N. Statistical Yearbook* (1971), table 12.

In summary, the critical variables in estimating world energy reserves at any point of time are the deposits in place, the technology and the costs of exploitation, and the level of energy prices. Unfortunately, the available estimates of world energy resources generally give insufficient information about these critical variables, so we have to do the best we can with some highly imperfect information. We turn now to a summary of the available information about resources, after which we return to the effects of changing technology, costs and prices.

(1) *Coal reserves*. More is known about world coal reserves in place than about reserves of other fossil fuels. Most of the potential coal-bearing regions of the world are believed to have been surveyed (though estimates for different regions are

frequently not consistent with one another) and surveys are made easier because coal occurs nearer the surface than do oil and natural gas, so that geologists are able to make reasonable estimates of reserves in place by drilling a relatively small number of holes.

One source of information is the World Power Conference Survey of Energy Resources published every six years, the last issue being for 1968.[9] It lists both measured and 'indicated and inferred' coal reserves by countries and gives the proportion of measured reserves which is economically recoverable. Unfortunately, the value of the Survey is reduced both by the absence of estimates for a number of countries and by the ambiguity of the term 'economically recoverable': in making returns, countries were simply asked to state the proportion of reserves considered to be of economic value, and this is obviously open to a variety of interpretations. The total of measured and inferred reserves of coal, brown coal and lignite given by the 1968 Survey is just under 9×10^{12} metric tons (ignoring countries which gave no reserve estimates), the most part of which is contained in three countries – the Soviet Union, the United States and mainland China (for which the latest estimate of coal reserves relates to 1913). The world total for economically recoverable reserves cannot be given because several countries with large reserves did not record the economically recoverable proportion of their coal.

Another estimate of world coal reserves has been given by Paul Averitt of the U.S. Geological Survey,[10] based partly on the World Power Conference figures, but including some additional inferred reserves, and relating to 'original coal reserves' which are the reserves estimated to have been in the ground before mining began. Averitt gives a figure equivalent to $15 \cdot 2 \times 10^{12}$ metric tons. This estimate has been used by Hubbert[11] to calculate future world coal production, taking account of past output and assuming that 50 per cent of Averitt's figure (that is, $7 \cdot 6 \times 10^{12}$ metric tons) represents minable coal.[12] On this basis Hubbert calculates that world coal output could rise to around eight times its present level by the middle of the twenty-second century before beginning to decline. He also shows that a lower world reserve estimate of $4 \cdot 3 \times 10^{12}$ metric tons (roughly the minable coal established by mapping and exploration) would support a world coal output rising to about six times more than the present level before decline begins around the year 2100. On these figures, coal appears to be a relatively plentiful natural resource, in terms of the number of years reserves are expected to last, compared with the reserves quoted for most other raw materials.

(2) *Oil and natural gas reserves.* Estimates of oil and gas reserves are considerably more difficult to make than the corresponding estimates for coal. Figures are readily available for 'proved reserves' but these are of limited value. Proved reserves are the proportion of reserves already located by the drill which can be recovered profitably at prevailing cost and price levels; thus they are no more than an assessment of the working inventory of crude oil the oil industry is confident it possesses and it is not surprising that proved reserves appear rather meagre. It would be quite uneconomic for oil companies to spend scarce funds on drilling holes for oil or gas which will not be brought into production for two decades or more. For what they are worth, at the end of 1972 world proved reserves of oil were estimated at around 670×10^9 barrels (91×10^9 metric tons),[13] or approximately thirty-five years' supply at the 1972 world annual production rate of about $2 \cdot 6 \times 10^9$ tons. World proved natural gas reserves were 1883×10^{12} cubic feet,[14] or over forty years' supply at the 1972 world rate of production of about 46×10^{12} cubic feet. Table 2.2 shows that in the past there has been a very big increase in proved oil reserves, which are now almost four times as high as in the mid-1950s: the reserves/production ratio has remained approximately constant over this period.

TABLE 2.2   Estimates of World Proved Reserves of Oil

End year	Million metric tons	Years' supply*
1947	9478	22
1950	11,810	22
1955	25,969	33
1960	40,788	37
1965	47,687	30
1971	85,442	34
1972	91,376	35

* Proved reserves estimate for a year divided by production in that year.

Source: *Institute of Petroleum Information Service.*

There is less information about proved natural-gas reserves than about proved oil reserves and the available estimates from various sources show quite substantial differences, but it is clear that estimates of world proved gas reserves have grown considerably in recent years (Table 2.3). In 1961 proved reserves appear to have been estimated at about 720×10^{12} cubic feet which was approximately forty times annual production in that year[15] and the reserves/production ratio seems to have remained roughly constant since then.

TABLE 2.3   Proved Reserves of Natural Gas

End year	10^{12} cubic feet	Years' supply*
1968	1332	37
1969	1498	38
1970	1588	39
1971	1725	38
1972	1883	41

* See note to Table 2.

Source: *Oil and Gas Journal*, various issues.

Alarm is sometimes expressed because of the apparently 'limited' supply of oil and natural gas indicated by proved reserves. The authors of *The Limits to Growth*, for example, appear to believe that proved reserves represent all the oil resources of the world. Indeed the estimate they quote for world oil reserves (455×10^9 barrels) appears to be substantially in error since it is only about two-thirds of estimated proved reserves.[16] There may or may not be cause for alarm about oil and natural gas supplies, but the proved reserves figures are no basis for judgement, for the reasons already given. To draw any useful conclusions about world resources of oil and natural gas one must examine estimates of ultimately recoverable reserves which are on approximately the same basis as those for coal discussed above – that is, they must refer to the reserves estimated to have been in place before production began – though estimation is significantly harder than for coal. It is possible to identify sedimentary basins where oil and gas *may* be present and it is possible to prove reserves by drilling, but computing the total volume of reserves in an area generally proceeds by fairly crude analogy with other known producing territories.

With these limitations in mind, we can consider some of the assessments made of ultimately recoverable oil and gas reserves. The 1968 World Power Conference Survey of Energy Resources is of little help because for many important oil-producing countries (for example, the Soviet Union) only proved reserves are quoted. However, an estimate by Hubbert of world ultimately recoverable oil reserves gives a range of 1350×10^9 to 2100×10^9 barrels or about two to three times the size of world proved oil reserves.[17] By comparison with the estimates of ultimately recoverable coal resources, these figures are fairly small; 1350 to 2100×10^9 barrels of oil is about equal to 0.3×10^{12} to 0.4×10^{12} metric tons coal equivalent (m.t.c.e.),[18] whereas the Hubbert range for coal mentioned earlier was 4.3×10^{12} to 7.6×10^{12} m.t.c.e. Thus estimates of ultimately recoverable oil are at best less than 10 per cent of estimated ultimately recoverable coal.

An interesting comparison has been made by Warman[19] of changes in estimates of world ultimate oil reserves over time. He shows that in the early 1940s such estimates were in the region of 400×10^9 to 600×10^9 barrels (that is, rather less than the reserves which by about 1970 had been proved); they then rose to 1000×10^9 to 1500×10^9 barrels in the early 1950s, but since the late 1950s the estimates have tended to stabilise around 2000×10^9 barrels. Warman considers that this consensus about the size of ultimate reserves is significant and suggests that 'our knowledge has increased to a point where future continued expansion (in ultimate reserves estimates) on the same scale seems unlikely'. Both Warman and Hubbert agree that if the complete cycle of world oil production is assessed in the same way as we have already outlined for coal, the peak of world oil output is likely to be around the year 2000.

Ultimate natural-gas reserves, according to Hubbert, are of approximately the same order of magnitude as oil – 8000×10^{12} to $12,000 \times 10^{12}$ cubic feet, which is about 0.4×10^{12} to 0.5×10^{12} m.t.c.e.[20] Estimated ultimate reserves of natural gas liquids amount to some 250×10^9 to 420×10^9 barrels, equivalent to rather less than 0.1×10^{12} m.t.c.e.

In addition to these 'conventional' oil and gas reserves, there is a substantial amount of oil locked in tar sands and shale. A calculation by Hubbert which is apparently very conservative, puts these at 490×10^9 recoverable barrels (equivalent to about 0.1×10^{12} m.t.c.e.). Some very much larger figures of oil from tar sands and shale have been quoted.[21]

(3) *Total fossil fuel reserves.* Putting together the above estimates for fossil fuel reserves gives the results shown in Table 2.4 – that the aggregate of our estimates of ultimately recoverable fossil fuel reserves is of the order of between 5×10^{12} and 9×10^{12} m.t.c.e. and that the bulk of estimated reserves is in the form of coal. (Table 2.1 showed that at present nearly two-thirds of world energy consumption is of liquid and gaseous fuel and only just over one-third is coal.) In terms of the current level of world energy consumption of about 7×10^{9} m.t.c.e. the lower and upper bounds shown in the table amount to 600 and 1100 years' supply, respectively, after making allowance for the relatively small quantity of past consumption of fossil fuels. To allow for expansion, if we assume that the recent growth rate of world energy demand of around 5 per cent per annum persists and if there were no other energy resources and no improvement in recovery rates, then fossil fuel reserves would be exhausted by about the middle of the twenty-first century. In practice, production of fossil fuels would not rise to a maximum and then cease, but would decline for some years from its maximum point: therefore the peak of fossil fuel output would occur *before* the middle of next century, given our assumptions about reserves and demand growth. Some doubts are expressed later about whether world energy consumption

TABLE 2.4   Estimates of Ultimately Recoverable Reserves of Fossil Fuels

	10^{12} metric tons coal equivalent	10^{15} kcal
Coal	4·3–7·6	25,400–44,900
Oil*	0·4–0·5	2400– 3000
Natural gas†	0·4–0·6	2400– 3500
	5·1–8·7	30,200–51,400

† Including natural gas liquids.
* Including conservative estimate for tar sands and shale.

Sources: Hubbert, 'Energy Resources' and 'The Energy Resources of the Earth'.

will increase as fast as 5 per cent per annum in the future, but whether it does or not it is clear that some other energy source will be needed in the not too distant future. This brings us to reserves of uranium, the principal fuel for nuclear fission reactors.

(4) *Uranium reserves.* In estimating uranium reserves there is an additional difficulty when compared with estimates of reserves of the fossil fuels: because of its military and political significance one has to treat reserve estimates with an extra amount of caution. Furthermore, the reserve estimates usually quoted do not include Communist countries.

Another complication is that the energy equivalent of any given quantity of uranium reserves varies enormously according to the type of reactor used for power generation.[22] More advanced reactors, such as the H.T.R. and especially fast breeders, use uranium resources much more efficiently than the early reactors, as Table 2.5 shows. The table compares the energy contents of various estimates of world uranium reserves according to whether they are used in light water reactors or breeders.

Thus it is not very meaningful simply to quote uranium reserves in terms of tons of uranium oxide, as is frequently done. It is necessary also to specify what reactor technology has been assumed. If one takes the view that by the mid-1980s there will probably be a substantial breeder-reactor programme in Europe and the United States so that many of the new nuclear stations will be breeders, then uranium reserves begin to look very large. A study presented to the Fourth U.N. Conference on Peaceful Uses of Atomic Energy in 1971[23] concluded that the estimated world total of uranium reserves recoverable at a price of up to $30 per lb (excluding the Communist countries) contains almost as much energy as the higher estimate we have already given for ultimate world coal reserves, if used in breeder reactors. The same study also pointed to the enormous volume of uranium which could be extracted from sea water, calculating that if only 1 per cent of the uranium in the sea were extracted and used in breeder reactors this would give a volume of energy equivalent to about nine times our higher estimate for ultimately recoverable coal. The uranium resource estimates from the study are summarised in Table 2.5.

B

TABLE 2.5   Estimates of Energy Content of World* Uranium
Reserves

	Metric tons	10^{15} kcal
Reasonably assured[a]	$1·4 \times 10^6$	
Light water reactors		190
Breeders		14,300
Estimated total[b] (excluding sea)	$4·0 \times 10^6$	
Light water reactors		600
Breeders		41,000
From sea[c]	$40·0 \times 10^6$	
Light water reactors		6000
Breeders		410,000

[a] At prices up to $15 per lb
[b] At prices up to $30 per lb
[c] 1 per cent of the estimated total uranium content of about 4×10^9 metric tons

* Excluding Communist countries

Source: L. W. Boxer *et al.*, *Uranium Resources, Production and Demand*, Fourth U.N. International Conference on the Peaceful Uses of Atomic Energy (Geneva, Sep 1971).

(5) *Other energy sources.* Several other sources of energy at present make relatively small contributions to world energy supplies – for example, non-fossil sources such as hydro, geothermal, tidal, wind and solar power. The scope for further hydro-electric development is very limited in most industrialised countries, though there are greater possibilities in the underdeveloped world. Power from geothermal sources, the tides and the wind – all of which are being used on a small scale in various parts of world – should be capable of considerable expansion, though at present it is difficult to see any of these contributing to world energy supplies by more than a few per cent.

A much more likely major energy source is the sun, which provides most of the world's energy income. Apart from agricultural uses, solar power is already being tapped in various parts of the world in the form of house collectors which provide heating and cooling, and there appears to be considerable scope for expanding this kind of diffuse collection of the sun's energy.[24] Centralised collection to generate electricity is likely to be more difficult and costly and may mean devoting large areas of land to trapping an energy source which is so dispersed. However, research is now being directed both at efficient collection and at means of overcoming the problem of cloud cover (for instance, by collecting solar energy by satellite and transmitting it to earth). Solar energy has so many advantages – for example, world-wide distribution (though not all countries are equally blessed), safety, freedom from significant effects on the environment, and enormous size – that it is unlikely to be long before we begin to make widespread use of this near-ideal energy form. To give an idea of the order of magnitude of solar energy, it can be calculated that in a favourable desert location a square with sides of less than 100 miles (about 9000 square miles or one-quarter of 1 per cent of the area of the Sahara) receives energy from the sun equivalent to present world energy consumption. Even allowing for relatively inefficient collection of solar power, it is clear that this is potentially a huge source of energy income which even the wonders of compound interest will not cause us to approach in the remotely foreseeable future.

Though in this paper we are merely giving a passing mention to possible future energy sources, it should be pointed out that there are two other 'novel' energy sources which may be in use next century, both of which seem likely to be large scale and relatively non-polluting. One is fusion,[25] the hydrogen bomb type of reaction produced from the fusing of light atoms, the probable materials for which (deuterium and lithium) appear to be available in very large quantities from sea water: however, fusion has not yet been demonstrated even on a laboratory scale. The other is the use, as an energy carrier, of hydrogen produced from the electrolysis of water.[26]

(ii) *World energy demand*

Assessment of future demand is at least as difficult as estimating reserves. Statistics of world energy consumption[27] are not very reliable since, apart from the aggregation problem of attempting to add together fuels measured in different units and with varying efficiencies of use, the statistics normally used include only 'commercial' sources of energy; they exclude wood, dung and other miscellaneous sources used particularly in under-developed regions (about which there is little information), and also human muscular power and the use of domesticated animals. Thus some of the increase in recorded world energy consumption is merely a changeover from these more primitive energy forms to coal or oil rather than a true rise in consumption.

In addition to these statistical problems, there are obvious difficulties in constructing a forecasting model for world energy consumption. Many people take refuge in naïve trend projections, assuming, for example, that world consumption will continue to increase at a compound rate of about 5 per cent per annum (the average for the last twenty years). Others make trend projections for individual countries and then add the 'forecasts' together, and some use simple regressions of energy consumption per head on real G.N.P. per head. These non-causal models may have appeared to give reasonable forecasts during a period in which world economic growth was proceeding fairly steadily and in which there were no sharp movements in energy prices, but it is unlikely that they will be of much help in the future because of the changes which are now taking place in the world energy market.

The most significant of these changes will probably be a substantial rise in energy prices. Briefly, the reasons for expecting much higher prices over the next ten years or so are:

(*a*) higher cost deposits of 'conventional' fossil fuel will be exploited (for example, offshore oil will be produced in deeper water) and production of oil from unconventional sources (tar sands, shale or coal) will incur substantially higher costs than those to which we have been accustomed;

(*b*) the movement to 'make polluters pay' by regulations or internalising the costs of pollution will increase costs in fuel industries; and

(*c*) most important, the oil-producing countries have considerable power to raise prices for some years yet.

This change to a world of higher energy prices seems likely to be of much greater importance than has yet been realised. During the 1960s oil prices remained relatively stable in the industrialised world. Indeed heavy fuel oil prices fell for a time despite the general inflation. Table 2.6 gives the example of Britain, where industrial fuel oil prices declined in the first half of the 1960s despite the imposition of a tax of £2 per ton in 1961: in 1970 prices were little higher than in 1955. Only in the last three years have oil prices begun to increase substantially.

What we are now observing is a transformation from a world

TABLE 2.6   Industrial Fuel Oil Prices in Great Britain

	£ per ton
1955	9·00
1960	8·30
1961	7·60
1962	8·50
1963	8·00
1964	7·50
1965	7·00
1966	7·40
1967	8·60
1968	9·40
1969	9·30
1970	9·30
1971	13·90
1972	13·30

Source: *Digest of U.K. Energy Statistics* (1973), table 100.

in which oil prices were falling relative to the general price level to a world in which the prices of oil and other energy forms will probably increase at least as fast as prices in general and probably a great deal faster for a few years. What is more, the enormous publicity which surrounds changes in energy prices has heightened consumers' and suppliers' awareness and has clearly generated expectations of further large price increases in a way which has probably never occurred previously. There are certain time lags in the adjustment system in the energy market – for example, because of the need for investment in equipment in the factory or the home – but the stimulation of these expectations may well make adjustment much faster than past experience would suggest.

In these circumstances forecasts of energy demand which take little or no account of price effects are likely to be misleading. Some of the predictions of the growth of U.S. energy demand which have appeared in the last two years fall into this trap: they assume that energy demand will continue to increase as rapidly as in the past even though a growing energy 'shortage' is predicted, which presumably means higher prices.[28]

What is needed is some econometric evidence on the likely response of aggregate energy demand to higher prices, but unfortunately there is nothing available; even for individual fuels there is little evidence on price elasticities. We intend to pursue this at the University of Surrey but the difficulty of the task must be recognised because there does not seem to have been any period in recent history in which energy price expectations have undergone a sustained and substantial increase of the magnitude which seems probable over the next few years. The basis for reliable estimates of price and other elasticities may therefore not exist.

The best that can be done at present is to put forward some statistics which give an indication of *potential* for price responsiveness in the energy market, though we cannot be sure what the response will actually be. Some months ago it was often difficult to convince people (especially engineers) that there is any significant scope for fuel saving as prices change – there was a strongly ingrained belief that individuals and companies use what they 'need' – but the effects of the Arab oil restrictions have made it obvious to all that the amount of energy we consume is capable of variation within wide limits, even in the short run, as the variables which determine consumption change.

The first piece of evidence on fuel saving is a U.S. study[29] which explored in some detail the scope for energy conservation and reached the conclusion that by 1980 U.S. energy demand could be reduced by as much as 7·3 million barrels per day oil equivalent (M.B./D.o.e.), which is around 16 per cent of forecast U.S. energy consumption in that year. The main sources of this large cut in consumption would be better insulation in houses, more efficient air conditioning, various shifts in transport (for example, freight from road to rail and urban passengers from cars to public transport), and more efficient industrial processes and equipment.

Then it is useful to try to classify the ways in which savings may occur as prices rise. Some of these are likely to occur 'naturally' as consumers respond to current or expected higher prices: others will occur because governments which expect higher prices will take action to encourage energy saving (such as insisting on improved domestic insulation standards). The savings are classified under three headings: (1) greater efficiency in converting primary to secondary fuels; (2) improved efficiency in fuel usage by consumers; and (3) substitution of other goods for fuel. British statistics are used to give examples.

(1) *More efficient use of fuel in conversion.* A given demand from
fuel consumers can be met by a reduced input if the efficiency
with which 'primary' fuels (such as oil and coal) are converted
into 'secondary' fuels (such as electricity and gas) can be increased. The amount of primary fuel used by the secondary fuel
producers in the United Kingdom is extremely large – about
37,500 million therms in 1972 or roughly 45 per cent of the
total fuel input into the U.K. economy. As Table 2.7 shows,
almost 60 per cent of this input is 'lost', principally because
conversion to secondary fuels is less than 50 per cent efficient
but also because of losses in distribution and use of fuel by the
secondary fuel producers themselves. These losses of nearly
60 per cent of fuel input to the secondary fuel producers amount
to no less than 26 per cent of the total fuel input to the U.K.
economy.

Within the secondary fuel production section, most of the
losses occur in public electricity generation. Consumers
receive, in the form of electricity, only just over one-quarter of
the electricity supply industry's energy input of primary fuels
(coal, oil, hydro and nuclear power) mainly because of conversion losses which amount to nearly 70 per cent of input. It
seems highly probable that as primary fuel prices rise and the
cost of losing energy in conversion therefore increases there
will be a strong incentive in electricity generation to raise

TABLE 2.7   Fuel Input and Output: U.K. Secondary
Fuel Producers,* 1972

	Million therms	*% Of fuel input*
Fuel input	37,515	100
Losses in conversion to secondary fuels	19,475	52
Secondary fuels produced	18,040	48
Losses in distribution and use by secondary fuel producers	2395	6
Secondary fuels available for domestic consumers and export	15,645	42

* Electricity supply, gas supply, coke ovens and manufactured fuel
plants.

Source: *Digest of U.K. Energy Statistics* (1973), tables 7 and 8.

conversion efficiencies by using more efficient cycles, though there may well be long time lags before the necessary technology can be fully developed and applied. In addition, there will be pressure to find means of using the large amounts of waste heat produced by existing methods of generation.[30]

(2) *More efficient use of fuel by consumers.* There is also scope for increasing the efficiency with which fuel is used by consumers. A given input of therms of fuel to consumers (in the form of secondary fuels such as electricity and gas or primary fuels such as oil and coal) can be used more efficiently so as to produce a larger output of 'useful' therms: this will generally mean changes in appliance or process design since the demand for fuel is derived from the ownership of fuel-burning equipment.

Transport is one area where large energy savings seem likely as prices increase. In motor transport it is probable that higher fuel costs will have effects both on mileages travelled and on car design: in the United States, in particular, there may well be a reaction against the heavy and thirsty types of vehicles now being produced. Annual consumption of petrol per car in the United States is about 2 tons compared with about 1 ton in the major Western European countries where mileages travelled are somewhat less and smaller, high-compression engines are used.[31] It may also be possible to reduce oil consumption for air transport (which at present is a much smaller user than road transport[32]). In the transportation sector as a whole, one would expect shifts away from the comparatively energy-intensive transport forms (such as aeroplanes and the private car) towards public surface transportation. It can also be expected that in the long term there will be a move away from oil as the principal road transport fuel.

Outside transport it is probable that additional large efficiency gains can be made, though it is difficult to quantify these, except for the United States, because of the lack of information on appliance efficiencies. The U.S. conservation study to which we have already referred[29] concluded that there is great potential for improved equipment and process design, especially in industry. Its estimated 1980 saving of 7·3 M.B./D.o.e. is split about equally between transportation (2·3 M.B./D.), industry (2·6 M.B./D) and the domestic/commercial sector (2·4 M.B./D.). In the domestic market the study identified the most important source of savings as being improved insulation standards, which is considered next.

(3) *Substitution of other goods for fuel.* In addition to efficiency improvements, there is considerable scope for the substitution of other goods for the direct use of fuel and for the greater use by consumers of natural energy forms. For example, consumers may decide to heat their houses less, substituting warmer clothing for direct fuel use and they may eat more warming foods. Standards of lighting may decline. Some of the most important changes in a world of higher fuel prices probably concern building design.[33] In recent times it may not have mattered that large amounts of heat have escaped from buildings and that only limited use has been made of natural sources of light and heat, but this situation is unlikely to continue as the economics move in favour of substituting insulation and changed building design for fuel.

(iii) *Some conclusions on energy depletion*
Any conclusions one draws about the future supply and demand situation in the energy market must be tentative. As is so frequently true of forecasting problems, we have a limited amount of information – much of it not in the form we would wish – about past trends and present stock and income levels. The supply information is deficient in that it is based principally on geological surveys and inferences drawn from them; in particular, assumptions about future recovery rates from our energy stocks are usually rather arbitrary. Our knowledge of the other key variables influencing fuel supplies – future exploitation technology and future energy cost and price levels – is very limited. Though we can see some new energy sources on the horizon, we are not clear whether they will be developed nor how long development would take; moreover, there may be quite new sources of which we are not yet even aware. On the demand side we are not sure how elastic world energy consumption will be with respect to price nor how long it will take for demand to respond to higher prices.

What we can say with a high degree of certainty is that one cannot describe the energy depletion problem in terms of a simple model in which a fixed stock of resources is being depleted at a known rate, as the simpler forms of the materials balance model imply. There are possibilities for substituting different forms of energy stocks for those which now dominate supplies (oil and natural gas), thus increasing the supply capacity of the environment, and for using less energy-intensive methods of production and consumption, so reducing energy consumption per unit of output. In addition, there is a vast income source of energy in the sun. The extent to which these possibilities will be exploited will depend on some highly complex feedback mechanisms in the system, involving the abilities of individuals, companies and governments to receive and react to signals which indicate to them that circumstances are changing. Broadly, there are two sources of these signals. One is the price system, which will provide financial incentives for the restriction of demand and the expansion of supply. The other is the shock effect of all that has happened in the energy market since conditions began to change about 1970 and which has been transmitted through the media – for example, the more aggressive attitude of the oil-producing countries and the realisation that oil and natural-gas prices will most probably rise substantially for a number of years. This barrage of information and speculation is now clearly affecting the behaviour of consumers and suppliers. The newspapers are full of schemes to save fuel and to exploit new sources of energy; though the occasion for the suggestions has been a short-term crisis, these demand-reducing and supply-increasing movements in the energy market should far outlast our immediate supply difficulties. In a sense this shock effect is just an improvement to the functioning of the price mechanism, with 'information' about future rising prices being fed in and speeding up the adjustment process. However, it may be rather more since people are now acting on an accumulation of all manner of ill-defined fears about future shortages. The more extreme and dogmatic statements about long-term fuel shortages need not be taken seriously in themselves; they are better seen as part of the adjustment mechanism, because of their effect in stimulating man's adaptive capacity, even though it is hardly likely that most of the authors would think of themselves as instruments of some invisible hand.

Given the complexities of the energy situation, one can do no more than make some probabilistic statements about the future and this we now do. The 'most probable' scenario which is set out below may seem optimistic, and indeed it is compared with the general gloom about energy shortage which is reflected in popular conversation, and which has been accentuated by the Arab oil restrictions, though these have little relevance to the long-term supply problem (see section (ii) below). However, the pessimistic view is usually very badly documented. Frequently it is based on inadequate evidence about energy resources, a failure to take into account the likely influence of costs and prices in determining the supply of and the demand for energy, and a lack of imagination about new energy forms, both stock and income. Moreover, it is usually rooted in fears about an *oil* shortage, which is now becoming evident and will be inconvenient but which is quite different from the physical shortages of energy in general which some people fear. Then there are subsidiary confusing factors. A good deal of the crisis atmosphere has been exported from the United States where there are some special reasons why a shortage of energy at prevailing prices should have occurred – for example, the low natural-gas prices enforced by the Federal Power Commission and the successful pressure by 'environmentalists' to delay construction of energy production and distribution facilities.

A probable view is that if we abstract from the geographical distribution of energy resources and from the pollution which may arise in using them and consider only the adequacy of global energy resources, the idea of a world energy famine in the foreseeable future seems rather far-fetched. Such evidence as we have set out suggests that the adjustment *potential* of the system is very considerable. It seems probable that the prophets of doom about energy have mistaken for a real crisis something which is a normal part of the process of economic change – a transition phase in which existing fuels are replaced by novel forms of energy and prices rise substantially for a time. The rest of this century will probably be such a phase, during which the world moves away from dependence on fossil fuels to the increased use of atomic fission and perhaps towards atomic fusion and the trapping of solar power. This will cause adjustment problems, but this is hardly anything new in the fuel market where since the last War coal has been supplanted on a massive scale by oil and natural gas, mainly as a consequence of relative price movements. It is conceivable that there may have to be a temporary move back to coal (through liquefaction or gasification) during the transition phase, because as we have seen coal reserves appear to be much larger than oil and gas reserves. It is also likely that adjustment to large-scale use of nuclear fission will not be smooth; for instance, there may be problems in bringing in sufficient nuclear capacity at the speed required from the 1980s onwards.

Without wishing to belittle these transitional problems, they fall well short of the global catastrophe stemming from fuel resource depletion which has been predicted in some quarters. Though low-cost fossil-fuel resources (especially oil) will probably become scarcer during the transition phase, incipient shortages will tend to be mitigated by price effects, including the important influence of price expectations. The impact of higher prices on demand has already been described. On the supply side rising prices should stimulate greater recovery from existing fuel resources, the exploitation of previously uneconomic and inaccessible reserves and the use of known unconventional fossil fuel reserves such as tar sands and shale oil. At the same time, there will be an incentive to invest in the more rapid large-scale development of nuclear fission, 'synthetic' fuels (such as hydrogen) and very large energy sources such as fusion and solar power. Given the potential for expanding supplies and economising on demand, it seems highly probable that the price system will prove a powerful adjustment mechanism in the energy market, even though it will probably take some years for investment in new sources of energy and in energy-saving methods to take place and thus for adaptation to higher prices to work itself out. One must hope that governments will be willing to allow fuel prices to rise so that the adjustment process will work: one danger, which we mention only in passing, is that commitments to prices and incomes policies will make governments try to hold down energy prices. If they do, the result may be a period of administrative allocation of fuel supplies which would probably be a very inefficient way of dealing with supply problems.

On a very long view, of course, it may be that energy resources will one day become insufficient whatever happens to energy prices. Continued economic growth for several centuries might exhaust the earth's stock of energy (including possible new sources such as fusion power) and we might by then be using all the solar power we can exploit. Consequently, we might have to move to a 'spaceship economy' as advocated by Boulding[34] in which, in so far as energy is concerned, the world is restricted to a consumption level equal to energy income (mainly solar energy). But, as we have already pointed out, the level of energy income is likely to be so high that it would seem premature to be worrying about conservation now (assuming that our only concern is resource depletion). Furthermore, once one begins to look a very long way ahead past experience would suggest that we probably have very little idea what energy forms future generations will be using: apart from the very large new energy sources which we now see on the horizon, it would be surprising if entirely new forms were not to appear. Frequently the conservationists are very vague about the time-scale on which they are thinking and their view seems to be merely that the world will come to an end sometime, which is no more than a statement of the obvious.

4. Other energy problems

The relatively optimistic view put forward above is, of course, incomplete because the depletion of energy resources is not the only issue in the energy market. We now consider briefly the two other matters mentioned at the beginning of this paper – pollution and the monopolisation of oil reserves.

(i) *Pollution*

Production, transportation and consumption of energy give rise to substantial pollution – for example, emissions of sulphur and nitrogen oxides and particles into the atmosphere, thermal pollution of water, oil spills in rivers and seas, and all the unpleasant possibilities associated with nuclear fission power.[35] The question arises whether the output of such wastes will strain the assimilative capacity of the earth. Though this is a matter on which an economist can hardly be expected to give a definitive answer, a few summary comments may be useful.

As a generalisation, it might be said that many of the problems of *local* pollution of the air and water from energy appear to be technically soluble and the remaining difficulties are those of identifying sources, instituting pricing or regulatory systems and ensuring that the necessary legal processes are efficient. The levels of pollution which have been reached have stemmed from relatively free use of the environment, and there now appears to be a clear case for dealing with this kind of market failure by internalising external costs or imposing anti-pollution regulations. In some cases, action against pollution has been remarkably successful – for instance, the U.K. Clean Air Act.

However, some energy pollution problems may be rather intractable. The market will not deal with them unaided and we cannot be sure they will yield to the marginal adjustments to company and consumer behaviour which economists expect to follow from imposing charges and setting standards. There seem to be at least two forms of pollution which may fall into this category.

First there is the cumulative effect of rising energy consumption on world climate. Fuel consumption on earth produces waste heat, which some scientists believe will eventually raise the temperature of the earth, giving rise to various unpleasant effects through global thermal pollution, and there are other possible effects of higher energy consumption on world climate (such as rising particulate and carbon dioxide contents of the atmosphere).[36] These kinds of global problems are not easily susceptible to control for at least two reasons – the absence of property rights in the earth's atmosphere and lack of knowledge about the climatic effects of rising energy use. It will be difficult to detect any adverse effects because of the mass of variables affecting world climate; even if effects were detected, because no one owns the atmosphere there would have to be international agreement on what the effects are, how to set charges or standards and how to enforce them. It is conceivable, though by no means certain, that by the time the effects were discovered and agreement reached an irreversible climatic change would have occurred.

Another difficult case is the safety of atomic fission power. Though most of the conventional forms of emissions are absent, there are many potential dangers associated with fission – accidents at power stations or fuel processing plants, mishaps with stored radioactive waste, hijacking of nuclear fuel, sabotage and so on.[37] The main problem is a serious accident leading to severe local or even global pollution: it is not just a matter of making marginal alterations to the manner of operation of nuclear power plants so as to control normal discharges (though that is required too). It is difficult to see how one could internalise the costs to society of a nuclear accident since there is no agreement on what these effects would be and there is a remote possibility that some types of accidents could annihilate the human race. The way out which has been adopted is for governments to impose apparently stringent safety standards.

There are, of course, physicists who will argue that fission power is so dangerous that it should not be developed any more. Apparently impressive cases can be made out for this argument and also for the opposite case.[38] It is not for an economist to try to pass judgement on what is essentially a scientific dispute but on present evidence it does seem rather unlikely, for safety reasons, that fission power will ever achieve the dominance in world energy supplies that (say) oil has now. Most probably we should see atomic fission essentially as a stopgap to cover the awkward transitional years as we move away from oil and natural gas to relatively non-polluting energy forms such as solar and (possibly) fusion power.

A personal view of the two forms of pollution discussed above is that they appear to be potentially much more difficult to solve than the energy supply problems which are so much in the news. Furthermore, there is an interrelationship between the depletion and pollution issues. The comparatively optimistic view of future energy supplies given earlier depended on the assumption that atomic fission, and especially breeder reactors, would be developed rapidly for a few decades. This seems the most likely outcome, but an alternative, if less probable, contingency is that if there were a major accident in the nuclear power industry in the next few years this might set back the development of fission power and would obviously lead to a more difficult supply position than has been suggested.

A less dramatic but still important point is that present concern with energy supply difficulties is leading to a relaxation of pollution controls all round the world: though this may not matter for a short period, it is to be hoped that this relative neglect of pollution from energy will not continue into the long term.

(ii) *Monopolisation of oil reserves*

One can hardly do justice in a brief space for comments on the attempt by some oil-producing countries to use their ownership of a large part of world oil resources for both economic and political ends. We shall merely review very briefly some of the major issues.

Although the oil exporters formed OPEC as long ago as 1960,[39] only in the last three years have they made serious efforts to use the power which they have through control of 50 per cent of world oil output, 66 per cent of world proved oil reserves and over 90 per cent of world crude oil exports (Tables 2.8, 2.9 and 2.10). Between 1960 and 1970, although there were various changes in the structure of taxation and in the forms of contractual agreements with oil companies

TABLE 2.8   World Oil Production 1972

	Million metric tons	*% of world total*
OPEC members		
Saudi Arabia	285·5	10·9
Iran	251·9	9·7
Kuwait	151·2	5·8
Iraq	71·6	2·7
Abu Dhabi	50·6	1·9
Qatar	23·2	0·9
Libya	106·7	4·1
Algeria	52·0	2·0
Nigeria	88·8	3·4
Venezuela	170·8	6·6
Indonesia	51·9	2·0
Total OPEC	1,304·2	50·0
U.S.A.	532·2	20·4
Canada	89·1	3·4
U.S.S.R.	394·0	15·1
Eastern Europe and China	48·8	1·9
Rest of world	241·3	9·2
Total	2,609·6	100·0

Source: *B.P. Statistical Review of the World Oil Industry* (1972).

TABLE 2.9   World Proved Oil Reserves, End 1972

	% of total proved reserves
OPEC members	
Saudi Arabia	21
Iran	10
Kuwait	10
Iraq	4
Abu Dhabi	3
Qatar	1
Libya	5
Algeria	7
Nigeria	2
Venezuela	2
Indonesia	1
Total OPEC	66
U.S.A.	5
Communist countries	15
Rest of world	14
Total	100

Source: *Oil and Gas Journal* (25 Dec 1972).

which were generally favourable to the producing govern-ments,[40] the 'posted prices' of crude oil (on which taxes are based) remained constant. Persian Gulf posted prices for light crude were held at about $1.80 per barrel, which was sub-stantially less than the 1948 posted price of $2.17 per barrel, and realised prices for crude oil fell well below posted prices during the 1960s. Since 1970, however, changes in market conditions have allowed the producing governments to raise crude prices substantially and to take greater control of oil operations in their territories.[41] The Teheran and Tripoli agreements in 1971 resulted in higher prices immediately and further planned increases up to 1975, but these agreements were soon breached. Prices rose sharply between 1970 and the summer of 1973 (Table 2.11) so that the Persian Gulf posted price went to around $3 per barrel. Then towards the end of 1973 further increases were imposed by the producing countries,

TABLE 2.10   OPEC Exports of Crude Oil 1972

	Million metric tons	% of world total
OPEC members		
Saudi Arabia	267·3	21·8
Iran	177·7	14·5
Kuwait	147·4	12·0
Iraq	67·2	5·5
Abu Dhabi	50·7	4·1
Qatar	21·5	1·8
Libya	106·4	8·7
Algeria	50·1	4·1
Nigeria	86·4	7·1
Venezuela	104·6	8·5
Indonesia	40·7	3·3
Total OPEC	1,120·0	91·4
Total world	1,224·6	100·0

Sources: *Petroleum Times* (27 July 1973); *Institute of Petroleum Information Service;* and *B.P. Statistical Review of the World Oil
Industry* (1972).

which raised the posted price of light Arabian crude in early
January 1974 to some $11.65 per barrel or about four times the
price in early October 1973. These increases will raise the price
of crude oil imported into western Europe to nearly $10 per
barrel (about £30 per ton), which is about three times the

TABLE 2.11   Crude Oil Posted Prices

	January 1970	August 1973	% increase
	$ per barrel		
Persian Gulf			
Iranian Light 34°	1·79	3·050	70
Kuwait 31°	1·59	2·936	85
Mediterranean			
Libya	2·21	4·582	107

Note: °API is an American Petroleum Institute measure of specific
gravity. The higher the number, the lighter the crude.

Source: *Petroleum Press Service* (May and Aug 1973).

import price in October 1973. Some producing countries have auctioned crude oil at even higher prices.

The other manifestation of the new-found assertiveness of the oil-exporting countries was, of course, the supply restrictions imposed by some of the Arab countries during the Middle-East War in October 1973 with the apparent aim of making the United States, Western Europe and Japan put pressure on Israel to give up its war gains.

We are not concerned here with the immediate issue of how the industrialised countries will fare during the period of restricted oil supplies, but with the power of the oil producers in the longer term. Though some economists have doubts about the strength of the producers,[42] the probability is that the OPEC countries have gained a strong semi-monopoly position which will now last for a number of years. The actions they have taken are obviously partly political but they are also consistent with what economists would expect given the market situation. Oil output is likely to reach a maximum some time in the next twenty years and it must appear to its owners that such a scarce resource should be conserved in the interests of price appreciation. Moreover, because a relatively small number of countries control such a large proportion of world oil exports and because some of these countries have strong political ties, formation of a cartel to regulate supplies is not too difficult and it has clearly been of benefit to members in the last few years. The market demand for crude oil appears to be inelastic with respect to price in the short term, because it takes time to substitute other energy forms on a large scale for a fuel which supplies over 40 per cent of world energy consumption. However, the price elasticity of demand for crudes from different sources (which, though not homogeneous are close substitutes) is much higher and the individual producing countries seem to have much to gain, at least in the short term, from suppressing competitition and combining to exploit the inelasticity of demand in the market as a whole.

It has been argued by Adelman[42] that it is in the nature of cartels that they are broken by 'chiselling and cheating' by members, but this seems unlikely to happen to OPEC in the next few years. Though one should not make OPEC appear more monolithic than it really is – clearly there are differences between Arabs and non-Arabs, countries which are already well on the road to development and those which are not, countries with ample reserves and those whose annual output may already have reached its maximum – there are a number of reasons why significant competition among the producers during (say) the next ten years is improbable.

(*a*) Group action has been successful so far and is likely to be so until competition from non-OPEC energy sources raises the elasticity of demand for OPEC oil. A price war at present would probably cause losses to the producers as a mass, because, since demand is inelastic, their revenues in total would fall.

(*b*) Despite the expectation of losses to OPEC as a whole, it is, of course, possible that individual members could gain extra revenues from competition. However, there are differences among the larger producers which may mean that for varying reasons they will not want greatly expanded output. Both Saudi Arabia and Abu Dhabi, which have abundant oil reserves (about 25 per cent of world proved reserves between them) will have difficulty in finding uses for funds which will accrue to them anyway over the next few years.[43] Thus oil in the ground may seem preferable to still more money. Some other countries are not anxious to expand production greatly because they are already concerned about the prospect of declining reserve/production ratios and therefore favour conservation: Iran, Kuwait and Libya (with about 25 per cent of world proved reserves between them) are all in this position.

(*c*) An expansion of output would mean increased producing capacity in most countries. This would be expensive and take time to bring into operation so that there is probably not much scope for competition in the short run.

(*d*) As well as economic interests, there are strong political forces – Arab nationalism and anti-Israel feelings – which bind together some of the most important oil producers. About 50 per cent of world proved oil reserves are in Arab hands.

For these reasons, it seems unrealistic to regard OPEC as a normal kind of cartel. The *internal* condition which often causes the break up of a cartel – belief by a member that it can gain more from competition than from continuing its membership – appears to be absent at present. Moreover, the *external* means of breaking up a cartel – by anti-trust action is, of course, not available in this case. Finally, it is quite wrong to see OPEC as just an organisation pursuing the *economic* interests of its members: there are strong political motives, such as changing U.S. policy towards Israel, behind the actions of the Arab producers.

Therefore, the industrialised countries – which have been used to a rapidly expanding supply of oil at low prices – will have to live for some time with a group of suppliers with considerable monopoly power which is more intent on obtaining capital for development than on trading in oil, which will almost certainly expand output more slowly than the oil companies would have done, and which will probably increase prices a good deal more. However, if one looks ahead to the late 1980s and 1990s, the oil-producing countries do not seem likely to have a particularly strong hold on the market; the demand for crude oil from OPEC sources is likely to be much more elastic in the long term than in the short term because of the substitution possibilities mentioned earlier in this paper. Given time, oil from OPEC sources can be partially replaced by oil from 'unconventional' sources such as tar sands or shale, by coal, by nuclear fission, or (in limited areas) by geothermal power. There is also the possibility of a really large oil find in a country which does not join OPEC, possibly in a new offshore area.

One of the easier substitution possibilities is oil from the Athabasca tar sands, which have been worked for many years but which have now been brought to the verge of profitability by the rise in crude prices. It is generally believed that Athabasca will be profitable at a crude price in the range $4–6 per barrel and investment in the area is now being increased.[44] Athabasca recoverable reserves are generally stated to be about 300×10^9 barrels or roughly half world proved reserves of 'conventional' oil. However, as pointed out earlier, this may well be a conservative estimate especially in a situation of much higher crude prices. Though oil from shale and from coal will probably be somewhat more expensive,[45] it seems likely that further substantial increases in OPEC crude prices will make both profitable in the next few years (though exploitation of shale may be held back for a time by environmental objections). Fission power will, of course, also look more attractive under a regime of higher crude prices.[46] Much further ahead, it may be that fusion and solar power will replace OPEC oil.

Thus there are already substitutes for OPEC oil which are on the verge of being competitive. The problem is to develop them on a sufficiently large scale. In the long run when they probably will be developed, the OPEC countries will be operating in a competitive market. People who look back from the early twenty-first century will most likely see the exercise of bargaining strength by OPEC in the 1970s and 1980s as a last effort by oil producers to assert themselves. By the turn of the century world oil output may well have passed its peak (less than 150 years after the drilling of Colonel Drake's first well in 1859 in Pennsylvania) and other forms of energy should be in widespread use. The more the OPEC countries raise prices and the more frequent are their actual or threatened reductions of oil supplies to the industrialised world, the greater the stimulus they give to research into forms of energy competitive with oil, to attempts to conserve energy and to the search for oil in non-OPEC areas. Consequently, at the same time that they are increasing their revenues in the short term, they are also shifting the demand curve for their product to the left in the long term.

Whether or not this is a sensible strategy for OPEC is not easy to judge, but it may be that in the end the oil producers will suffer losses from their attempts at 'conservation'. The popular view appears to be that conservation will pay even in the long term because oil prices will rise so that oil held in the ground will appreciate: though this is a widespread opinion in the producing countries, it should be obvious that oil prices will not forever increase rapidly. It is likely that the price of crude oil (though not necessarily of oil products to the consumer) will increase at a rate faster than inflation in the industrialised countries during the next ten years or so; by the early 1980s Persian Gulf crude prices could well be double what they are now. However, this will probably raise crude prices well above the prices of competitive energy forms and beyond that time it is conceivable that the advent of effective competition for oil from other energy forms will reduce oil prices drastically. The large rent element in the oil price means that prices could be cut a long way before the cost floor is reached: production costs in the Middle East are at present only of the order of 10c. per barrel. This is more likely to be the beginning of the price-cutting effect expected by Professor Adelman than intra-oil industry competition, although once the other energy sources begin to compete the oil producers may well start to cut prices against each other; as Adelman has argued, with the oil companies much less powerful than in the past, the competition could be fierce.

5. Conclusions

The conclusions of this paper can be summarised as follows:

(*a*) Fears about severe energy shortages in the long term resulting from a run down of world fuel resources seem to be exaggerated, provided the pollution problems associated with energy can be overcome. The probability is that what we are now observing is no more than a transition from oil and natural gas to new energy sources, during which energy prices will increase substantially.

(*b*) Fears about pollution from energy are tending to fall into the background because of excessive concern about energy supplies, but if one is looking for 'physical limits' to growth it is likely that the earth's capacity to assimilate wastes will become a constraint before there is any question of 'running out of energy'. Two awkward energy pollution problems may be global thermal pollution and the safety aspects of atomic fission.

(*c*) The most immediate issue in the world energy market – the power of the oil-exporting countries – is probably the least serious matter in the long term, provided a major war can be avoided. For a few years some or all of the OPEC members will be able to restrict the expansion of supplies and raise prices, thus accelerating the switch from oil to other energy sources which would, in any case, have been taking place. However, on a long view this will most likely appear as just a passing phase in the history of world energy – a last gasp from the owners of an asset which is likely to be exhausted in the foreseeable future.

3 SOME ISSUES IN THE CURRENT DEBATE ABOUT ENERGY AND NATURAL RESOURCES

A. J. SURREY and WILLIAM PAGE

Economics has always contained an element of schizophrenia with regard to natural resources. The view that market forces should be left to equate the demand and supply of natural resources through changes in costs and prices glossed over the effects of market imperfections and the long lead times in developing new supply sources; but it was tenable as long as it could be assumed there was no practical limit to the total supply of natural resources which could be tapped. Increasing recognition that the earth's resources are ultimately finite, combined with the expectation that world consumption will continue to expand at compound growth rates, throws doubts upon this sanguine view.

The inherent contradiction between these two propositions has usually been ignored. Over 100 years ago Jevons sounded an early warning in arguing that British coal reserves would run out if demand continued to grow at 3·5 per cent a year; but this fear was allayed by the development of new types of fuel, a large international trade in primary fuels (especially oil) and by technical progress in the use and production of energy. These factors made it reasonable to assume that there was no practical limit to global supplies of natural resources. This key assumption was implicit in the policies pursued by the United States, Western Europe and Japan throughout the 1950s and 1960s: any deviations from their adherence to 'competitive' energy policies were due to considerations of national security, the balance of payments and social costs and benefits. British energy policy, as expounded in November 1967, rested upon the assumption that coal and nuclear power would have to fight for a share of the long-term energy market, in which the price level would be determined by plentiful and cheap supplies of petroleum. Until the early 1970s the general view among economists and policy-makers was that the exhaustion of world mineral resources was a possibility too remote to contemplate.

Over the past two years public anxieties have arisen with numerous predictions of a world energy 'crisis', although it must be pointed out that these anxieties have stemmed partly from confusion between physical resource depletion and the dramatic shift in political bargaining power and economic rent to the resource-producing countries. A 'crisis' stemming from monopolistic exploitation of resources is potentially no less dangerous than one stemming from fears of longer-term physical resource depletion. But for policy formulation the difference is vitally important.

What factors have brought about this abrupt change of mood? As far as we can see there is no single cause, but several contributory factors:

Many young people, especially among the better educated and more articulate sections of the rich, industrialised countries, are profoundly challenging the goal of ever higher standards of material welfare and the structure of their society. This contrasts starkly with the great bulk of mankind still struggling to escape from poverty. They have no such illusions: for them, economic growth is the only way forward.

There has been an upsurge in doomsday literature, stemming largely from preoccupation with environmental issues. This is especially characteristic of contemporary American thought, and it is linked with the moral challenge to materialism.

Big changes have occurred in the world economy in the past two to three years, coinciding with and tending to reinforce the doubts about the desirability and feasibility of continuing economic growth. In the case of crude oil, especially, there has been a major shift in bargaining power from the resource-importing to the resource-producing countries, which may well mark the end of an era when the control and ownership of resources – and consequently the lion's share of the economic rent – has been in the hands of the industrialised countries. Meshed in with this are the effects of global inflation on an unprecedented scale; a series of international monetary crises and exchange-rate movements, which have had an unsettling effect on business confidence; poor grain harvests, which have affected the supply and price of many farm products; and a shift to more nutritious types of food in parts of the world where dietary habits were so long constrained by poverty.

Great publicity has attached to attempts to apply computerised 'systems dynamics' methods to simulate the future of the world. The most notable case has been *The Limits to Growth* work of Meadows and others in the United States, where a combination of what can only be described as Malthusian assumptions and the apparent immutability of their doomsday predictions has had a startling impact – not least among some of those concerned with policies for population, agriculture, mineral resources and international aid, and those unable to submit *The Limits to Growth* work to rigorous examination.

1. The limits to growth

Given the highly controversial impact of *The Limits to Growth* work and the apparent intellectual and numerical support it has provided for those who believe that economic growth is wrong or cannot be sustained, it is appropriate to discuss it briefly.

Much of the impact of this work derives from the fact that it was the first publicised attempt to encompass the problems of population, food supplies, natural resources and pollution within a single computerised world model – in short, to deal with the world as a single system and to use the computer to devise consistent solutions to interrelated problems. It comprises five interdependent subsystems – population, agriculture, non-renewable resources, pollution and capital. The links between them are such that a change affects both the subsystem in which it occurs and the other subsystems. The model treats the world as a single entity without geographical subdivisions and assumes that food supplies and non-renewable resources are each homogeneous. It ignores the political and economic subdivisions which exist in the real world, and the important differences which exist between various types of foodstuffs and between various types of natural resources. Despite these serious deficiencies, the model has the merit of providing a framework for analysing the impact of developments in one part of the system upon the whole. To the extent that it helps to make national governments more aware of the international implications of their policies, to break down the jealously guarded, watertight compartments which divide so much research effort, and to stimulate debate about the composition of economic growth and the distribution of its fruits, *The Limits to Growth* is to be welcomed. In other respects, however, it is dangerous.

The popular appeal of *The Limits to Growth* lies in the apparent inevitability of its main conclusion that the world 'system' will collapse in the time-span of many people alive today, owing to over-population, resource depletion and pollution. Even if action is taken to avoid two of these modes of collapse, the third will get us. Therefore, according to *The Limits to Growth* team, the only common solution is to adopt policies for zero growth to preserve the stability of the world system. Tinkering with the system will at best only slightly delay collapse, and at worst (if it leads to higher population and living standards) accelerate it.

The novelty of *The Limits to Growth* lies simply in the power of the computer to quantify when and how collapse will occur. But its theoretical foundations can be traced back to Malthus nearly 200 years ago. Malthusian doctrines left their mark upon social and economic policies in Britain long after events had invalidated them. The danger with *The Limits to Growth* doctrine is that it too may divert attention to false 'doomsday' predictions and away from the economic, social and technological possibilities for improving the condition of man. Also, unless zero-growth policies were accompanied by a massive international redistribution of income and wealth, they would perpetuate the current extreme inequality in living standards and commit the bulk of humanity to permanent poverty. A more divisive and politically-explosive remedy for world problems is difficult to envisage!

Our main concern here, however, is with the non-renewable resources subsystem rather than with the mechanics of the model as a whole. It must be noted that this subsystem rests upon three highly contentious suppositions: all non-renewable resources are homogeneous and therefore perfect substitutes for each other; the total stock of these resources is equivalent to 250 years' supply at the 1970 level of consumption; and the costs of discovery and extraction (measured as the proportion of total world capital invested in mining and resource-processing activities) will increase rapidly as the stock of non-renewable resources diminishes. From these suppositions it is axiomatic that if world industrial production continues to grow at current compound growth rates and if there is little scope for technical progress and recycling, then increasing demands would be placed upon dwindling reserves. 'Collapse' of the whole system would follow as insufficient capital was available to meet other basic needs and as supplies of non-renewable resources ran out.

Adherents to this doctrine tend to rebut criticism – for example that their resource estimates are too conservative, that future economic growth will be less rapid than they predict, or that the long-run marginal cost curves for resource discovery and extraction may rise less steeply than they predict – by arguing that quite large changes in these assumptions would have only a slight effect on the timing of the collapse which is bound to occur unless zero-growth policies are pursued. It is our view, however, that these criticisms cannot be brushed aside so lightly. How the reserves are measured is not unimportant. Technological possibilities cannot be discounted. Exponential growth in demand is not a foregone conclusion.

2. Concepts and measurement of reserves

Economists have always realised that the measurement of reserves cannot be divorced from prices and techniques of production. A particular deposit counts as part of the reserves only if it can be recovered economically at a given price and with given techniques of production. Published reserve estimates of various mineral resources usually contain the assumption of prices and technologies not greatly dissimilar from those previously or currently in operation.

Because of accidents of history or politics, exploration has sometimes concentrated in particular well-endowed areas. In such cases the published 'world' reserves are little more than estimates for those particular areas, for no systematic effort has been made to find new reserves elsewhere.

For crude oil, coal and certain minerals where more systematic exploration has been done, the published figures are usually divided between 'proven' reserves of reasonably well-known size and content, and 'inferred' reserves thought likely to exist from knowledge of the general geology of particular areas. For obvious commercial reasons, exploration has usually concentrated on areas where the reserves are most accessible and easy to extract and transport. 'Inferred' reserves, although subject to great uncertainty (especially for those resources which occur in deep isolated pockets rather than as continuous beds over large areas with occasional surface outcrops), are frequently estimated to be much larger than the 'proven' reserves. The latter are usually little more than what it has so far been in the commercial interest of an industry to discover.

The profit motive implies that commercial exploration has aimed to find sufficient new resources to meet an industry's requirements over its forward planning period (typically eight to twelve years, allowing for lead times to develop new production capacity) and any new reserves which promise to be more profitable than previous discoveries. Admittedly, chance discoveries have sometimes occurred further afield or deeper than could be economically used with current techniques and price levels, but it remains generally true that no systematic effort has been made to find every deposit which might be economically recoverable in the unknown and probably different economic, technical and political circumstances of the distant future.

Even with their own definitions, the published estimates are often unreliable. Different standards of calculation are often used. They frequently contain a conservative bias stemming from geological uncertainties when a deposit is first discovered and from commercial considerations. And in most cases little or nothing is known of the resource potential of the U.S.S.R., China and other Communist countries. In some cases the same applies to the developing countries.

Crude oil provides a good example. Between 1951 and 1971 estimates of 'proven' world reserves increased by a factor of 5·7 and those of the Middle East (which contains over 60 per cent of the world total) increased more than sixfold, in spite of the large quantities which have been extracted. During this period new discoveries and extensions to known oilfields were made, but a good deal of the increase came from revisions of earlier estimates. Given the current political circumstances surrounding the oil industry, the scope for deliberate under-reporting will probably be smaller than in the past; but some upward revision will continue to be necessary as knowledge accumulates on particular oil reservoir conditions. The fact that oil exploration has concentrated on finding the biggest and most profitable fields is reflected in the fact that 75 per cent of the total crude oil discovered to date comprises individual fields with reserves of at least 300 million barrels.

Although the international search for crude oil is much more systematic than that for other resources, petroleum geologists have only a hazy idea of the size of ultimately recoverable reserves. Discounting past production and possible reserves beneath the oceans, none of the forecasts made by leading petroleum geologists over the past twenty years suggests that ultimately recoverable reserves are less than 1,300,000 million barrels – three times the crude oil reserves quoted in *The Limits to Growth*.

Since published reserves are usually the sum of past successful exploration undertaken in relation to price levels and technologies then current, they rarely indicate the quantities that could be economically produced at different price levels. Generally there is no way of knowing what new reserves would become economic in future if prices and technology change dramatically.

This can be illustrated by reference to published uranium reserves. Of the published reserves recoverable at prices up to $10 per lb, 95 per cent are in the six non-Communist countries that the Western nuclear weapons powers considered politically reliable suppliers. This is also where the bulk of world exploration has been undertaken. By and large, commercial exploration has concentrated on locating low-cost deposits because uranium prices have remained low. Although estimates are made for reserves minable at prices up to $15 per lb, they are unreliable because price trends have not justified systematic exploration for higher cost reserves. In the late 1950s and early 1960s uranium exploration virtually ceased owing to earlier over-production for weapons purposes, and over the whole post-war period additions to the reserves have been closely correlated with exploration activity. Some guesses have been made about long-term availabilities if uranium prices rose above $15 per lb, but they are highly speculative. Moreover, there is no way of knowing how long the reserves will last: fears about diminishing availabilities, reflected in rising uranium prices, would encourage both more exploration and the introduction of the fast breeder reactor, which is incomparably more efficient in its use of uranium than current thermal reactors.

'Known' reserves of many mineral resources have expanded greatly over the past twenty years, owing to more intensive exploration. In addition to the examples of crude oil and uranium quoted above, it is worth noting that known world reserves of bauxite increased ninefold between 1950 and 1970. Those in Jamaica alone, estimated at 300 million tonnes in 1950, were successively revised until in 1970 they stood at 800 million tonnes – despite 104 million tonnes having been extracted since 1950. Several cases are on record where quite recent individual discoveries have significantly increased the size of known world reserves. For example, a recent discovery at Sar Chemah in Iran is said to have virtually doubled known world reserves of copper, which stood at 308 million tonnes in 1967. A recent discovery in Brazil raised known world reserves of iron ore by 10 per cent. Australia, a major producer of uranium, increased its known uranium reserves recoverable at prices up to $10 per lb by over 50 per cent during the year ending June 1973. None of this means we can assume that the reserves will go on being extended indefinitely, nor that future additions will necessarily match world demand projected at compound growth rates, but it strongly suggests that it is unsafe to assume that the end of commercial resource exploration is in sight.

Even if there was evidence of a general increase in the real costs of exploration per ton discovered, it would not necessarily increase prices, for example, if the new discoveries were of higher quality or situated closer to the market, with correspondingly lower transport costs. Exploration costs per ton of reserves discovered can be misleading; for example, due to the fact that recent discoveries tend to be under-reported and that exploration costs tend to be higher in entirely new areas than in areas where drilling is essentially a matter of extending out from known deposits where the geology has been fairly well defined by previous activity. It is worth noting here that although North Sea oil exploration is said to have involved costs per ton discovered many times greater than the 1.5 U.S. cents per ton of the Middle-East discoveries in the 1960s, this will be offset by lower transport costs and (on present policies) by lower taxes and royalties. The point is simply that exploration costs generally represent only a small portion of the total cost and price of the refined product.

Petroleum geologists believe it unlikely that individual discoveries will be as large as those of past finds in the Middle East and that the recent massive crude oil discoveries in the North Sea, Alaska and Siberia are each small in relation to requirements over the next twenty years estimated at compound growth rates. Nevertheless, as far as most mineral and fuel resources are concerned, man's knowledge remains fragmentary and superficial. Large areas of the earth's land surface have yet to be properly surveyed, let alone tested with the drill. For instance, 74 per cent of Argentina has been classified as mineral-rich, but only one-third has been explored.

The oceans cover 71 per cent of the earth's crust, and exploration has only recently begun on a few sections of the continental shelf. The technology required for marine exploitation is in its infancy, although salt, magnesium and bromine have been extracted from sea-water on a commercial basis for several decades. Methods are being investigated to enable vast quantities of, amongst other things, uranium to be extracted (viable, it would seem, if the long-term price of uranium reaches $20 per lb). The offshore oil industry is currently limited to a maximum of 700 ft for exploration – much deeper than only a decade ago – but commercial exploitation of the manganese nodules covering ocean floors, at depths of thousands of feet, has already been started by a Howard Hughes subsidiary; other groups hope to follow.

3. The influence of technology

Under the impact of successive economic and technical changes the size of particular items in the basket labelled 'reserves' keeps changing, as does the variety of the items in the basket and expectations of how long each will last. Anyone attempting to forecast whether the reserves are sufficient to meet long-term needs cannot escape the obligation to display imaginative judgement about future economic and technical circumstances and the measurement of the resources which might then constitute useful reserves. To base long-term forecasts upon current concepts of usable 'reserves' is tantamount to ruling out possibilities for future economic and technical change. If we glance back thirty, fifty or 100 years it is quite clear that no one could have foreseen the changes which have fundamentally altered the size and composition of world 'reserves'. It would be irresponsible to assume that technology will always provide timely solutions against resource depletion, but if there is any truth in the adage that necessity is the mother of invention, it would appear excessively pessimistic to assume that technical progress will halt.

At any given time opportunities to improve existing technologies appear limited, for example, the thermal efficiency of current best-practice fossil-fuel power stations appears to be close to the theoretical limit imposed by the steam-condensing cycle. But few are gifted with the necessary imagination and insight to predict the introduction of techniques not yet invented. In practice the forecaster is usually restricted to considering new technologies which are theoretically possible and those which are practically feasible if their costs fall or if prices rise.

To put this argument in historical perspective it is necessary to point to a few of the countless examples of the effect that technical change has had in the comparatively recent past. It is salutary to recall that until the advent of commercial nuclear power, which is still in its infancy, uranium did not figure in the inventory of usable resources. Crude oil drilling began about 100 years ago, but at first the market was restricted almost entirely to kerosene for lamps. With technical change, the expansion of the market, and great exploration, the size of the economic reserves has steadily increased. The same is true for many other resources. Aluminium, now second to steel in terms of annual production volume, became commercially usable only after the invention of the Hall–Heroult electrolytic extraction process in 1886. Its subsequent commercial development has been linked closely with the development of cheap electric power sources, especially hydro-electric power.

The energy required to produce 1 lb of aluminium by electrolysis has fallen from a 1939 average of 12 kWh to a present-day figure of 8 and a best practice of 6·5; Alcoa is claiming a further 30 per cent reduction for its new process. Early blast furnaces consumed 8 tons of coke for 1 ton of pig

C

iron produced. This fell to 5 tons during the first half of the last century, and is now below 1. Comparing the blast furnace of the mid-1940s with today's, 150 tons of limestone now replace the previous 500 (per 1000 tons of iron produced).

In addition to the introduction of entirely new technologies, the quantity and life of economically recoverable resources has been greatly extended by incremental technical improvements which have reduced the input of ores and fuel per ton of output or permitted the use of ores of lower grade and higher impurity content which were formerly ignored. For example, the average grade of copper ore used in the United States in the 1880s was around 3 per cent. Today it is around 0·6 per cent, and some plants are said to use ores of 0·3 per cent. Taconites are now a commercial source of iron ore, whereas before the Second World War there was no way of commercially extracting iron from these rocks.

There is, of course, no way of stepping thirty, fifty or 100 years into the future to see what techniques will then be available. All we can do, bearing in mind the changes which have occurred in past decades, is to point to technologies which have a reasonable chance of being developed on the basis of current knowledge. It has long been known that non-conventional sources of hydrocarbons exist in very large quantities. Athabasca tar sands alone are estimated to contain 635,000 million barrels of oil – 11 per cent more than current world proven reserves of crude oil. Oil shale deposits in Colorado alone are estimated to contain 1,800,000 million barrels – more than three times the size of world proven reserves of crude oil. Taking a 1965 estimate by the U.S. Geological Survey of world oil shale deposits and assuming a recovery factor of 50 per cent and a yield of 10 gallons of oil per ton of shale, world recoverable reserves from oil shales would be 6,850,000 million barrels – twelve times the size of proven world reserves of crude oil. If conversion techniques are improved to permit the production of 4·5 barrels of synthetic oil from 1 ton of average grade bituminous coal, as engineers have predicted, some idea can be derived of the huge potential supply of oil theoretically obtainable from the estimated 16,800,000 million short tons of world coal reserves.

It may seem superfluous to add further possibilities, but we do so to challenge the concept of 'non-renewability' and the finite nature of fuel and mineral resources. Recycling scrap metal and the use of hydro-electricity are current examples, although it could be argued that their potential is small in relation to future demands extrapolated at compound growth rates. Among the possibilities for escaping from the conceptual straight-jacket of fixed energy resources, the principal ones are fusion, solar and geothermal power. If any of these new sources are developed on a large commercial scale in the next thirty to fifty years, it would in effect remove the constraint of depleting finite fossil fuel reserves. In citing these examples of unconventional sources of hydrocarbons and new energy technologies we do not belittle the technical and environmental problems which may be encountered in developing them. Indeed we would urge that before new technologies are introduced commercially in response to forecasts of imminent world shortages, great care should be taken to examine the environmental and other hazards which these new technologies may present.

4. Conclusions and policy implications

Knowledge about the ultimate size of world mineral resources is fragmentary, and is largely the outcome of commercially-orientated exploration related to past and present costs and prices and to past and present techniques of production and transport. There is simply no way of accurately assessing world reserves of so-called 'non-renewable' resources, nor of anticipating which materials will constitute usable resources in the distant future. Attempts to forecast how long the reserves will last ultimately reflect the forecaster's subjective pessimism or optimism about the future. It would indeed be tragic if policies were based upon false assumptions regarding future consumption levels projected at compound growth rates in ignorance of the long-term effects of changes in relative prices and utilisation efficiencies and the possibilities of substitution and saturation.

The legacy of Malthus on nineteenth-century economic and social policies should make us beware of the impact that neo-Malthusian predictions may have on policies during the remaining quarter of the twentieth century. Computer models can be a useful tool in the social sciences for analysing complex relationships and for portraying possible future scenarios. But we must avoid accepting their predictions as the basis for long-term policy – or worse, as a substitute for it. They can be dangerously misleading to the extent that they encourage the substitution of mathematics for knowledge and computation for understanding. Our Unit's detailed critique of *The Limits to Growth* work points to these dangers.[1]

The real world is so complex that the computer modeller has to simplify and make assumptions and judgements about the nature of complex relationships and often also about the choice of data. His judgements are inevitably, if not deliberately, coloured by his own attitudes and values as well as by his working environment. The validity of the model is only as good as the assumptions and data on which it is based. It is extremely difficult for the modeller to specify all the value-judgements incorporated in a complex socio-economic model and even more difficult for others to rebut any of his more tendentious assumptions.

Complex socio-economic models tend to convey a spurious accuracy with regard to relationships and quantities which are really unknown and are sometimes unknowable. This applies especially to the 'Non-renewable resources' and 'Pollution' subsystems of *The Limits to Growth* model.

The most fundamental and controversial judgements in a socio-economic model purporting to represent long-term trends lie in its assumptions with regard to innovation and technical change, substitution possibilities, human values and policies.

Perhaps the greatest danger of all springs from what we have called 'computer fetishism' – the tendency to endow computer models with an independent power transcending the concepts on which they are based, and thus to assume their predictions somehow predetermine the future.

The key ingredient missing from *The Limits to Growth* work is that of man's ability, through individual and collective choices, to influence his future. Whether such models are biased towards an optimistic or pessimistic view of the future, there is a grave danger that their spurious precision and apparent immutability will divert attention from what can and needs to be done to solve the pressing current problems of the world, e.g. regarding income distribution, resource allocation and social policies.

The central problems in the debate about resource depletion, we believe, are uncertainty and risk: the impossibility of gauging even the approximate size of the world's various types of mineral and fuel reserves which might be usable in the long-term future; the difficulty of gauging how demand will respond to perhaps substantial price changes over a long period and of gauging future substitution possibilities; and the risks that new technologies which now appear promising will prove socially unacceptable or unfeasible to introduce commercially.

One thing is certain, however; while the debate about resource depletion continues to rage important decisions will have to be taken. What practical advice can economists offer to policy-makers?

Believing that market forces will not necessarily provide socially desirable solutions to the important problems surrounding the use of natural resources and that attempts to predict how long the reserves will last will generally not provide reliable guides for long-term policies, we suggest several courses of action which appear relevant to the nature of the problems, including their inherent uncertainties.

(i) *Long-term demand forecasts and substitution possibilities*

Because the root cause of the current pessimism about resource depletion stems from the assumption that demand will continue growing at high compound rates and because long-term extrapolative forecasts tend to be self-fulfilling to the extent that investment decisions are based on them, the first essential is for a searching examination of the factors likely to affect the future growth and composition of demand and for analysis of the scope for policy choices and their respective social costs and benefits, including the possibilities for altering the long-term growth and composition of demand, an examination of substitution possibilities, the more efficient use of materials, methods to prolong product life, and recyling. This approach of investigating the scope for policy choices is inherently more useful than one of relying upon mechanistic long-term projections.

(ii) *Identification of critical minerals and promotion of systematic exploration*

The need for two other courses of action is also self-evident. One is to identify critical minerals whose proven reserves appear low relative to potential demand and for which no immediate substitutes are available. This information is needed as a basis for deciding whether to concentrate scientific effort on developing substitutes and whether some form of rationing is necessary. Also governments and international agencies should give priority to systematic exploration programmes to improve knowledge of the quantities of various mineral resources likely to be recoverable at various costs and prices. Only when knowledge has greatly improved will it be possible to make rational judgements about the need for global resource policies.

(iii) *Research and development (R & D)*

Our third suggestion is perhaps more controversial. R & D on mineral and energy technologies should not be left entirely to market forces. Nuclear power has been brought to its current stage of development largely by government support for R & D. Given the crucial importance of adequate supplies of mineral and fuel resources to maintain and improve living standards, the probability that the lead-times involved in developing new supply sources and substitutes will be long, and the need to regard this type of long-term research and development *up to a point* as a kind of global insurance policy to safeguard the quality of life for future generations, there is a strong case for increasing the level of public funding and also for a more international approach to this type of R & D than has been evident in the past.

There is, of course, much room for debate about how far government support should go, whether it should include the development work necessary for commercial application as well as basic research, and about the criteria for allocating public funds between alternative R & D projects. Important as these questions are, they are subsidiary to the argument for giving priority for public support for R & D in these areas.

Also important is the need to recognise that R & D should not be confined to 'big' path-breaking technologies (e.g. fusion power), but that it should include resource-saving techniques, e.g. recyling mineral wastes, batteries for electric vehicles, public transport and better insulation of buildings and plant.

The need for a more international approach to R & D in these areas is threefold. Unless they get this type of assistance the resource-poor developing countries will be in danger of being crippled by rising world prices, which would not only be highly undesirable in itself but would severely reduce the value of the traditional forms of aid and assistance they receive from the industrialised countries. An international approach to the accumulation and dissemination of scientific knowledge is likely to be more beneficial for the developing countries in the long run than the present policies of the industrialised countries of maintaining proprietary control over scientific and technical knowledge whilst extending financial aid (often with strings attached). The second reason is that each industrialised country stands to benefit from new resource-supplying or resource-saving technologies whenever they are applied. The point is that a major technical development or discovery of new sources, wherever it takes place, will both leave more mineral or fuel resources available for other countries and help break the monopoly power now wielded by OPEC. A third reason is to avoid wasteful duplication in very costly areas of R & D (but *not* to stifle competitive innovation) and to pave the way for a competitive international supply structure when the new techniques reach the point of commercial application.

5. Polarisation between resource-rich and resource-poor countries

Recognising the dangers of an increasing polarisation between high- and low-income per head countries and between resource-rich and resource-poor countries, we urge the need for studies of future conflicts which may arise from these inequalities and ways of avoiding them. If poorly endowed countries cannot attain their reasonable aspirations owing to inability to acquire assured natural resource supplies, this will be a fertile breeding ground for future conflict. The current Middle-East situation has highlighted the fact that the industrialised countries are dependent upon the willingness of the oil-producing countries to supply ever-growing demands rather than leaving oil in the ground to appreciate in value; but the problem has much wider significance. In particular it will require that the resource needs of the developing countries are not submerged in the scramble by the industrialised countries to gain control over natural resources for their own use.

On the other hand, the industrialised countries could help the resource-poor developing countries by pursuing policies to reduce the monopoly power of resource-exporting cartels, such as OPEC. If the industrialised countries became less dependent upon OPEC, leading to a fall in the international price of oil, the resource-poor developing countries would benefit. In the case of a number of minerals such as copper and tin, a higher and more stable price than has often prevailed in the past is necessary to support economic and social development programmes to enable the producing countries to attain acceptable living standards.

6. The institutional framework

A number of factors are likely to require changes in the institutional framework with regard to resource use, especially energy. The most radical proposal so far is that to create an association of big oil-importing nations to exert countervailing power against OPEC, but this has had a lukewarm reception among the importing nations that would stand to lose most in the event of a confrontation which led a united OPEC to withhold its supplies. If the recent massive oil price increases are to be prevented from driving many oil-importing nations into heavy balance-of-payments deficits followed by world-wide deflation and perhaps by competitive devaluations, it may well be necessary to adapt the role of the international economic institutions to provide special credits for countries with oil balance-of-payments deficits and to encourage the oil-producing countries to make their surplus revenues available to the deficit nations in the form of loans or direct investment. No one has a vested interest in creating world-wide recession.

Moves by the resource-producing countries to extend their control over resource supplies, combined in the case of oil with moves by several large importing countries to enter direct deals with the producing countries, seems likely to erode the role of the multinational companies. The primary aim of government policies should be to develop stable international supply arrangements for mineral and fuel resources which satisfy the legitimate interests of both the producing and consuming countries, rather than to preserve a possibly outmoded form of entrepreneurship. Should the multinational companies lose control over production and possibly refining and marketing activities, they could perhaps retain a useful and profitable role in service management (e.g. design engineering, project co-ordination and transport) and through diversification, including the development of substitutes for the resources they previously owned and controlled.

The consuming end may also require institutional changes, perhaps towards greater public control and ownership of energy suppliers and moves by electricity and gas regulatory agencies to replace promotional selling by tariffs which reflect the long-run costs of supply and discourage profligate consumption. In certain cases it may also be necessary to alter existing statutory regulations where they confine public or quasi-public energy suppliers to existing techniques, to enable them to enter different fields such as district heating and solar energy.

These suggestions reflect our view that the physical exhaustion of global resources is only a remote possibility and that it would be gross folly to jettison the aim of better living standards on the supposition that the end of the world is nigh. Certainly there is much room for argument about the desirable pattern of economic growth and how its fruits should be distributed. Equally it is necessary to take a view of possible long-term developments, and prudent to set in hand long-term R & D as a form of global insurance against the uncertainties of the future. Above all, however, it is necessary to recognise that the important questions surrounding the use of mineral and fuel resources involve economic, social and political problems whose solutions are likely to be at variance with the austere zero-growth solution advocated by the neo-Malthusian school.

4 COMMENTS ON THE PAPERS BY ROBINSON, AND SURREY AND PAGE

MICHAEL COMMON

I propose to concentrate on the long-run issues discussed in these papers, in which context both can be regarded as a rebuttal of *The Limits to Growth* proposition that mankind faces the prospect of economic and social collapse due to resource exhaustion. This is not the only source of collapse considered by the Meadows group, and neither of the preceding papers seems to go for an unconditional 'no collapse' forecast. Professor Robinson is more worried about pollution than resource depletion, particularly thermal pollution. Surrey and Page seem to want to identify social and political factors, rather than physical limits, as the critical areas. The interconnections between such problems as resource depletion, pollution, population growth and social conflict are something which we should bear in mind in any discussion of the economics of resource depletion.

It has been said of *The Limits to Growth* that it has had the effect of diverting attention away from the real problems we face. In one respect at least I think this criticism is valid. The debate about economic growth and the environment now seems to be approached by many people as a problem in forecasting the date of world collapse. Robinson and Surrey and Page rather follow this all-or-nothing line: considering only resource depletion, they put the collapse date far into the remote future, so far that it is not something which we need to worry about now. However, concern for future generations is not just a question of whether they have positive or zero stocks of natural resources, or of whether they exist or not. Short of exhaustion and collapse there exists a problem of allocation over time. Economists have long been interested in problems of this sort: marginal adjustments in depletion rates are feasible and may be important. It seems more fruitful to enquire into the allocative consequences of different depletion rates than to dispute the date of collapse. What really worries many people is not that man will not survive the problems raised by Meadows and others, but rather what kind of people the survivors will be. 'The quality of life' is something which economists are wary of discussing, and in so doing they neatly define an area of enquiry. But neat areas of enquiry are just that, and economists should be equally wary of dismissing as foolish the problems raised by those whose perspective is different from their own.

The main argument of both papers can be characterised as follows. The Meadows group is wrong when it forecasts resource exhaustion in the twenty-first century, and hence there is no physical problem of resource availability in the long run. There are four specific reasons cited as the sources of the Meadows group's error:

(1) An understatement of the size of ultimately recoverable stocks of natural resources.

(2) A failure to allow for the augmentation of commercially exploitable stocks which occurs as prices rise with depletion.

(3) An insufficient allowance for the effects of rising prices on the demand for natural resource-based products.

(4) An insufficient allowance for the resource stock–augmenting effects of technical progress.

While I have no intention of defending *The Limits to Growth* on any of these points, I do wish to consider them further, since they raise questions which the contributors have either ignored or glossed over.

In order to fix ideas, it will be useful to consider the production of raw materials (inputs to production for final consumption) from natural resources *in situ*. Specifically, consider the production of a usable primary energy source from fossil fuels in the ground. This requires inputs of labour, capital, and the resource, according to say

$$Q_t = A\, L_t^{\alpha_1} K_t^{\alpha_2} M_t^{\alpha_3} \qquad (1)$$

where Q is the raw material output, measured in energy units;

L is labour input; K is capital input; and M is resource input. The use of the Cobb–Douglas form here is purely illustrative. The total, ultimately recoverable, stock of the natural resource can be measured in several ways. However measured, it is in the nature of the case that it is finite. This finite total stock can be denoted by $\bar{M}$.

The first of the points raised in the preceding papers concerns the size of $\bar{M}$. This is relevant to an argument about the date of exhaustion, but is not relevant to the question of whether there exists an intertemporal allocation problem. The production of Q is subject to the constraint

$$\sum_{t=0}^{T} M_t \leqslant \bar{M}$$

For any finite $\bar{M}$, this constraint means that the higher is Q during t, the smaller must the sum of Q for all future periods be, inputs of labour and capital being held at their period t levels. The allocation problem is complicated by the fact that fossil fuels can alternatively be used as inputs to the chemicals and plastics industries. In some such uses there exist possibilities for recycling, in which case the constraint imposed by the initial stock endowment does not apply. (The fact that fossil fuels have uses other than energy provision appears to be ignored by Professor Robinson, especially in his remarks on the medium-term prospects for oil.)

It is quite conceivable that $\bar{M}$ is so large that the finite stock problem is not one we need worry about very much. However, it is also true that the stock is not homogeneous. $\bar{M}$ exists as 'stuff in the ground', and $\bar{M}$ consists of deposits of crude oil, natural gas, tar sands, oil shale and coal. These deposits vary in the quantity of resource-bearing material which it is necessary to process to get one unit of Q. They also vary in their effective proximity to locations where raw materials are used, and from whence the labour and equipment for extraction come. Where a resource stock is non-homogeneous, it has to be assumed that the basic pattern is one of exploitation down a decreasing quality gradient. (Exceptions to this trend are, of course, to be expected.) This is precisely the point which has been made in these papers in identifying the second source of error in *The Limits to Growth*. Both papers argue that as a stock is depleted, so the price rises, making the exploitation of lower quality deposits commercially viable. Both papers overlook the implications of this for the physical aspect of the allocation problem.

The effect of declining quality can be incorporated into equation (1) by writing it as

$$Q_t = AL_t^{\alpha_1}K_t^{\alpha_2}M_t^{\alpha_3}\left\{\bar{M} - \sum_{i=0}^{t-1} M_i\right\}^{\alpha_4} \qquad (2)$$

It is clear that if capital and labour inputs are held constant, Q_t falls with t. Alternatively, to maintain Q_t constant, inputs of capital and/or labour have to increase with t. At time t, considering future periods these effects will be the greater the greater is M_t. Where a mineral resource is exploited down a decreasing quality gradient it must also be expected that the volume of residuals per unit of raw material output will increase over time.

The implications of the varying quality of fossil-fuel deposits do not lie in the remote future, as two examples will show:

(*a*) It is currently accepted that rising oil prices will lead to some substitution of coal for oil, as a primary energy source. Typically, digging coal out of the ground is a less pleasant and convenient way of getting an energy source than pumping oil out of wells. This is reflected in relative extraction costs: U.K. miners now appear to be seeking to have it reflected even more markedly.[1]

(*b*) Reference has been made in the preceding paper to the large quantities of oil available from tar sands and oil shales, and to the fact that the price of conventional crude oil is now such that the best of these deposits are on the margin of commercial viability. In the United States the highest quality oil shales contain about 1·5 barrels of oil per ton of shale: in 1972 the United States produced 3885 million barrels of oil. A very quick calculation indicates that producing this oil output from the best oil shale would involve processing 2590 million tons of shale! This implies that a rather serious residuals problem is associated with any switch to exploiting oil shales: it is not clear how far process costings include any allowance for handling the residuals to meet any environmental requirements.[2]

Resource exploitation down a decreasing quality gradient is not necessarily inconsistent with economic growth, as that is currently measured. If in successive periods, a constant output of the primary energy source is maintained by increased inputs of capital and/or labour, then G.N.P. will rise, all other things being equal. It is, of course, unlikely that other things will remain equal in the face of a rising price for the primary energy source. This is the third point at which *The Limits to Growth* is said to err. Changing relative prices would be expected to lead to changes in the total demand for energy as a raw material, and to changes in the way that energy gets used. But, as Professor Robinson notes, this is a complicated question about which we actually know rather little. Forecasting the demand for primary energy sources and the actual depletion rates for fossil fuels is very difficult, and it seems certain that any forecast now existing will, *ex post*, prove to be wrong. But the impossibility of long run depletion forecasts does not imply that there does not exist an intertemporal allocation problem.

There are several dimensions to this problem, as can be seen from equations (1) and (2), where capital and labour can be substituted for the resource in the production of the raw material. It is usual to consider the labour input as constant, and concentrate on substitution between capital and natural resources. With capital as foregone final consumption, we can, to some degree, choose now among alternative combinations of resource depletion and savings for a given endowment to the next generation, specified in terms of Q. If the problem is looked at in this way, it turns out, not surprisingly, that the key question is the degree of substitutability between capital and natural resources in the production of raw materials. I suggest that this is something about which we actually know rather little. I would also suggest that the actual problem has an important feature which typically does not appear in the economist's model of it. Depleting finite stocks of fossil fuels closes our future options in a way that depreciating a capital stock does not, in that the former is irreverisble while the latter is not. Given labour and natural resources, capital equipment can be created from scratch: if, today, the world's entire capital stock were destroyed, it could be recreated. Given labour and capital equipment, natural resources cannot be created: if, today, the world's entire stock of fossil fuels were destroyed, it could not be recreated.[3] This asymmetry between capital and resource stocks, and its significance, is perhaps obscured by the tendency to analyse these problems in the context of one-good models.[4]

Thus far, I have been guilty of taking the state of technology as given and fixed. A few general, and perhaps obvious, points seem in order on this subject. First, technical progress is not a free good: its provision requires that, at some point in time, inputs be diverted away from other uses. When looking at a particular productive activity this is sometimes overlooked because it is not that activity which bears the cost. What is relevant here is not just government-financed research and development, but also some proportion of the costs of the industrial and educational infrastructure. This opens up another dimension of the allocative problem: it would be nice to know how far the future effects of resource scarcity can be offset by investment in research, but we really have very little idea. It would seem unwise to extrapolate past experience of cost and benefits in this area. I am quite prepared to believe that it is possible, by investment programmes for capital equipment and the state of knowledge, so to arrange things that the physical effects of declining resource quality can be offset. I am not prepared to believe that this must necessarily be the case.

Economists have done a great deal of work on technical progress which reduces labour and/or capital inputs per unit of output. In the present context, resource-saving technical progress is at least as important, but rather little work appears to have been done on this. Some interesting work is now being done on energy inputs to production. One thing which emerges from some of this work is the dangers inherent in assessing alternative processes solely on a monetarised basis: process rankings depend on relative prices, and can change with a changing price structure. This is obvious, but appears to be frequently overlooked. An example can be taken from agriculture and technical aid to the less developed countries.[5] In advanced arable farming systems, high labour and land productivities are achieved largely by supplementing human and solar energy inputs with fossil-fuel based energy inputs. This is obvious where farm machinery is concerned, less obvious, but perhaps more important, where fertilisers are concerned. Such systems are 'advanced' only where labour and land are expensive relative to fossil-fuel based energy inputs. Their exportation to less developed countries makes sense only if accompanied by a commitment to ensure that those countries have, and will continue to have, access to cheap non-human energy. In the absence of such a commitment, the 'green revolution' may well become a sick joke of horrific proportions.

Finally, it is necessary to say something about the completely new energy technologies which have been mentioned, of which the most interesting appear to be solar energy and nuclear fusion. As regards solar energy, tapping this source of income (other than by agriculture and forestry) would obviously be a 'good thing'. It has been pointed out that, once installed, a solar-energy system involves low running costs, zero pollution and zero depletion. As far as large-scale secondary energy provision applications are concerned, the snag appears to be in the installation and is such that solar-based electricity, for example, would not be cheap. To quote a NASA report: 'it is shown that even for optimistic projections of technology, electric power from large-scale terrestial use of solar cells is approximately two to three orders of magnitude more costly than current electric power generation from either fossil or nuclear plants'.[6] This assessment uses 1971 U.S. prices for inputs (land costs being excluded!), so is subject to modification as these prices change. Unfortunately, the input breakdown in the report is not fine enough to make it possible to say how the solar/conventional cost ratio would move for likely price changes. As regards nuclear energy and electricity generation, Professor Robinson has indicated the problems which go with fission and the advantages of fusion. It appears to be the case that it has yet to be shown, in principle, that fusion is a viable way of generating electricity.

5 DISCUSSION

MR HARRISON (Open University): I am very worried that in fact many of the questions that have been answered in papers that we have heard are not the right questions to be asking in this situation. If I may just go through some of these things. We have had some slight mention of a lead time, but I think this is an absolutely crucial point. It is all very well to say that we can make use of tar sands, that we can make use of fission energy, and so on, but you have to ask yourself: what is involved in actually making this come about? Some of the sums that I have seen done on this are absolutely horrific. There are not enough material resources, nor enough manpower resources to do it in the sort of time scale that is envisaged. I have come across very few people who seriously question the near exhaustion of oil over the next twenty to thirty years, and that is a very short time indeed in which to get these massive new industries under way.

Secondly, I think there is a factor going to come in which has not really appeared in the past, which is connected with the sheer scale of operations which industrialisation has now reached. It is one thing to say 'all right, we want to double our power supplies; we have one power station and we need to build another'; it is a completely different operation, a different order of magnitude altogether, to say 'all right, we have 100 power stations, we want to double them, therefore we have to build 200'. The relationship between the amount of capital available and current rates of consumption is different; the manpower ratio is different, and so on. This is something that economists ought to be looking at very carefully indeed.

Thirdly, I would say that there are, I think, going to be serious limitations of manpower. We have talked of the use of tar sands. Tar sands have to be mined and, so far as we know at the moment, it is not a matter of just drilling holes in the earth, which you leave. I have seen an estimate that something like 100,000 or 200,000 miners would be required to produce the sort of oil supplies that the United States requires. Where are these men going to come from? Are a sufficient number of people going to be prepared to undertake what is probably not a particularly attractive job? How are you going to get them into what is a fairly inhospitable part of the world and create what will now be considered reasonably civilised conditions for them? These are important factors. If you want to exploit nuclear energy, where are you going to get trained engineers from? This could be a very serious problem.

I think it is a very great pity that most of the papers at this conference are concentrating on energy rather than on other materials, because I have a very strong suspicion that it is the shortage of other materials used in comparatively small quantities, but which are crucial to various industrial processes, which will turn out to be the real limiting factor.

All that I can say is that there has been far too little work done on this subject, as far as I can see. I think that far too much has been said too glibly about the possibility of substituting one material as we go short of something else, because in many cases one can say already that it is not a matter of substituting one material for another in the same type of application; you will have to find a completely new way of doing something. To take one simple, trivial and obvious example: if mercury is no longer available for making thermometers and you cannot find another suitable liquid, almost certainly you would have to devise some sort of electronic device. These substitution problems are enormous. If you already have one very large industry which is dependent on one source and you then have to switch over to another industry with a completely different source, how are you going to make that switch? What sort of inefficiencies are going to result while you are trying to run the two in parallel? It is going to put up costs – at least for a short time – enormously. I imagine that if the cost barrier is too great the economic forces will not work.

The next point is that it was suggested that efficiency in using energy will increase. I am not at all sure that this is true, because if we cannot get the raw materials that we require we may not be able to run, say, power stations at such a high temperature, because we have to use less efficient materials, and therefore we get less power out. Certainly the amount of extra energy required just to get energy out of tar sands, compared with getting energy out of oil, is by no means negligible. So I think that one of the things going against us will be a decreasing efficiency in the use of energy and probably also in the use of other materials.

PROFESSOR ROBINSON: On the long lead times I think that a source of confusion here is the idea that one day you will have to replace *all* your oil. Clearly the system does not work like that. It is not a question of one day replacing American crude oil by shale oil; the thing will take place gradually. Consequently, there is a much longer lead time than one might imagine.

The second thing is the *size* of the change that takes place. Many people have said that the system is bigger and consequently it is much more difficult to change. As a simple arithmetical point, if you look at expansion in a growing system and compare a point later in time with one early in time a given percentage change inevitably is a lot bigger. But why is it that we assume now that the size of the change that we have to cope with in the future is going to be impossible to deal with, whereas in the past we have managed to deal with it?

MR JOHN DAVOLL (Conservation Society): It seems to me that the first two speakers have a very abstract sense of what goes on. It does not seem to relate at all to the real world in which terribly unpleasant things happen. Professor Robinson seems to think that substitution can bring in other energy sources with relatively little trouble; but really it is not like that at all, because what we have become conditioned to, and dependent on, is the continual rise in energy consumption of material throughput that our industry consists of; so that your trouble arises not when you are compelled to change over in a smooth way to something else but, rather abruptly, as has happened now. Let us take the case where nuclear energy might be substituted for oil. Have you tried to work out just how many nuclear reactors you need to install merely to continue your rising energy consumption and keeping our present supply as it is? You find that the number is quite unfeasible. So that one has the situation where there is tremendous difficulty in maintaining the growth that one has depended on hitherto to suppress social problems of inequality, and the evidence now is that when this happens you get very difficult social tensions which may be so severe that either social disorder or break-down will occur.

The difficulty really arises from the fact that economists have become so conditioned to growth – and I except certain honourable members of the profession – that they are quite unwilling to work out other ways of responding to the situation other than going for more energy. So really they make a tremendous and parochial underestimate of the difficulties of switching from one energy source to another.

The other thing that I find completely absent from the economist's mind is any idea of just where we are going; although Professor Robinson did admit that we might actually, by using fission reactors, expose the human race to the risk of extinction, this was passed over rather lightly towards the end of the talk, just as a man who has developed some synthetic food might add as a throwaway line: 'It was violently poisonous, but we are still working on it.' It was quite wrong to suggest, I submit, that if we get deep into nuclear reactors we shall at some point say: 'Enough; we now have enough – we will cut off.' Once we get a little pregnant with this idea, that will be it.

So we have an ethical decision here which cannot be re-solved by cost–benefit analysis but which is a very simple one, and that is, do we trust the bloody-minded and incompetent human race to master just the installed reactor and the process-ing plants, let alone the accumulating nuclear wastes, for ever? This is really only one part of the other scenario, which is implicit, in that we are going to build up this tremendously industrialised planet which will depend for its survival, its employment and its food supply on the management for ever of these resources and phasing a new world in an attempt to prevent people from starving and from going to war when the previous one runs out. I suggest that there could be few more irresponsible recommendations.

6 OPTIMAL DEPLETION OF A REPLENISHABLE RESOURCE: AN EVALUATION OF RECENT CONTRIBUTIONS TO FISHERIES ECONOMICS

JOHN BUTLIN

1. Introduction

The theory relating to optimal rates of depletion of stocks of non-replenishable natural resources has been developed, if a little sporadically, throughout this century. The theory of optimal rates of use of *replenishable* resources does not seem to have had any such comprehensive development, and the work that has been undertaken has been specifically directed towards one or other of the two main replenishable resources – forestry and fisheries. It is to the latter of these that this paper is devoted. More specifically it is confined to the major developments that have taken place in fisheries economics over the last five years.

There was a time when the fish resources of the sea were considered 'inexhaustible'. Increased total demand for animal protein, as a result of increased global population and of increased *per capita* demand, has meant that the pressure on the world's agricultural and fishing industries to provide protein has increased. These two major sources of protein are not totally unrelated, as high-quality protein (usually fish-meal) is an important ingredient in most animal feeds. Thus fisheries have been required to supply an increasing proportion of the increased total demand for animal protein. As a consequence, known commercially viable fish stocks have been exploited more intensively, the increase in price making lower-valued species and less dense stocks commercially viable at the extensive margin. The problems of potential over-fishing raise problems both for the economist and for the biologist involved in fisheries management. For the economist the main problem is the over-allocation of productive factors to the exploitation of an unappropriated resource. The need to define the socially optimal catch per unit time over the life of the fishery (that sequence of catches which will maximise the discounted present-value of the Ricardian rent from the fishery), and to recommend policies which will achieve this without causing further misallocation of factors to the industry, is the *raison d'être* of fisheries economics.

It has been noted elsewhere[4] that the theory of the economic behaviour of fishing units, acting individually or as a fleet, on a particular fishing ground or on a series of grounds, has a relatively short history. Although Marshall[20] (pp. 166–7 and 369–72) addressed himself to the problems of diminishing returns to inputs into fishing, the first article that directed its attention explicitly to the economic basis of the over-fishing problem (the observed tendency, paradoxically, for fishing fleets to exploit a commercially viable stock to the point at which the existence of the stock, and thus its commercial viability, are threatened) was by Scott Gordon in 1953.[14] From then until the late 1960s, the work in fisheries economics either refined or qualified the work of Gordon (see, for example, Scott,[28] Crutchfield[8] and Turvey[34] or undertook empirical investigations into particular commercial fisheries, developing the model from the basic theory as presented in Gordon's paper (see especially the work by Crutchfield and Zeller[11] and by Crutchfield and Pontecorvo.[10]

The last quinquennium has seen a resurgence of interest in fisheries economics. Although theoretical developments have thus far outnumbered empirical improvements in models for evaluating existing fisheries' management policies, the direction and extent of the progress made can be usefully assessed by using the Scott Gordon model as a standard against which to evaluate recent contributions. In the next section a stylised version of Gordon's model is presented, and the remainder of the paper is devoted to evaluating the more recent work on the basis of this.

2. Uncontrolled exploitation of an unappropriated fishing ground

The essence of Gordon's explanation of over-fishing is that it is attributable to the absence of ownership of the fishing ground. In the absence of private ownership, the objective of each individual exploiting the fishing ground will be to maximise his *current* profit. With free entry, boats will enter the fishery until all rent potentially attributable to the fishing ground is dissipated. It is useful to compare this situation with commercial agriculture, an industry with some similarity to fishing except that some individuals hold title to all factors employed. In an agricultural system where the land is worked by tenant farmers, the existence of super-normal profits will encourage expansion of the industry until these profits have been completely competed away. (Each producer will produce only a small proportion of the total output.) In this situation all factors are earning their marginal social product and there is no misallocation of factors. If, however, we now regard land as common property, and include the previous payment to land as being part of the surplus then there will be an over-allocation of factors in expanding the industry to the point at which supernormal profits *plus* the payment to land have been competed away. If, in the former situation, factor allocation was efficient, then increasing the inputs of factors other than land must result in factor misallocation, that is privately owned factors will be used beyond the point at which their social marginal product is equal to their factor cost. (Once the rationale has been developed, it can be seen that the possibility of using factors of production to the point at which their marginal productivity is negative cannot be discounted.) The explanation has been developed in an agricultural context, but it transfers directly to any intra-marginal fishing ground. In the long run, fishing grounds will be exploited to the point at which the marginal cost of catching an extra unit of fish equals the *average* revenue product of the extra unit of fish caught, i.e. all rent, plus the factor payment potentially attributable to that ground, have been competed away.

The reason for dissipation of the rent during the uncontrolled exploitation of a common-property resource has frequently been a cause of confusion when first encountered. The important part of the analysis, and that worth repeating for emphasis, is that if the resource is privately owned, the rent to the resource is a cost of production. If the resource is not privately owned, the rent potentially attributable to it is a residual, and each individual exploiter of that resource wishes to maximise his share of the rent remaining when he enters the industry. With perfect competition, the marginal product of each input to the fishery to an individual producer is equal to its factor cost With free entry to the common-property fishery, an individual fisherman will enter the fishery as long as the residual earnings per unit output exceed the opportunity cost (factor cost) of the inputs.

The explanation of over-fishing was thus shown by Scott Gordon to be due to unlimited access to the resource. He developed a model in which the economic and biological aspects of fisheries could be interrelated, thereby providing an analytical tool for evaluating alternative modes of exploitation of the fishery. The model comprised four equations:

$$P = f(L) \tag{1}$$
$$L = g(P,E) \tag{2}$$
$$C = h(E) \tag{3}$$
$$C = L \tag{4}$$

Equation (1) indicates that *ceteris paribus*, the size of the population, P, of a given species of fish on a particular fishing ground is determined by the quantity of fish, L, taken from the ground at a point in time. (Other biological factors, such as natural mortality of fish, are assumed constant.) The second equation is the production function of the fishery, landings (output) of fish being dependent on the fish stock and the level of variable inputs used, E. (E is a mnemonic for fishing effort, which in turn ought to be regarded as an aggregate index of inputs into the fishery.) Implicitly (from the accompanying diagrams in Gordon's article) $g_P, g_E > 0$ and (from the existence of a maximum rate of landings from the ground that is sustainable over time, achievable with a particular level of effort) $g_{PP}, g_{EE} \leqslant 0$. The third equation is the cost function. It is assumed that, with the supply of factors being perfectly elastic to the fishermen on this ground, cost is proportional to the level of effort. The factor of proportionality is the per unit cost of effort. Finally, it is assumed that the landings from this ground have no effect on the price of fish. Hence, the fourth equation expresses the equilibrium condition in an uncontrolled fishery, where the fishery will be exploited to the point at which total cost is equal to total revenue (or, average cost equals average revenue). It is also possible, using Gordon's model, to define for this ground, the optimum fishing intensity, i.e. the level of E that maximises $L - C$.

Gordon labelled this category of model 'bio-economic', indicating that, in the model, an attempt had been made to incorporate the characteristics of the fish stock as well as the behaviour of the economic units concerned. As the first complete model of a fishery it was to revolutionise the approach taken in fisheries economics. However, it can be seen in retrospect that the model was deficient in several ways.

(*a*) It was not explicitly dynamic. The adjustments of the fish stock to a greater or lesser level of fishing effort, and the feedback from this to the rate of increase in stock biomass was not allowed for. Also, there was no explicit attempt to include the reaction of the fishing fleets to changes in catches between seasons.

(*b*) Whilst, implicitly, the failure of the unregulated fishery to allocate factors efficiently is an example of Bator's 'ownership externality' or 'failure by enforcement'[1] the more general problem of the ways in which certain external effects hamper efficient factor allocation are not dealt with thoroughly.

(*c*) The model, as developed, did not allow for the uncertainty inherent in fishing. Although the subsequent empirical investigations into fisheries management[8, 9] must obviously have had a stochastic specification, the manipulation of error structures is inadequate as a means of incorporating the effects of uncertainty upon factor allocation in the fishery.

(*d*) Whilst Gordon's model advanced significantly the analysis and prescription of fisheries' management programmes, it was of limited use as a tool on which to base policy decisions relating to any particular fishery.

(None of the foregoing should be considered as detracting from the progress represented, *at the time it was published*, by Scott Gordon's paper. Let it be emphasised again that these four limitations are being discussed with the benefit of considerable hindsight.)

The four limitations to Gordon's analysis provide a useful

basis from which to evaluate recent developments in fisheries economics. However, before moving to the recent literature, it is worth noting, in general terms, the changing environment of the world's fisheries against which these papers have been written.

3. The state of the world's fishing industries

In 1970 global consumption of fish, for all purposes, was approximately 65 million tons, having grown at an average annual rate of 5·5 per cent per annum from 1949 to 1951. Much of the increase in world consumption of fish since 1950 has been in the form of 'reduced' fish (fish-meal and fish-oil). Of the total consumption of fish in 1970, the developed countries accounted for about one-half, the remainder being distributed in approximately equal shares between the less developed countries and the centrally planned economies. (The differences in *per capita* intake of fish protein that are implied when relative proportions of the world's population are set against these figures are sufficiently striking as to require no further comment.)

The pattern of global demand, as described above, has changed over the post-war period. The supply situation has changed more dramatically, and may be more indicative of the concern now frequently expressed concerning an industry which, for many countries, is peripheral (both in terms of its contribution to G.N.P. and in terms of the proportion of the labour force it employs). Consider that part of the world's fish stocks which are commercially viable, but not yet fully exploited, as being a measure of the global excess supply of fish. Robinson[25] estimates that in 1966 the unharvested potential of all such stocks of marine and freshwater species, as a proportion of the total stocks available, was almost 58 per cent. By 1970 this figure had fallen below 46 per cent. He further estimates that by 1980 the proportion will have fallen to 30 per cent, and that the total potentially available supply will be taken by the year 2000. Whilst we have all (hopefully) learned to be wary of accepting, too readily, global estimates and predictions since the recent spate of interest in 'world models', these figures help to illustrate the severity of the problem.

In the light of this information, it is not surprising that this decade has seen the appropriation of contiguous continental-shelf fishing grounds or contiguous spawning areas by states off the east and west coasts of South America, the north coast of Africa, by Iceland, and by several other states; nor is it surprising that the Law of the Sea Conference, to be held this year in Caracas,* is expected to ratify some form of agreement on coastal state custodianship of contiguous fishing grounds; nor, given the world shortage of fish protein, and its consequent increase in value, is it surprising that, in the absence of effective regulation to limit the total catch taken from the fishing grounds involved, many fisheries have 'failed' in the past five years.

With this background information in mind, it is appropriate now to examine recent contributions to fisheries economics in the light of the four limitations to the Scott Gordon model that were listed above. It will be recalled that these are:

(*a*) that the model was essentially static;

(*b*) that the problem of factor misallocation due to the pervasiveness of externalities was not adequately handled;

(*c*) that the problem of incorporating the uncertainty inherent in fishing was not tackled, the model being deterministic; and

(*d*) that the model as developed was not potentially able to provide an adequate basis with which to formulate policies towards particular fisheries.

(i) *Dynamic models of the fishery*

Theoretically, perhaps the most successful extension of the theory of the fishery over the last five years has been the development of a fairly explicit dynamic model of fisheries behaviour. For the most part, the developments have been effected by applications of the recent extensions of neo-classical capital theory to this aspect of applied economics. The most complete exposition of this is to be found in the contribution by Quirk and Smith.[23] Others who have used this approach are Plourde,[22] and Thompson *et al.*[33] The first part of Quirk and Smith's paper compares the competitive general equilibrium model of allocation in an economy with two consumer goods (fish, harvested competitively from an open access ground, and

* 1974 (Ed.).

one other consumer good produced by independent firms), and one non-reproducible input which has to be allocated between the two industries. Comparing this model with a dynamic welfare-maximising model indicates that the former does not maximise welfare because of open access to the fishing ground, Bator's 'ownership externality'. However, a unit tax on fishing firms corrects this. An alternative solution is to appropriate the fisheries. Extensions of the model later in the paper include the inclusion of two independent fish species and the production of one 'other' good that can either be allocated to consumption or production. Again, the competitive model does not maximise social welfare due to the externality that arises because of open access to the fishery, and again one possible corrective measure is the imposition of a lump-sum tax on catches in both fishing industries (the proceeds being returned directly to consumers). An alternative efficient solution is for the fisheries to be appropriated in such a way that only one firm exploits each ground. If more than one firm exploits each appropriated ground then the competitive solution does not maximise social welfare and the appropriate lump-sum taxes have to be applied to the catches of each firm exploiting the ground. In all the above cases the taxes imposed reflect the marginal social user cost per unit of fish caught for each particular species. (A tax imposed on a party bringing about an external diseconomy, at the level at which the marginal increment in social welfare due to the reduction in the diseconomy is equal to the marginal cost of effecting this reduction by the party responsible, is the easiest way of controlling an activity the full cost of which is not borne by the producer. That is, as long as the tax proceeds can be redistributed solely to the parties experiencing a loss in welfare.) The paper does proceed to other extensions of the model, but these need not concern us here. The question that needs to be posed is: 'What contribution to the economic behaviour of fisheries does this paper make?'

The first contribution that this paper, and others in the same vogue, make is that they enable one to examine the behaviour of the fishery out of equilibrium. Prior to the work of Quirk and Smith, the behavioural theory of the fishery had been formulated entirely in terms of equilibrium solutions (with the exception of Crutchfield and Zellner's work[11]). Maybe this had been a result of the attempt that had been made by most workers in this field to incorporate the maximum sustainable yield (M.S.Y.)* curve into their analyses to evaluate the effect of fishing pressure on the stock level. However, by definition the M.S.Y. curve is an equilibrium relationship and when incorporated into models of fisheries gives only long-run equilibrium solutions. Smith[32] noted this shortcoming of traditional models in a paper to which reference will be made below. The reduction of the solutions to the constrained dynamic optimisation problem to phase space diagrams enables the stability of certain input/stock combinations to be examined. One important aspect of this is that the conditions under which fishing pressure can lead to the commercial extinction of a species can be easily recognised. (Gould[15] has shown that this is not explicitly excluded from traditional models of commercial fisheries.)

The third principal advance in theory that comes out of Quirk and Smith's paper is the attempt to integrate, into an economic model of a fishery, interactions between species. Fisheries biologists have been trying to understand interspecies relationships (or relationships between different levels of trophic chains) for some time, and the work of Garrod[13] is especially worth noting. It is to be considered a significant advance to the behavioural theory, however, when a model is developed into which various types of species interaction can be incorporated.

This is by no means all that one could find to appraise in this particular piece. We shall return to it briefly below in connection with other matters. However, other pieces of work which are explicitly dynamic deserve attention.

An evaluation of recent literature on fisheries economics would be incomplete without reference to the work of Smith.[32] He developed a model that specifically incorporates the several types of externalities that are to be found in fisheries. He emphasises that these arise solely because of the common-property nature of the fishery. The incorporation of a general growth function into the model, the assumption of profit maximisation on the part of each fisherman (who is assumed to be homogeneous in every respect) and a condition that permits the industry to expand and contract (if necessary at different rates) complete the model. The formal solution of the model

---

* See Gould[15] for a thorough exposition of this concept.

again allows the system to be reduced to two autonomous equations, thus enabling the complete system to be represented in phase space. The model is capable of extremely diverse interpretations, including the conditions under which exploitation of the fishery is not commercially viable, situations under which there is only one stable combination of fish stock and industry capacity, and again a comparison of sole owner versus competitive recovery. It is also extremely useful in that it allows the effects of the several common types of externality to be incorporated into the model, and their effects upon the fishery to be examined separately. Reference will be made to this in more detail below, however.

Hanneson's work[17] is particularly interesting. It is not possible to do it justice in such a brief survey of the literature but its essential features can at least be outlined. There are two parts to his paper. The first is a relatively simple application of the dynamic theory of the fishery, but with several important modifications. The first is that it allows for fish of different ages, and attempts to take into account the age–class aspect of the composition of a fish stock. Secondly, a rather more specific biomass* growth curve is incorporated into the model whereas previous models have used only extremely general growth functions in which the rate of growth of the total weight of fish in the stock is a function of the size of the stock.

Hanneson formulates this problem as an optimal control problem and solves the system in the prescribed manner as an intertemporal welfare maximisation problem. The necessary conditions for an optimum imply that under certain conditions there exists an optimal strategy that involves exploiting the particular year-class for a finite period that is shorter than the average life of the species. If the social rate of discount is decreased (*ceteris paribus*) then the period during which the stock should be exploited is diminished, and the age at which the year-class should initially be exploited is postponed. The former effect is entirely consistent with rates of extraction of natural resources as reflected by the social rate of time preference, but the shorter 'harvest' period needs further explanation. To some extent the result is inherent in the model, but there is

* The term 'biomass' simply means the total weight of fish in the stock.

an intuitive explanation which sheds some light on the problem. The end of the exploitation of the year-class (in isolation) is denoted as the time at which the cost per unit of fishing mortality (the defined opportunity cost of fishing effort in this context) is equal to the value of the catch from that particular year-class. The time at which exploitation of the fishery is terminated is therefore fixed, and postponing the start of the fishing of the year-class inevitably results in a shortening of the period over which the stock is exploited. Although this result may appear to be contrived, it has important implications. It is the first attempt that has been made to incorporate the possibility that a constant rate of catch from the fishery may not be the optimal policy. It seems that it has taken a long time for this to percolate through from the theory of extraction of other, non-renewable resources.

However, the more interesting part of the paper is that in which Hanneson introduces a fishery with several year-classes that are indiscriminately fished (that is, caught with gear that takes all the fish it encounters, regardless of age, once they have been recruited into the fishery). The optimal policy is not that all year-classes should be fished at their optimal age, as might have been expected from the first part of the paper. This result would, of course, conform to the concept, commonly accepted amongst fisheries biologists (and inherent in the concept of the equilibrium yield curve) that the harvest from the fishery should not vary from year to year under optimal management conditions (when the stock was being fished to maximum sustainable yield). The concept of an indiscriminate fishing technology indicates that the concept of a eumetric regime, that is, fishing with equipment that can select different year–classes of fish is being ruled out. However, the optimal policy, even under the eumetric regime, is not a time-invariant catch rate. Hanneson's explanation is:

> If fish of optimal age are left to grow . . . the total biomass will grow at a rate that is lower than the social rate of discount, and if there was nothing else to be considered, this would be an inoptimal policy. But if the fishery has been halted for one year, then two year-classes will be available, one of optimal age and one a year older. Since the cost per ton of fish caught is inversely related to the size of stock from

which it is taken, it may be optimal to let some year-classes grow beyond optimal age.

This result is entirely plausible, and one suspects that the application of the theory of optimal replacement of capital of different vintages ought to have yielded similar results. (The only reason for which the results may not have been similar is that it is easier to distinguish between different vintages of capital for the purposes of replacement than it is to distinguish between different year-classes of fish for the purpose of selective capture.)

An application of this more general model to the data on Icelandic cod stocks gives interesting results. Assuming a constant natural mortality of fish, and a constant opportunity cost of fishing as well as a constant fish price, shows that 'periodic' fishing yields both a greater total catch and a higher capitalised value of the resource rent than does sustained fishing. The reason for this is that the periodic regime reduces the effect of using non-selective fishing gear. Reducing the opportunity cost of fishing effort still produces the same quantitative result, but the periodicity is now more regular, and the time during which the stock is not fished conforms more closely with the optimal age to exploitation than was previously the case. This result can be explained by the fact that strong year-classes (above-average cohorts resulting from better than average survival from the first year) are more important in determining the size and rate of growth of the stock. Again, changing the rate of discount produces qualitatively similar results.

Although not yet published, this piece of work is of considerable importance. It changes the nature of the management problem completely. The problem is no longer to find that regime under which the application of a certain level of fishing effort over time to a particular resource produces the optimal level of catch and resource rent, but rather to find that particular periodic regime that effects this. On a practical level it makes the management problem that much more difficult, unless the fishing fleets can be rotated around the stocks so that the fishing fleet is fully utilised, whilst at the same time each fishery is fished under an optimal periodic regime. It is necessary under such an arrangement that the cost of rotating the fleets around the stock is not significantly higher than that of keeping them fishing at a constant average rate on particular grounds.

This section can be concluded with a brief summary of the advances in the dynamic theory of the fishery that have been made over the past five years.

(*a*) The use of certain formal techniques of dynamic analysis has made it possible to examine the fishery in disequilibrium states.

(*b*) There has been more precise specification of the conditions under which inefficient competitive exploitation can be remedied.

(*c*) At least two attempts have been made to incorporate into the models explicit stock growth functions.

(*d*) Results from recent developments in capital theory have been applied to render more tractable the problems that arise when theoretical models are modified to make them more nearly approach 'real world' situations.

(*e*) There has been an attempt to incorporate into the problem of optimal rates of exploitation of a particular stock the fact that the fish comprising any particular stock are of different 'vintages'.

(The question as to whether these developments have addressed the important problems in the environment of fisheries exploitation that was evolving whilst they were being produced is left to the concluding section of the paper.)

(ii) *Externalities and the theory of the commercial fishery*
The recent literature on fisheries has included many references to the external economies that are inherent in the open-access resource problem. The pieces that contain the more significant contributions are those by Smith,[32] Bell[2] and Rich.[24] We have already had cause to refer to Smith's work, and noted briefly that in the paper that he co-authored with Quirk[23] and in his own paper the externalities that are inherent in the fisheries problem are comprehensively incorporated into the models. Analytically, it is often felt unnecessary to list the externalities that impinge on a particular industry. For the fishery, however, the exercise is not irrelevant due to the pervasiveness of such problems. A brief consideration of the externalities identified by Quirk and Smith and by Smith will illustrate the point.

D

Between the two papers the following sources of effects external to the decisions of the individual skipper are identified:

(*a*) stock externalities, which arise if the cost of catching fish increases as the fish population falls;

(*b*) gear externalities, which result if the type of fishing gear used affects the rate of growth of the population;*

(*c*) crowding externalities, resulting from congestion of vessels on grounds where the stock is concentrated in a small area; and

(*d*) 'fish-stock' externalities, which result from the fact that, in many cases, predation by man is a disturbance in the trophic chain, or food cycle, of a complex ecological system.

This list is by no means exhaustive. (Another possible externality in the fishery has been identified. It arises partly from the fact that, whilst fishermen usually seek one or at most two species, presumably in order to maximise the return to their effort, the ratio of desirable to trash fish is to some extent a random variable that does nevertheless affect the value of the catch, see Butlin[4]. This apart, the analyses developed by Quirk and Smith, and by Smith, indicate that the existence and effect of a particular externality have a crucial implication for the stability of their models (in the sense that a particular input/stock combination may or may not lead to a stable equilibrium in the fishery depending on the externalities postulated) Bell develops the long-run industry cost functions from a model of the Maine lobster fishery into which 'technological' externalities have been incorporated. Because of these externalities, the industry long-run average cost curve is rising throughout, and is backward-sloping for effort beyond maximum sustainable yeild because of the shape of the yield curve. (Copes had derived this property of the industry cost curves in an earlier article[6] and uses it in an article to which we shall refer below.) In a similar paper (at least at a theoretical level) Rich develops a model for estimating the gains and losses in the various surpluses that would come about under the alternative partial effort limitation schemes that have been suggested by bodies responsible for the regulation of particular fisheries in the past. He specifies the externalities rather more

* For a more thorough discussion of the problems raised by non-selective gear, see Turvey.[34]

carefully, but reaches essentially the same analytical conclusions. However, by a careful examination of the model,
Rich is able to isolate the effects of the growth and congestion
externalities that he identifies as being important in the context
of the fishery with which he is directly concerned (the Pacific
Halibut Fishery) and, furthermore, suggests a way in which
these effects can be quantified. (One should note that exercises
such as this have already been undertaken, and yield startling
results. For example, Crutchfield and Pontecorvo[10] estimated
that approximately 50 per cent of the gear being used in the
salmon fisheries off the west coast of North America was
unnecessary. Similarly, Bell estimates that a doubling of the
price of lobsters to the Maine fishermen would result in an
increase in the number of traps used by 60 per cent but a fall
in the catch by 20 per cent. Such estimates as these help to
illustrate the importance of externalities in explaining the
essentially economic nature of the over-fishing problems.)

4. The development of stochastic models of the fishery

The inclusion of this section in the paper is to illustrate a major
gap in the literature on the fishery, rather than to discuss a
series of papers that have addressed themselves to this problem.
The importance of stochastic factors in the fishery is great.
Anyone with any experience of the fishing industry in any
country cannot but be impressed with the importance of
'fisherman's luck' in fishing (although personal observation
suggests that in many cases this term is used as a proxy for
other factors, such as the ability and experience of the skipper).
Also some of the major innovations in fishing over the past two
decades have been in techniques adopted to increase the
probability of encounter with a commercially exploitable shoal
of fish. All this notwithstanding, only the work of Thompson
et al.[33] attempts to deal explictly with the problem of uncertainty in the context of fisheries.

Broadly speaking, one encounters uncertainty in two aspects
of the fishery. First, it arises in the problem of whether any
fish will be caught on a particular trip. *Ceteris paribus* (which
implies mainly that one is assuming that the availability of the
stock does not change from season to season) this is largely a
function of the experience of the skipper and the sophistication

of the stock-locating equipment carried. In one sense, then, one could say that those few models that have tried to incorporate the experience of the skipper into their analysis (usually by means of a subjective ranking of those still in the fishery by the most successful of the skippers who have recently retired from the fishery) have implicitly taken this aspect of uncertainty into account. This seems to be taking an altogether too *ad hoc* an approach to incorporating stochastic elements into the theory of the fishery, and such attempts seem poor substitutes for a thorough exposition of the optimal decision rule (in terms of time spent searching and investment in stock-locating equipment) for an individual boat 'producing' under a primitive 'encounter' technology.

The other aspect of uncertainty that is encountered in fisheries problems is that which arises when one removes the *ceteris paribus* assumption made above for the individual boat on an individual trip. That is, what is the optimal strategy for a vessel owner when the problems of stock fluctuations from season to season are admitted into the analysis? This is the problem addressed by Thompson *et al*. They limit their model to a vessel owner whose objective over time is to stay in the industry. The model that is applied is one that had been developed previously by the two senior authors to derive an investment rule for a 'survival conscious' firm. In the authors' words: 'The model . . . is concerned with the effect of survival considerations on the growth in net worth of an economic unit involved in sequential and irreversible acquisiton of capital stocks with uncertain future yields.'

Again the model used is dynamic, with a random variable incorporated to represent 'unknown net revenue per unit of capacity in each year'. Under definitions of firm survival and 'survivable' investment decisions, the investment strategy of the firm is derived. The rule is that the firm will purchase additional capacity in any given year if the marginal product of that capacity under the worst conceivable outcome is positive. This survival rule is compared with a rule derived when the survival requirement is not imposed, and whilst some similarity in the rules is seen, the two are so formulated that the effect of the survival requirement can be measured.

The model, set up as a dynamic programming problem; was applied to a shrimp fishery, with various runs being made to simulate differences in initial equity, differences in ability of the skipper, inflation in the cost of equipment and improved technologies (largely more powerful vessels in this case). The survival requirement affects investment decisions both through the values of the random variables and through the length of the time horizon over which the decisions apply. The major effect in the case of the Texas shrimp fishery seems to have been to produce only modest increases in capacity even when expected returns from additional capacity are relatively high.

Whilst this analysis has limitations (which the authors make quite explicit) it is an important contribution to the theory of the fishery. It indicates that, for the fishery studied, the relatively slow rate of growth that has been observed in the industry during periods of favourable returns to the fishermen involved can be explained in terms of the survival model. Given that this phenomenon is not unique to the Taxas shrimp fishery (see, for example, the slow rate of growth in the British distant-water fleet during the past several years despite considerable increases in the price of white fish) its application may be more general than the authors imply.

(i) *The political economy of fisheries regulation*
Whilst theoretical developments have been made to a significant degree in all branches of economics over the past several years, many areas of economics have not paid much attention to the problems of effectively implementing the policies that theory indicates are appropriate, or the general political acceptability of such policies. A few economists associated with fisheries are to be commended in that they have paid attention to what may be labelled the 'political economy' of fisheries control (that is, the problem of implementing the indicated policies within the political, as well as the economic, constraints of the environment within which the policies have to operate).

Four pieces of work will be considered in this context; those by Cheung[5], Scott and Southey[30], Copes[7] and Crutchfield[9]. Cheung attempts an economic-cum-legal analysis of the problem of the fishery. He maintains that any contract implies a 'set of contractual stipulations chosen by the participants are such that the return to all resources be maximised subject to the constraint of competition'.

Cheung explains, at greater length than we need discuss

here, that the absence of property rights defined over the fishery affects not only the factor allocation to the fishery, but also the costs of policing private investment inputs into the fishery. He elaborates on these effects in terms of choice of product, rate of use of certain inputs when returns from them are not appropriable, and the capitalised value of the asset. An analysis of the concept of externalities in terms of different property-right systems is developed concluding that the concept of 'externality' is imprecise in the absence of a well-defined system of property rights. It is worth quoting Cheung on this:

> Every economic action has effects. . . . [It is not] illuminating to view the damage as external or internal to a firm, for the firm is but a holder of contracts for the transformation of one type of right to another. *The same applies to all decisions on resource use.* . . . The problem is general because for every gain there is a cost. A more useful approach . . . is through a theory of contracting: whether the right to contract is recognised by law, and to what extent transaction costs affect contractual arrangements and resource allocation.

Anyone reading this cannot help but be struck by its distinctly 'Coasian' flavour and must also recall that there are limits to this approach.[19, 21] However, it is as well to bear in mind that from a more pragmatic viewpoint there appears to be a great deal of sense in this approach. In essence, many of the policies that are proposed for the regulation of fisheries are in the form of defining property rights over a particular fishery.*

What, then, is to be made of Cheung's contribution? Its intuitive appeal has already been noted. However, an analysis of costs of enforcement of particular contractual arrangements that would, in a frictionless world, remedy the resulting misallocation of resources has more power than this. It is at the heart of Cheung's argument that transactions and policing costs

---

* It is also worth noting *en passant* that this article contains a significant theoretical development of the received theory in the explanation that is given for the dissipation of rent under open access. This will not be touched on here, except to note that it provides a much more satisfactory explanation of the dissipation of rent on a particular ground than does Gordon's theory (which was carefully formulated to handle the explanation of the dissipation of rent on two grounds of differing productivities).

may be so high as to exclude the explicit conferring of property rights on a particular group of participants in the fishery. (It is also noted that the economic system is much more responsive to changing conditions than is the legal system.) This raises two further questions.

(*a*) Is the government likely to be more efficient in correcting resource misallocation when the costs of conferring the enforcing property rights are prohibitively high? The answer, as Cheung indicates, is broadly in the affirmative, although there are some qualifications that have to be noted.

(*b*) What are the implications for Cheung's seemingly neat exposition of a theory of externalities based on a theory of contracting? The theory still holds, of course, but the practical usefulness of the approach is lost. The problem is that for different sizes of organisation of groups of fishermen and consumers and also for different sizes of resource (whether in terms of area of the ground or abundancy of the stock) an effect may be 'external' or 'internal'. It would seem preferable to have uniform definition of externalities if the problem of policy formation to eliminate the distortions brought about by their existence is to be tackled effectively.

The piece by Copes stands apart from the other articles being considered in this section in that it analyses the alternative policies for control of a fishery in terms of the direct and 'incidental' effects on producers' and consumers' surpluses that would result from alternative management regimes. It is not necessary to discuss the theoretical aspects of Copes's paper, in that it is a fairly explicit and straightforward application of partial equilibrium welfare analysis to the problem (although the insight into the problems that Copes derives using this approach are extremely clear). The importance of the paper (in the context of this evaluation) lies in the policy implications that follow quite naturally from the analysis. These are, as the author indicates, that over-fishing problems in developed countries are exacerbated by improved technical efficiency and low rates of outward mobility of factors from the industry. Two results of this are, firstly, increased fishing pressure (which would be irrational in all but the open access situation), and secondly, low returns to factors in the industry. However, some governments have attempted not to cure the symptoms but to attack the root causes – excessive inputs into the industry – by controlling entry into the fishery. Copes notes, however, that the objective of government regulation of the fishery is not ubiquitously the maximisation of the rent to the resource: 'In deciding how far to proceed with entry limitation it behoves the government not only to pursue an increase in resource rent. . . . It is also necessary to watch for the retention of producers' surplus, particularly where the low incomes of producers are so central to government concern.' Copes spells out some of the difficulties of implementing restricted entry policies, but indicates, that, to a large extent, the problem revolves around the shape of the average social cost curve of the fishery: 'The critical ingredients of social cost calculation in respect of a fishery would seem to consist of an estimation of the value of alternative employment opportunities for factors engaged in the fishery and a measurement of the varying efficiency of different fishing units.' Copes seems to think that this is a task of small dimension to the economist. On this one would take issue with him, but the reasons for disagreement can best be left to the conclusion. At this stage it is sufficient to indicate that the concept of opportunity cost is by no means clear in the context of a fishery. Even if it is accepted that a definition along the usual lines is acceptable, Professor Copes's own experience with the fisheries of eastern Canada should have taught him that the opportunity costs are extremely low for many fisheries' inputs. Also, the problem of producing consistent indices of fishing effort is by no means the straightforward task that Professor Copes suggests.

The contribution of Southey and Scott is in the same vein as that of Copes. It considers the regulation of a fishery by three alternative mechanisms that represent differing degrees of central authority control over the fishery. The first is that typically favoured in theoretical models, in which a central authority responsible for the control of the fishery levies taxes at the rate of the marginal social user cost of the catch per vessel (see, for example, Quirk and Smith[23]). However, as the authors point out in the paper, the identification of such fine tax structures is often not operationally possible. Hence reinforcing measures have to be appended to achieve efficient fishery regulation (these are usually labelled 'partial effort' controls). Under such a system of management the central authority has to control effort directly (*de facto*), and so a series of problems of a practical nature present themselves. The implication is that in a world of less than perfect knowledge the tax/subsidy system does not supplant the other partial effort measures that, of themselves, have been shown to be ineffective in the control of a fishery (see Crutchfield and Zellner[11] and Crutchfield and Pontecorvo[10]). Rather, they become part of this set of partially effective controls on the fishery which, if implemented in the correct combination, may optimise the social rate of extraction from the fishery.

The second regulatory mechanism to be considered by Southey and Scott is a perfectly competitive solution – a free market in rights to fish the ground. In effect, a licence is issued to each participant in the fishery that confers on the licence-holder the right of access to the ground. Such rights would be transferable. In this case the authors suggest that the reason for the failure of such a regulation is that there would still exist effects external to the individual licence-holder, the implication being that an optimal rate of extraction cannot be achieved. (It is not entirely clear what external effect would result from exploitation by a limited number of licence-holders.) It appears that Southey and Scott have not taken this argument to its logical conclusion, because the intra-marginal licence-holders will, in a competitive market, buy up the rights from the marginal licence-holders, and this will occur until all external effects have been eliminated by absorption. This is essentially a solution after the manner of Coase. It is likely to result in a fishery being exploited by a sole holder of all the rights to fish the ground (if the ground has a small surface area but an abundant stock).

The third scheme of regulation that is referred to (and the list is, intentionally, not exhaustive) is the system of sole ownership. Scott indicated in an earlier article[28] that there are several *a priori* reasons why sole ownership will not necessarily result in a socially optimal rate of fishing. To this, Southey and Scott add a series of reasons of a more practical nature which further confirm their belief that sole ownership is not likely to produce the optimal solution.

The discussion that produced this rather dismal prospect for fisheries regulation was based on an extremely simplified fishery, undifferentiated over time and space. The introduction of either one of these complications serves to illustrate the complexity of real-world fisheries management problems. The cost of the search for the *optimum optimorum* becomes socially prohibitive. This rather negative conclusion appears to be the main outcome of this paper.* However, this is not to say that the paper does not serve a useful purpose. It is pragmatically orientated, and it serves to put the papers which we have already identified as being fairly major theoretical developments into perspective.

Crutchfield's paper is an excellent résumé of the state of the arts in fisheries conventions to date, and indicates that in only one international fishing convention is there any substantive economic content. The set of controls that he chooses to discuss are those that are currently internationally most palatable, i.e. international quote allocations. These form the basis of the recent settlement between Iceland and the other countries that fish the stocks on the Icelandic continental shelf. However, in the light of the Law of the Sea Conference and the outcome that is being predicted by many experienced observers, one feels that the other forms of international fisheries control ought to have been examined by economists. However, discussion of this issue must be postponed until the latter part of this paper.

5. An evaluation of recent developments

In the text thus far, the various pieces mentioned have been evaluated individually, and their contribution to eliminating one or more of the limitations of the Scott Gordon model noted. It now seems appropriate to take a broader view. Given the discussion in the first part of the paper, there are two bases from which this can be undertaken. The first is the extent to which the more recent models are improvements on Scott Gordon's. The second is the degree to which the developments enable models to be constructed for the purpose of policy

* The paper is mainly concerned with the more practical aspects of fisheries management. It is worth noting, however, that the appendix to the paper gives an excellent analysis of the effects of partial regulation of the fishery, and the reasons why partial effort regulation may not be second-best solution to the efficient regulation of a fishery.

analysis and prescription in particular fisheries within the world fisheries environment as described above.

From the discussion in the body of the paper, it is apparent that the application of dynamic analytical techniques to the theory of the fishery has extended it considerably. The work of Smith, Quirk and Smith, Hanneson, Plourde, and Thompson *et al.* is all in this vein, and a rich variety of testable hypotheses has been derived. It seems that the problems of testing these hypotheses, derived from the behaviour of fleets in fisheries in explicitly disequilibrium situations is an extremely difficult one, and there is little evidence in the literature as yet that the problem is likely to be overcome in the immediate future. Both Hanneson and Thompson *et al.* had to resort to simulation methods, which must be regarded as a second-best approach as there is no means of indicating statistical confidence in the models. (Other work not reported here has also found the only feasible approach at the moment to this category of problems is via simulation.) However, compared to the Scott Gordon model, the work discussed above is to be considered a significant theoretical improvement.

The second major limitation of the Scott Gordon model was that the externalities that are frequently encountered in the fishery had not received adequate attention. It was further suggested that, although such a task might be of little value in many industries, in fisheries, due to the diversity and pervasiveness of externality problems, it was necessary and potentially fruitful (in terms of the possibility of reducing factor misallocation). The most obvious externality, that of 'failure by enforcement' as Bator describes it, has been quantified for particular fisheries by Rich, Bell, and Crutchfield and Pontecorvo. The resulting inefficiency in factor allocation found has been sufficient to justify the exercise, and to cause concern. (The fact that the misallocation of resources is often compounded by measures taken by authorities charged with control over the particular fishing grounds, to prevent over-fishing, gives further cause for concern, see Butlin[4]. For the problems stemming from other externalities the degree of misallocation is, *a priori*, not likely to be so serious. (It is not clear to what extent, when attempting to measure the inefficiency of factor utilisation brought about by open access to an individual fishery the effects of other externalities are captured. It is likely that those due to crowding of vessels are likely to be included in any such estimate.) It is also going to be extremely difficult to quantify those external effects which arise because of interference, by fishing, in the growth rate of the stock at least until the effect of exploitation on fish populations is much better understood by biologists. Once again, theory can provide several alternative hypotheses, but these hypotheses have not been satisfactorily tested.

Concerning the problem of introducing the uncertainty inherent in a capture process the one available piece of work was found to be extremely useful, but limited in its approach (necessarily so, because of the 'survival' condition imposed on the firms.) It is not solely in situations where production is by exploitation of a free-moving species that the problem of uncertainty in production is to be found. However, the economics literature contains very few pointers to the direction in which applied economists ought to be moving if this problem is to be overcome. (Some recent work by Rothschild and Stiglitz[26] offers a possible indication of the approach that ought to be taken.) That the problem of uncertainty in fisheries is extremely important is evidenced by the sophisticated electronic stock-locating equipment now installed in most vessels that fish commercially important stocks. It is possibly in this area that the theory of fisheries economics has made least headway in the past two decades. However, it would seem that the problem lies in the lack of appropriate fundamental theory, and until this is satisfactorily developed little progress can be expected in any aspect of applied economics in which uncertainty of production is important.

The final limitation of the Scott Gordon model mentioned was that it was not well-suited for policy prescription. On this front, progress has been made. In the case of particular fisheries the work of Crutchfield and Zellner, although not within the terms of reference of this paper, was explicitly orientated towards a particular fishery, as was the work of Crutchfield and Pontecorvo, Hanneson and (to a lesser extent) Thompson *et al.* The work of Southey and Scott suggests that policy prescription, when extremely fine tax structures can neither be identified nor imposed, becomes a much more complex process, and that of Copes illustrates quite clearly and elegantly that the policy objective is not always to maximise the rent to the resource. The latter further indicates that 'incidental' surpluses can play an important part in evaluating the effects of alternative policy objectives. Hence, the limitation in the Scott Gordon approach has been reduced both for more general considerations, and for policies relating to particular fisheries, by work presented during the past five years.

At this point it is useful to summarise the conclusions that arise fairly clearly from comparing recent developments with the limitations of the original model. Firstly, the major developments appear to have been theoretical rather than empirical. Given that the progress that has been made has been achieved with the aid of recently developed analytical tools, this is to be expected. However, in agricultural economics, an industry which we noted above is similar to fishing in many ways, empirical developments have typically followed closely on theoretical improvements, and it is to be hoped that major progress in empirical work in fisheries economics will be forthcoming soon. Secondly, although uncertainty is extremely important in the context of the fishery, very little progress has been made, either in theory or empirically, to further the understanding of the effect of uncertainty on factor allocation in fisheries (or any other natural resource exploitation process where the technology used is of the hunting rather than the husbandry type). Thirdly, problems of policy implementation are better understood. On the one hand, policy implementation in the context of the general applicability of particular policy measures in a world of less-than-perfect data, and where the costs of policy implementation and enforcement are positive, has received explicit attention and the complexity of the second-best solutions has been shown. On the other hand, models for assessing optimal management strategies have been developed, and improvements in these are to be expected.

It was suggested earlier that there are two possible bases for evaluating the recent literature, one being based upon the limitations of a particular model, the other upon the extent to which the work is of relevance to the particular problems that have arisen in the context of the world's fisheries. Using this second criterion, one cannot regard the literature so favourably. The overriding problem of world fisheries for the past decade (at least) has been the problem of international fisheries management. In spite of the existence of several international bodies charged with the responsibility of international regulation of fishing grounds, many bilateral fishing agreements, and three F.A.O. conferences on fisheries (1957, 1962 and 1973) there is little evidence of effective fisheries control on a global scale. Largely because of this, many countries have unilaterally extended their fishing limits, and there is every indication that the Law of the Sea Conference, which was to be held in 1974, will ratify some form of agreement on coastal state custodianship of contiguous fishing grounds. No where in the literature, however, is there evidence of serious economic work having been undertaken on the possibile economic effects of such an agreement. This must be a strong indictment of those economists involved in fisheries research. The indictment is the more justified when the tools necessary for the analysis of the problem are to hand and have been frequently used in economics. It will be shown below that, *a priori*, the qualitative economic implications of one analytical approach can be derived, but it is perhaps useful first to consider the extent of the problem. In January 1974 there were at least thirteen countries which had claimed fishing limits of between 12 and 200 miles, for the purpose of conservation of fish stocks near to the countries involved and of importance to their economies. More specifically, either the fish from grounds, together with the output of associated industries, comprise a significant proportion of the country's national product (and, more important, usually an even larger proportion of the country's foreign-exchange earnings), or alternatively, the countries concerned are low-income countries, and the diet of most of the population is protein-deficient. The fishing grounds adjacent to their shores were being exploited very intensively by foreign distant-water fishing fleets, with little of the benefit from exploiting these fisheries accruing to the countries concerned. A dramatic example of the former situation is provided by Iceland. When the herring fishery failed (due, almost certainly, to over-fishing) in the mid-1960s, reduction in the catch, in two successive years, of 25 and 35 per cent brought about devaluations of the krone by 24 and 33 per cent respectively.

Between 85 and 95 per cent of Iceland's export earnings come from the export of fish and fish products. As an example of the latter situation, one can consider countries like Senegal, on the west coast of Africa. Along the whole of this coast, Japanese, Russian, Korean and other countries' distant-water fleets are fishing indiscriminately for fish to be reduced to fish protein and fish oil either for use in their home countries or for sale on the world market. A comparison of protein levels in the diets of the two sets of countries concerned helps one to understand why countries such as Senegal would consider extending their fishing limits.

It is appropriate at this point to outline the approach that would seem most useful in attempting to assess the economic effects of global coastal-state appropriation. It involves the application of spatial equilibrium theory to the world market for fish. Consider the world market in fish for direct consumption. To a reasonable approximation it is perfectly competitive. No one country, or regional grouping of countries, catches a significant proportion of any one species of fish, nor is any one species of fish found predominantly on a particular fishing ground. A possible exception is salmon, although with increasing Japanese high-seas trawling for salmon the traditional dominance of the United States and Canada in this market has been considerably reduced. The regulatory system that is envisaged is that each coastal state should estimate, either unilaterally or as a member of a regional group, the quantity of fish that should be taken from 'its' ground. The quantity that could be taken by the indigenous fishing industry would be estimated, and the surplus (if any) could be exploited by foreign fleets which would pay annual licence fees to catch a certain quantity of fish (i.e. the coastal countries could 'rent' part of their fishing to foreign fleets). Under such a regime, the basic theorems of spatial equilibrium analysis imply that the cost of licences to exploit the surplus of fish on any country's ground will tend towards equality, and will differ only to the extent that countries 'renting out' some of their fishing are at different distances from the major distant-water fishing nations, or to the extent that proportions of species with different market values vary between fishing grounds. Thus the result that Smith[31] derived for equilibrium in competitive spatially separated markets can be used, i.e. that this equilibrium is the rent (surplus) minimising equilibrium in such a set of markets. The most interesting aspect of this conclusion, as Smith demonstrated, is that the solution is the dual of the Samuelson 'net-social pay off' maximisation problem.[27] It is worth considering these conclusions in rather more detail.

The immediate result of this analysis, that global net social welfare would be maximised under such a regime of fisheries control, is of itself completely synthetic. Nevertheless, a consideration of the possible outcomes of a coastal-state appropriation system of fisheries management, implied by the formal analysis, suggests that such a system would be Pareto-superior to existing schemes of international fisheries management for the following reasons.

(a) The ownership of the fishing grounds by particular countries implies that there would exist an incentive for each country, or regional grouping of countries, to settle on an optimal management scheme for 'its' fisheries. In this context, 'optimal management' means maximising the capitalised economic rent from the resource. (This is not to say that the optimal policy for all states will ensure the existence of the stocks into the indefinite future. It is not difficult to conceive of a situation in which the user-cost of a fish stock, i.e. the loss to future generations from taking fish now rather than at some future date, to a particular country is sufficiently low as to result in the exhaustion of this stock over a finite time horizon. The most obvious example is a low *per capita* income country with a rapidly growing population that is heavily dependent on fish for its food supply. If the stock is to be preserved indefinitely into the future, it may be preserved at the expense of the lives of people for whom it is the sole source of food.)

Whilst Smith demonstrates that a policy of equilibrium in spatially separated, competitive markets implies the minimisation of the total surplus to consumers and producers, it does *not* imply the total dissipation of this rent, which is the outcome under a system of open access to all stocks. The existence of this 'appropriable' rent is the incentive for efficient management.

(b) Following directly from the first point is the possibility that the costs of administering the management of each fishery will be kept to a minimum. Also, it is likely that regulatory action to prevent the over-fishing of a stock will be taken quickly. This is to be contrasted with the current system of international fisheries regulation which is cumbersome, expensive, and has yet to show that it is capable of speedy action. There is evidence that certain fish stocks have been overfished because of the dilatoriness of the regulatory authorities. Burd[3] has shown that the international body responsible for the control of herring fishing in the north-east Atlantic was first informed of the possibility of over-fishing many of the herring stocks in the North Sea in 1958. However, regulatory action of sufficient severity was not taken until ten years later, by which time most of the stocks concerned were no longer viable as commercial fisheries.

(c) Whilst the discussion thus far has been formulated in terms of fish for direct consumption, and whilst the world market for fish meal and fish oil is less competitive, the analysis is not entirely without relevance to this market. The market was dominated until recently by Peru and Norway. The number of countries involved is gradually increasing, however, both because of the failure of the Peruvian anchoveta fishery over the past three years, and because of the rapid increase in the world price for fish meal and fish oil. The result has been an increase in the number of grounds and diversity of species exploited for fish taken for processing into meal and oil. The implication is that the world market for fish meal and fish oil is becoming more competitive, which, in turn, makes the case for coastal-state appropriation even stronger.

6. Conclusions: the future development of fisheries economics

The paper has evaluated recent contributions to fisheries economics, both to the extent that they represent improvements on the seminal work of Scott Gordon and to the extent that they have made an effective contribution towards analysing the current problems facing the world's fisheries. On the former basis, the major developments appeared to be either in theory, or in the problems of managing particular fisheries. On the latter basis there has been no work published to date which sheds any light on the major problem facing the world's fishing industries, i.e. the most appropriate way of achieving an effective global fisheries management regime. Thus the needed future orientation of fisheries economics seems fairly clear: it is necessary, first, that the problems of incorporating uncertainty into the models of fisheries ought to be tackled with some urgency. Second, more appropriate empirical techniques ought to be developed so that those working with fairly advanced bio-economic models do not have to resort to simulation methods to give their models any quantitative substance. Finally, urgent attention needs to be given to the net gains from particular management regimes for individual countries or for regional groupings of countries, particularly with reference to coastal-state appropriation. Neither the literature surveyed nor the research priorities just indicated are exhaustive. However, this paper has been orientated towards identifying the most urgent of the problems that remain largely unresolved in fisheries economics twenty years after the initial work of Scott Gordon. One final comment is in order. Much of the progress in empirical research in agricultural economics has been made possible by extensive systems for collecting reliable data that have been established by individual countries' governmental statistics divisions. The state of data collection and collation in fisheries (and hence the quality of such data) in most countries is highly unsatisfactory for the required research in fisheries economics. Unless the collection and collation of data from fisheries is improved considerably in the near future, the next twenty years will again yield largely theoretical developments in fisheries economics. This will be of little use to the policy-maker during a period when the resolution of problems in national and international fisheries control is expected to become increasingly necessary.

7 DISCUSSION

DR R. LAWSON (Hull): It has been said recently that the pending competition for resources of the sea was going to make the Klondyke look like a kindergarten tea-party. So far as fisheries is concerned, this competition is now well advanced, to the point of extinction of some species and the near extinction of many other species.

It is against this background that I want to comment on the review of economic theories given by Mr Butlin. I sincerely hope that the review of the theoretical aspect of fisheries economics as given by Mr Butlin is not going to blind us to the realities of the situation.

The realities of fish production and fish depletion are founded very largely in politics and the main job of the law of the sea is to sort out, on some sort of legal framework, how resources can best be used, distributed and reserved for future use in a workable management regime.

In the east Atlantic, about 80 per cent of the fish which is taken is taken by the developed countries, from the coast of some of the poorest countries in the world – like Mauritania, and so on. The fact is that many of the developed countries have these tremendous fishery operations, using factory vessels, and factory operations.

In one operation undertaken by a South African organisation, which during this particular year flew under a flag of a Caribbean Banana State, 100,000 tons of fish were taken from the sea in one month. At this rate, the whole of the oceans of the world would be depleted with fifty such operations. That is the sort of scale of depletion of fish with which we are faced now.

The trouble is that these big operators from the developed countries are very highly mobile; it is very difficult to control it and to manage them. There is little return to the developing countries often in the waters that they are fishing. What I would really like to see fisheries economists thinking about is

less theoretical model building and far more practical examination of the political situation, the question of equity and the
question of distribution, which, of course, really is the nitty-
gritty of the law of the sea. I think that a lot more work has to
be done at a completely different level.

PROFESSOR R. H. BARBACK (University of Hull): Mr Butlin
has favoured, going into policy considerations, the appropriation by coastal states for some fisheries and he has favoured a
system of licensing for others, but these propositions that he
has put forward, in so far as he has discussed them, are deficient
in avoiding important and realistic questions. These questions,
true enough, are not purely economic, but the absence of
political/legal factors in this realm just does lead to the non-
operation of theoretically based policies. I would, therefore,
like to ask Mr Butlin the following questions, as samples of the
questions to which he ought to be exposed.

As far as licensing is concerned, who is to do the licensing?
As far as appropriation of sea areas by coastal states is concerned, who and which states shall appropriate exactly what
sea areas?

Then he should face the question: how shall the interests of
existing distant-water fishing countries be taken account of in
this regime and what shall be done about applying the doctrine
which carries substantial political force, when the resources of
the sea are the common heritage of mankind in general,
including even the non-coastal states?

By putting questions of this type, I think probably what I am
doing is asserting that in this realm institutional, social,
political and legal factors are neglected to everyone's peril
when he is propounding policy and I think that these factors
should always be in the forefront, even to a theorist, in this
field.

MR BUTLIN: In response to the question of coastal-state
appropriation and licensing, these, of course, go hand-in-hand.
If coastal states appropriate grounds, they will then determine
how much of the fish they want to extract for their fisheries and
they will license on that basis. There is no conflict between the
concept of appropriation and the concept of licensing.

Who should allocate licences? The answer to that one is that it should be the country who owns the resource. On the question of which states should allocate licences, as far as those fisheries within a certain distance of the coast are concerned, there is very little problem. For ocean fisheries, for countries like Indonesia, it is largely a function of the extent to which they can police these limits.

The third question, on the existing rights of distant-water fisheries, my simple response to that is why should they have access to any fishing grounds? The concept of historic access seems to me very often an argument for some countries not having direct investments in fishing fleets which enables them to exploit further grounds. This seems to be largely the problem of the British fleet and our insistence on the right to fish on Icelandic grounds.

The common heritage is a very emotive concept, but I think that we have to move away from emotive concepts and towards practical programmes. If we are going to do this we have the choice either of having a common heritage and no fish, or a management programme which cuts across some of our more nationalistic feelings and some fish.

For example, there are now basically four herring industries around the British Isles, all of which are having to have some control put on them and are in danger of being completely out-fished. The ultimate effect upon the price of herring and other fish, both in this country and in the Common Market, is fairly obvious. So if we want some system which is going to act sufficiently quickly, I think we have to move away from international bodies and towards national bodies which have a vested interest to ensure the conservation of stocks.

8 ECONOMIC ASPECTS OF NATURAL RESOURCE DEPLETION*

GEOFFREY HEAL

If one asks the question 'Will a market mechanism lead to a sensible allocation of exhaustible resources over time?' – and this seems a very pertinent question to ask in the present context – then in economic terms one is asking whether there are any reasons to suppose that examples of market failure are important in this field. Presumably the most clear-cut example of a market failure is a total absence of the appropriate market, and there are two general categories of market which in an ideal Arrow–Debreu world would play an important role in securing an efficient allocation of resources over time, yet which in practice are notable largely for their paucity. The categories concerned are clearly forward markets and contingent commodity or risk markets. Forward markets are of importance because the essence of the problem is that it involves allocating a fixed and unaugmentable stock between *competing* uses at different points of time: we are much more concerned about the allocation of oil resources between current uses and those a decade hence than we would be about the allocation of cars between such uses, because we know that in ten years' time we can always make more cars if it seems worth while. Contingent commodity or risk markets are important for the obvious reason that in any economic decision that has to take into account events in the relatively distant future, uncertainty will loom large, and also for the very topical reason that

* This paper is part of a larger work[1] being written by the present author and Dr P. S. Dasgupta, of the London School of Economics. We are grateful to A. J. Bromley, of the Science Policy Research Unit at the University of Sussex, for helping us to gather and interpret data relevant to the present paper.

operating in resource markets involves considerable political risks. What I hope to do in this relatively brief paper is to outline the consequences for resource allocation of the non-existence of these markets, and then compare these theoretical predictions with some data describing the actual operation of a resource market, to see whether the phenomena identified by the theory as important are also 'identified' in this way by the data.

Let me begin by discussing the consequences of the non-existence of forward markets. Traders will have to base decisions on their own expectations of future prices, rather than on definite information. The consequences of this are not clear, but it seems that a number of outcomes may be possible. One could, for example, argue as follows. As stocks of an exhaustible resource are depleted, it will become apparent to dealers that it will not always be possible to meet current levels of demand, and rumours of future shortages will cause prices to rise. The price increase, if it is expected to continue, will cause sellers to hold stocks off the market, and will cause buyers to economise on their use of the commodity and start searching for substitutes. These two moves reduce future demand and raise future supply, thus preventing the development of the anticipated shortages. The fact that buyers economise on their use of the commodity and develop substitutes will also serve to ensure a reasonably smooth transition from the resource to whatever is the best substitute when stocks run out.

The above is obviously an ideal scenario, the intertemporal equivalent of perfectly functioning, perfectly competitive markets. A lot could clearly go wrong. For example, sellers might not expect the initial price increase to continue, so that an initial price increase consequent upon rumours of future shortages might actually bring a wave of selling designed to take advantage of what are thought to be temporarily high prices. Whether this happens will obviously depend on how sellers form their expectations of future price; if they do this by extrapolating current rates of change, then an increase will have the desired effect of inducing them to hold stocks off the market, but if on the other hand they have in mind some idea of a normal price, an average of past prices, then they will regard a sharp rise as a temporary phenomenon to be taken advantage of by selling. Their willingness to bear risks will also come into the picture. If, as seems likely, they are not certain whether an upward trend in prices will continue, then the more risk-averse may well cash in on present high prices by selling, while the gamblers keep their goods off the market.

In order to examine these possibilities more closely, I shall set up and comment briefly on some simple models of price adjustment in a resource market. The first is remarkably simple, but is a useful building block: I suppose that the current price p adjusts at a rate proportional to the difference between current demand D and current supply S:

$$\dot{p} = D - S \qquad (1)$$

I assume that the level of demand is chosen so that the marginal payoff to resource consumption equals the price: thus if the payoff from consuming an amount C is given by $U(C)$, then D is chosen so that

$$U'(D) = p \qquad (2)$$

The rate at which supply changes is assumed proportional to the difference between the current price and the expected future price E, which for the moment is taken as given. Thus

$$\dot{S} = p - E \qquad (3)$$

and increase in the current price above the expected future price calls forth an increase in supply as sellers take advantage of attractive market conditions, and vice versa. Assuming the payoff function $U(D)$ to be logarithmic, this system can be written as

$$\dot{p} = 1/p - S \qquad (1a)$$
$$\dot{S} = p - E \qquad (2)$$

The solution to these equations depends on whether $E \geqslant 1/\sqrt{2}$ or $E < 1/\sqrt{2}$ these two cases are shown in Figures 8.1 and 8.2. The system converges to an equilibrium where $1/p = S$ and $p = E$ (demand equals supply and the price is at its expected level), and the convergence may be oscillatory (as when $E \geqslant 1/\sqrt{2}$ or monotone). The oscillatory behaviour is a clear illustration of the sort of behaviour referred to before, when I argued that an increase in the current price, if not expected to continue, could lead to a wave of selling and thus increase rather than decrease the depletion rate: a high current price

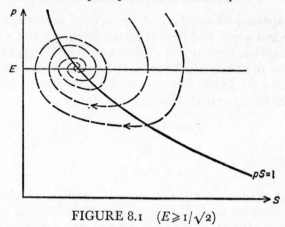

FIGURE 8.1 $(E \geqslant 1/\sqrt{2})$

leads to expectations that it will fall, so that there is a rush of selling and this forces the price down to a level that seems lower than an equilibrium value, at which point supplies are withheld and the process starts again.

The model of equations (1a) and (2) is clearly unconvincing for a number of reasons, with the fact that future price expectations are taken as given by no means the least of these. In any market expected future prices will probably be influenced by the history of past prices, and in a market for an exhaustible resource the balance between future supply and demand will also be influential. To reflect these factors I shall write

$$\dot{E} = a_1(p - E) + a_2 S \qquad (4)$$

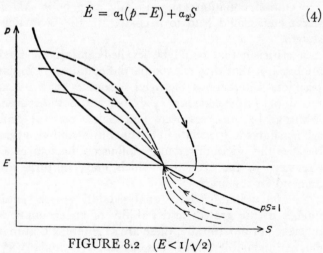

FIGURE 8.2 $(E < 1/\sqrt{2})$

Thus expectations are revised upwards if the present price exceeds that which had been expected for the present, and vice versa. The last term is (for a given stock) proportional to the inverse of the reserve–production ratio, and its presence indicates that a decline in this ratio boosts price expectations.

Augmenting the earlier model with this gives:

$$\dot{p} = (1/p) - S \tag{1a}$$

$$\dot{S} = p - E \tag{2}$$

$$\dot{E} = a_1 p(p - E) + a_2 S \tag{4}$$

Although the last equation is simple by comparison with many formulations one could have used, it is still sufficiently complex to make solving this system the kind of exercise one does not undertake lightly, particularly in a relatively brief talk. I shall therefore confine myself to a few general remarks about the solution.

(*a*) The only equilibrium to this new system occurs when $S = 0$, $p = E = +\infty$. In other words, the only equilibrium occurs when the resource stock is exhausted. That there should not be an equilibrium, in the sense of a constant price-expected price-output triple, whilst the resource is still being used, is I think fairly clear on intuitive grounds.

(*b*) The system can easily lead to oscillations in price and output: its behaviour is very sensitive to the parameters of the expectation equation (4), and any exogenous shift in these parameters could lead to a change in the behaviour of the system.

A criticism that could be levelled against the models just analysed, is that they are too partial equilibrium in nature: in practice, interactions between resource markets and the remainder of the economy are important, both because traders arbitrage between resources and claims on real capital (by selling shares to speculate in commodities, and vice versa), and because the prices of resources influence the returns available elsewhere in the economy, which may, in turn, affect the demand for resources.

Several writers[2,3] have analysed full general equilibrium models of the growth and stability of an economy with resources: not unnaturally, these are so complex that in order to derive intelligible results it is necessary to make very strong assumptions – for example, that markets clear instantaneously and that arbitrage between resource and capital markets occurs so rapidly that the rates of return on both assets are always equal. The model that I want to analyse next is a compromise between the general and partial equilibrium approaches: letting $\tilde{E} = \dot{E}/E$, it can be formulated as

$$\frac{\dot{S}}{S} = a(r - \tilde{E}) \tag{5}$$

$D(p) = S$ or equivalently

$$\frac{\dot{p}}{p} = \frac{-1}{\eta} \frac{\dot{S}}{S} \tag{6}$$

$$\frac{\dot{\tilde{E}}}{\tilde{E}} = \beta \left(\frac{\dot{p}}{p} - \tilde{E} \right) + \gamma \frac{\dot{S}}{S} \tag{7}$$

where r is the rate of return available from holding assets other than resources, and is the elasticity of demand for resources. Equation (5) embodies the idea that there is arbitrage between resource and capital markets, but that this is not sufficiently rapid to produce complete equalisation of returns: it is assumed that if the rate of return elsewhere (r) exceeds the rate of capital appreciation on resource $(\tilde{E})$, then resource owners sell resources to hold claims on real capital, and that the strength of this movement depends on the difference in returns.

For simplicity I am now assuming the resource markets to clear instantaneously (in view of the speed with which resource prices move, perhaps not a bad approximation), and equation (7) is the analogue of equation (4), except that it is stated in terms of rates of change rather than levels: this is required by the fact that it is the rate of change of the resource price that determines the return to holding it and thus appears in equation (5) as an explanation of sales policy. Substituting equations (5) and (6) into equation (7) gives

$$\dot{\tilde{E}}/\tilde{E} = r(a\gamma - a\beta/\eta) + \tilde{E} \tag{8}$$

The behaviour described by equations (5) and (8) can once again be analysed graphically: it is relatively easy to show that if

$$\frac{a\beta}{a\gamma + \beta} > \eta \geqslant 0$$

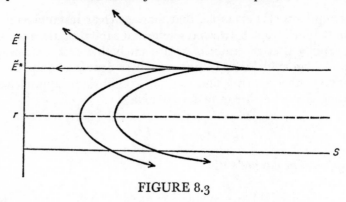

FIGURE 8.3

then the development of price expectations and supplies is as shown in Figure 8.3. Here $\tilde{E}^*$ is defined by

$$\tilde{E}^* = r/\{1 - \beta\eta/a(\beta - \gamma\eta)\}$$

Because of equation (6), it immediately follows that the behaviour of actual and expected prices is as in Figure 8.4.

Thus if the initial expected rate of capital appreciation is $\tilde{E}^*$, then this expectation remains unaltered, so that expected prices grow exponentially at a rate $\tilde{E}^*$: actual prices also grow exponentially at a rate $(\tilde{E}^* - r)a/\eta$, and the level of consumption falls exponentially at a rate of $(r - \tilde{E}^*)$, so that the reserve–production ratio remains constant. This trajectory is an interesting one, as it mimics the long-run behaviour of an optimal depletion path: it can be shown that on such a path the resource price rises exponentially and in the long run the consumption rate falls in a similar fashion.[3, 4] But although

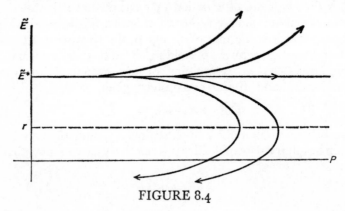

FIGURE 8.4

the system can generate an almost optimal outcome, it is also clear that this is very unstable: if initial price expectations are just infinitesimally different from E^*, then it moves cumulatively away from this well-behaved outcome. In this respect it demonstrates something akin to the saddle-point property discovered in both descriptive and optimal growth models.[5, 6] It is also true that this analysis has rested on the assumption that $\eta < \alpha\beta/\alpha\gamma + \beta$: if, however, the elasticity of demand is 'too great' in that this inequality is violated, then the resulting movement is as in Figure 8.5, with prices falling and consumption rising exponentially on the path on which $E = E^*$, which is this time a stable path.

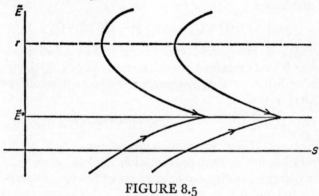

FIGURE 8.5

Having established rather tentatively the kind of behaviour that may result in a series of spot markets for exhaustible resources unaugmented by future markets, it is natural to enquire whether this class of outcome seems compatible with an efficient allocation of resources over time. Of course, the market structure postulated does not satisfy the sufficient conditions for efficiency, but this need not prevent the outcome from being efficient 'by chance'. I have, in fact, considered this issue at length elsewhere,[7] and so will just observe that an efficient allocation would be characterised by the property that the present value of the marginal product of the resource would be the same at all times when consumption is positive. For fluctuations in output to be compatible with such an allocation, it would be necessary for demand to fluctuate in anti-phase, an unlikely eventuality but not an entirely impossible one.

Having made some remarks about the likely behaviour of a set of unaugmented spot markets, I want now to turn to a similar discussion of the consequences of uncertainty and uninsurability. The easiest way of approaching this aspect of the problem is almost certainly via some examples, and this is the route I shall adopt. I shall consider briefly the problem of resource allocation in a two-period world where a stock Q of an exhaustible resource is available in the first period, and in period two there is probability θ that an extra amount X_1 will be discovered, and probability $(1 - \theta)$ that this discovery will be X_2. The social utility of resource consumption is given by a function $U(\ )$, so that an optimal resource allocation is one that maximises

$$U(Q_1) + \theta U(Q - Q_1 + X_1) + (1 - \theta)U(Q - Q_1 + X_2),$$

where Q_1 is first-period consumption. The solution to this problem is best examined graphically. Clearly $dU(Q_1)/dQ_1$ is a declining function of Q_1, whereas the expected second-period marginal utility,

$$\theta dU(Q - Q_1 + X_1)/dQ_1 + (1 - \theta)dU(Q - Q_1 + X_2)/dQ_1,$$

is increasing. If the marginal utility of resource consumption becomes infinite as that consumption tends to zero, only one of the marginal utility configurations can occur, as shown in Figures 8.6 and 8.7.

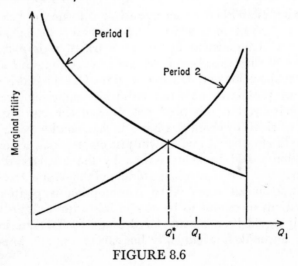

FIGURE 8.6

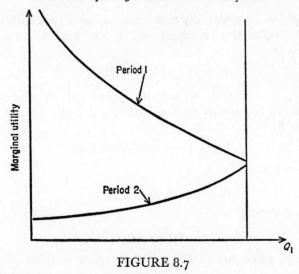

FIGURE 8.7

In the former case (Figure 8.6), the socially optimal level of resource consumption in period one is Q_1^*, whereas in the latter (Figure 8.7) one has a corner solution and it is optimal to consume all of the initial stock in the first period. Note that if either $X_1 = 0$ or $X_2 = 0$, so that there is a positive probability that none of the resource will be discovered in period two, then it will never be optimal to consume all of the initial stock in period one, as only configurations such as Figure 8.6 could arise. The reason for this is, of course, that the expected marginal utility of second-period resource consumption would become indefinitely large as Q_1 tends to Q, and there is a positive probability of having no consumption in period two.

In order to see how the resource would be allocated with a complete set of contingent commodity markets, we have to distinguish two states of the world:

State one: the resource stock in period one is Q, and an amount X_1 becomes available in period two.

State two: the resource stock in period one is Q, and an amount X_2 becomes available in period two.

Corresponding to each state of the world there will be two prices for the resource, one in each period: these will be labelled p_j^i, $i = 1, 2, j = 1, 2$, where i represents the state of the world and j the period. Letting q_j^i be the amount of resource sold in period j in state i, the seller who has a first-period stock q and who may discover either x_1 with probability θ or x_2 with probability $(1 - \theta)$ in period two, will have a certain revenue of

$$R = p_1^1 q_1^1 + p_2^1 q_2^1 + p_1^2 q_1^2 + p_2^2 q_2^2.$$

Clearly, $q_1^1 = q_1^2 = q_1$ because in period one it will not be possible to tell which state of the world has occurred. It is obvious that

$$q_2^i = q - q_1^i + x_i, \quad i = 1, 2$$

so that setting

$$p_1^1 + p_1^2 = p_1, \, p_2^1 + p_2^2 = p_2, \, R$$

can be expressed as

$$R = (p_1 - p_2)q_1 + p_2 q + p_2^1 x_1 + p_2^2 x_2$$

Assuming prices to equal expected marginal utilities,

$$p_1 = \frac{\mathrm{d}U(\Sigma q_1)}{\mathrm{d}(\Sigma q_1)}$$

where Σq_1 represents the sum of first-period sale, and likewise

$$p_2^1 = \frac{\theta \mathrm{d}U(Q - \Sigma q_1 + X_1)}{\mathrm{d}(Q - \Sigma q_1 + X_1)}, \quad p_2^2 = \frac{(1 - \theta)\mathrm{d}U(Q - \Sigma q_1 + X_2)}{\mathrm{d}(Q - \Sigma q_1 + X_2)}$$

where, of course, $Q = \Sigma q$, $X_1 = \Sigma x_1$, $X_2 = \Sigma x_2$, i.e. the individual firm's stocks and discoveries add up to the social totals. The profit-maximising sales policy is to sell all the first-period stock in period one if $p_1 > p_2$, and vice versa: only if $p_1 = p_2$ will the stock be divided between both periods.

We can now show that a complete set of markets will produce an optimal division of resources over time. Consider first the case shown in Figure 8.6 and suppose that $p_1 > p_2$. Assuming demand to be determined by equating marginal utility to price, this would produce a first-period demand of less than Q_1^*: however, sellers would clearly offer a supply equal to the entire stock, and markets would not clear. A similar argument shows that $p_1 > p_2$ is also incompatible with market clearing, so that the only market equilibrium is characterised by $p_1 = p_2$ and

$$\frac{\mathrm{d}U(\Sigma q_1)}{\mathrm{d}(\Sigma q_1)} = \frac{\theta \mathrm{d}U(Q - \Sigma q_1 + X_1)}{\mathrm{d}(Q - \Sigma q_1 + X_1)} + \frac{(1 - \theta)\mathrm{d}U(Q - \Sigma q_1 + X_2)}{\mathrm{d}U(Q - \Sigma q_1 + X_2)}$$

and is therefore socially optimal. Similar arguments can be used to reach the same conclusion in the case of corner solutions such as that shown in Figure 8.4.

If there are no markets for contingent commodities, then sellers have to trade on spot markets in each period, and in period one face a known present price and an uncertain future price. If they are risk-neutral, then the reader can easily confirm that maximisation of expected profits leads to a market equilibrium characterised by an optimal allocation of resources. Risk-averse sellers produce a different outcome. Consider first a utility function giving rise to the configuration of marginal utilities shown in Figure 8.6: if the first-period price were equal to the expected second-period price, then the whole first-period stock would be sold in period one – traders would have nothing to gain from storing it and would have to bear extra risks to do so. To have some of the first-period stock stored until the second, it would be necessary for the expected second-period price to exceed that in the first period, and this could be a market equilibrium only at a period-one consumption level such as Q_1, where second-period expected marginal utility exceeds that in the first. This clearly involves less than the optimal amount of conservation. If some traders are risk-neutral and some risk-averse, then it can be shown that provided that the stocks held by risk-averters do not exceed Q_1^*, in total, an optimal allocation will still result.

For the configuration of utilities shown in Figure 8.7, the situation is rather different. Here the ideal outcome is that all initial stocks should be sold in the first period, and with risk-averse sellers a sufficient – though not necessary – condition for this outcome is that the expected second-period price should not exceed the first-period price: any prices satisfying this condition will produce a market equilibrium at the appropriate corner solution.

The conclusions to be drawn from our discussion of uncertainty about future supplies when taken in conjunction with an inability to insure are clearly that if sellers are risk-neutral, the outcome will be satisfactory: if some are risk-averse and some risk-neutral, it will be satisfactory provided that the stocks held by risk-averters are small enough, and if all are risk-averters, then the allocation will be optimal only if the configuration of utility functions dictates a corner solution, as in

E

Figure 8.4. Although these conclusions are based on one particular specification of the nature of uncertainty, they can be shown to have a rather greater degree of generality than the model from which they were derived. Given that risk-aversion and uninsurability together may imply inadequate resource conservation, it would seem interesting to enquire whether there are simple government policies which might remedy the the situation. For example, where sellers are faced with uncertainty about future prices, are there grounds for price-support programmes?

In addition to uncertainties arising from an inability to predict market movements, there are important political uncertainties in the extractive industries. These are difficult to model convincingly, but perhaps the following situation captures much of what we have in mind when we refer to these. Consider a company with a concession to mine or drill for a resource in a foreign country. Formally, the concession is open ended – i.e. stretches to infinity. However, the firm fears that in practice the host government may at some future date end the concession without prior notice. It is obviously easy to think of examples that fit these assumptions. In formal terms, the company has a stock S of a resource of which it may sell an amount q_t at price p in year t. It wishes to choose a feasible sales profile – i.e. one satisfying

$$\sum_{t=0}^{\infty} q_t \leqslant S$$

which maximises the present value of a utility-of-income function

$$\sum_{t=0}^{\infty} U(q_t p)\, \delta^t, \quad 0 \leqslant \delta \leqslant 1$$

At least, this is the form the problem would have if it was certain that the concession would never be ended. But if the firm believes that there is a probability $a(T)$ that the concession will be ended in year T, then it will seek to maximise an expected utility given by

$$\sum_{T=0}^{\infty} a(T) \sum_{t=0}^{T} U(q_t p)\, \delta^t$$

which can be rewritten as

$$\sum_{t=0}^{\infty} U(q_t p)\, \delta^t \beta(t),$$

where

$$\beta(t) = \sum_{T=t}^{\infty} a(T).$$

It is easily shown that a solution to the second problem involves a higher rate of depletion than a solution to the first – basically because there is an additional discount factor $\beta(t)$ in the maximand. This then reinforces the earlier conclusions that uncertainty will raise depletion rates.

After talking for some time at a more or less abstract level about the kinds of factors a theorist would expect to influence resource markets, and the nature of the influences they might exert, I would now like to take a more empirical orientation. I want to look at data from one particular market – the oil market – and see whether our earlier discussion can throw any light on – or can be refuted by – observations from this market. Clearly there are no forward contingent commodity markets in oil, and there are also considerable risks of expropriation or contract termination, so that all of the earlier issues are relevant. In particular, sellers of oil will have to choose sales policies on the basis of expectations of future price movements, and in such situations the earlier discussions would suggest the likelihood of somewhat unstable price movements, with the form of market behaviour very sensitive to the nature of the expectation–formation process. Figures 8.8 to 8.10 provide some data that can be used to check the soundness of these suggestions. Figure 8.8 shows the movement of the posted price of Kuwaiti crude oil from 1954 to the end of the first quarter of 1973. All three curves show the real price, and they are measured in 1958 U.S. dollars, 1958 £ sterling and 1958 Deutschmarks. In view of the substantial changes in exchange rates that have occurred since 1967, it seems appropriate to consider prices measured in several different currencies: the effects of this can be seen clearly in 1967, and since 1970. Posted prices, as you are no doubt aware, are not determined by market forces: their main function is to determine the tax and royalty payment from oil companies to the exporting countries. During the period considered, these payments were proportional to the posted price, so that this price is a measure of the relative bargaining strengths of host countries and oil companies, and is effectively an index of the price at which the countries sell their oil to the companies. It is also one of the main determinants of the companies' marginal cost of oil, f.o.b. at the terminals, the other determinant being the marginal

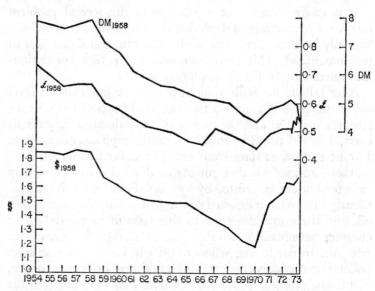

FIGURE 8.8   Posted Prices of Kuwaiti Crude Oil

extraction cost. As this latter is both small and stable, we can to a first-order approximation regard the posted price as an index of the f.o.b. cost of oil to the companies: of course, the c.i.f. cost will include transport costs, which are large and have been extremely variable. Figure 8.9, which again relates to Kuwaiti oil over the same period, shows the ratio of the market price to the posted price, and so provides a set of conversion factors with which to transform posted into market prices. Figure 8.10 shows posted prices for Saudi Arabian oil, again measured in 1958 U.S. dollars, 1958 £ sterling and 1958 Deutschmarks. Although it has not proved possible to construct a complete time series for the market/posted price ratio in this case, such

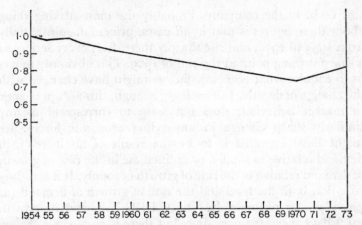

FIGURE 8.9   Ratio of Market to Posted Price of Kuwaiti Crude Oil

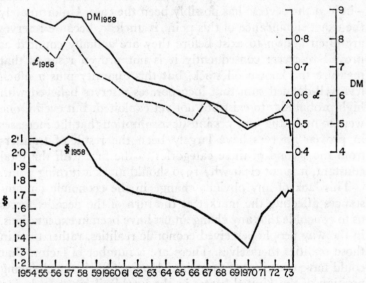

FIGURE 8.10   Posted Prices of Saudi Arabian Crude Oil

data as are available suggest that it would look very much like that for Kuwait.

For the two oil sources considered, the data displayed cover most aspects of price – the market price at which oil can be resold, the price received by the exporting country, and the cost f.o.b. to the company. Probably the most striking thing about these figures is that in *all* cases, prices fall substantially from 1954 to 1970, and rise sharply thereafter: every series has a sharp turning point at the end of 1969. This obviously moves us to enquire what economic factors might have changed with the change of decade. Interestingly enough, this abrupt change in market behaviour does not seem to correspond to any similarly sharp change in underyling economic forces: we might have expected it to be the result of an increase in demand relative to supply, or an increase in the rate of growth of demand relative to the rate of growth of supply. It is certainly true that both the level and the rate of growth of demand (as provided, for example, by O.E.C.D. G.N.P. and its growth rate) have increased over time, but there is no obvious change of trend in 1969–70. Nor has there been any decrease in the rate at which additions to proven reserves have been discovered – indeed the reverse has possibly been the case. Unfortunately the exact significance of this point is unclear, because reserves are often known to exist before they are actually counted as proved reserves: consequently it is not proven reserves that measure the known oil stock, but this quantity plus a much less well-defined sum that incorporates reserves believed with high probability to exist but not yet exploited. But even if one were to make the very pessimistic assumption that the increases in proven reserves have largely been the result of transfers from the second of these categories to the first with the total constant, it is not clear why 1970 should mark a turning point.

This lack of any obvious change in the economic circumstances affecting the market at the turn of the decade, forces us to conclude that any change must have been in expectations, in the way people perceived economic realities, rather than in those realities themselves. There are a number of factors that could have contributed to such a change. One is the changing position of the United States in the world oil market: during a relatively short period starting in about 1970 the United States moved from a position of substantial self-sufficiency in oil supplies to one of substantial dependence on imports. Two consequences followed from this – an increasing recognition of their bargaining power on the part of the oil-producing countries of the Middle East and South America, and a general realisation that the exhaustion of resource stocks, a possibility which had been in principle recognised but had been consigned to 'the long run', could, in fact, become a tangible reality. Another factor contributing to these changes in attitudes was the intellectual resurgence of neo-Malthusian analyses of the world's prospects: in spite of their well-documented short-comings, studies such as Forrester's *World Dynamics*[8] and Meadows's *The Limits to Growth*[9], undoubtedly had a substantial impact on the public's assessment of the likelihood and importance of resource shortages. Both of these studies argued that continuing economic growth and population growth would in the foreseeable future result in substantial shortages of important raw materials, shortages which would be sufficient to prevent further growth and possibly even lead to economic collapse: not surprisingly, these apocalyptic findings were given considerable publicity, and this once again had the effect of making oil suppliers more aware of the strength, and oil users of the weakness, of their respective positions, and also emphasised that 'the long run' in which stocks might be depleted stretched into, but possibly not much beyond, the foreseeable future.

A further contributory factor may be found in the changing financial position of some of the major oil-producing countries. There is evidence that in the 1960s a number of Middle-Eastern countries were engaged on development programmes that had high immediate foreign exchange requirements, and because of this were placing considerable pressure on oil companies to produce more royalty payments for them. Clearly the most sensible way for the companies to meet this demand, in a situation where, as was almost certainly the case in the 1960s, the price of oil exceeded the marginal production costs and revenue payments, was for them to increase production: the alternative would have been to pay higher royalties per barrel. In this fashion the foreign exchange needs of the developing countries contributed to the downward pressure on oil prices in the 1960s. By the early 1970s the position was rather different: although some oil-producing countries were still short of foreign exchange – Nigeria, for example – many of the major producing countries in the Middle East were by then sated with foreign currencies, particularly dollars. Foreign currency reserves were more than adequate to meet their development needs, and with highly unsettled world currency markets, a substantial devaluation of the dollar and rapid inflation in most industrial countries, their marginal valuation of extra foreign currency holdings was clearly very low: at least one Middle-Eastern foreign minister was heard to declare that oil in the ground was far safer than money in the bank. Because of these circumstances, some producing countries in the early 1970s were exerting pressure to reduce the production of oil from their fields. The Libyan government, for example, ordered substantial reductions in the production rates of all oil companies in Libya in 1970, as did the Kuwaiti in 1971. Pressure to reduce output or at least its rate of growth, would obviously help an upward trend in prices, and this was boosted by a number of random interruptions to supply, and an upsurge in demand in the United States in 1972.

On this interpretation of events, it seems that the change in market behaviour in the early 1970s followed, as asserted earlier, not from any fundamental economic changes but from changes in people's interpretation of the economic circumstances, and in particular from changes in their interpretation of the long-run balance between supply and demand in the oil market. From a situation of complacency in the 1960s, traders swung sharply to one of considerable concern in the early 1970s, prompted by changing American fuel balance and the extensive and rather alarmist public discussion of energy supplies. When referring earlier to the way in which traders' price-expectations are formed, we mentioned two important factors – the trend of past prices, which might *ceteris paribus* be expected to continue, and an index of the balance between the remaining stock of the resource and future demand for it. One could interpret the data discussed above by saying that up to 1970, the first of these factors was operative; prices in real terms had been falling and sellers, whose bargaining power at that stage was not thought to be very strong, operated on the assumption that they would continue to fall. This clearly gave them an incentive to increase, rather than reduce, their sales (see equation (1) above), which contributed to further falls in prices and to the 'glut' of the 1960s. This trend was reinforced by a strong desire for foreign exchange on the part of many producing countries. This mode of market behaviour only began to change when traders came to place increasing emphasis on the long-run balance of supply and demand, and during the early 1970s this factor began to dominate the formation of price expectations and hence the behaviour of prices. It was, of course, reinforced by the extrapolative mechanism: once prices seemed set on a rising trend, this provided sellers with an incentive to hold stocks off the market in order to realise higher future prices, and this, of course, contributed to the shortages and upward pressures. Confirmation of the importance of the incentive to hold stocks off the market is provided by the fact that in the early 1970s oil-producing countries were, for the first time on record, attempting to cut back the rate of production, explicitly in order to conserve their stocks but no doubt also to benefit from, and reinforce, the rising price trend.

It certainly seems to be the case that price movements in the oil market are compatible with the type of price-adjustment model suggested earlier: the factors recognised as important there have been operative, and indeed the market has displayed some of the instability that the earlier discussion suggested might be possible. The only difference of substance between the behaviour of the oil market and the models discussed earlier is that to explain the former fully it has been necessary to introduce factors such as the American energy balance or public concern about energy supplies, which are exogenous to the model as formulated.

In addition to being unable to sell oil forward, traders in the oil market are on the whole unable to insure against some of the most important risks that they face, and we now turn to an examination of this aspect of the problem. One form of risk is of course the risk that future prices will be different from those that were expected: this is an inevitable concomitant of the inability to trade forward, and in some measure its consequences have already been discussed. It is apt to produce a reliance on extrapolative forecasting, and a potential for instability: the reliance on extrapolative forecasting will mean that existing trends tend to be reinforced. The effect that an inability to insure against mis-estimating future prices will have on this picture, of course depends on the attitudes of traders towards risk: if sellers are risk-averse, then it will introduce a systematic bias towards selling now rather than storing. In a period such as the 1960s, when prices are on a downward trend, this will reinforce the trend: on the other hand, in a period when other factors are making prices rise, then this risk-aversion will tend to moderate the increase and reduce the extent to which traders are prepared to hold stocks off the market in order to gamble on a price increase.

The oil market does, of course, present risks other than those that are inevitably associated with price uncertainty – in particular, it is rich in political risks. As the bargaining position of producing countries has become stronger, and their economic independence has increased, they have asked for more favourable royalty terms: there is a clearly visible upward trend in the royalty terms they have managed to negotiate, and companies operating oil concessions must be aware of the possibility that this will continue. Obviously this provides an encouragement to increase the depletion rate: oil now is worth more in net revenue terms than oil in the future, and this is equivalent to an increase in the discount rate applied to future earnings.

Over and above the risk that higher royalties will be demanded, there is in many cases a non-negligible risk that concessions will be ended earlier than agreed, or that operations will be expropriated. This possibility was mentioned before, and it is hardly necessary to substantiate the point further. It was shown that the effect of such terminal-date uncertainty is to increase the rate of depletion that a profit-maximising firm will choose. According to this argument the fact that oil companies face an undoubted risk of expropriation in some countries will increase the rate at which they deplete oil fields in those countries. Although a plausible argument, this is, in fact, a difficult one to substantiate: the risk of expropriation is often difficult to gauge *ex ante* and data on the rates at which individual fields are depleted is often hard to find. However, there is very interesting evidence to show that the rate of depletion of oil concessions in Libya was increased sharply at a time at which President Gaddafi was making increasingly militant and threatening statements about foreign concerns operating in Libya. This seems a clear example of depletion rates rising as the risk rises: however, one should not jump too quickly to a conclusion of cause and effect, as other factors might have contributed to the change in depletion rates – for example, the proximity of Libyan oil to the rapidly growing western European market, particularly at a time when the Suez canal was closed. It may be worth noting that there is a possible feed-back effect here: an increase in the rate at which a concession is depleted because of a perceived political risk may well displease the host government, particularly if this had indeed planned to take control of the oil itself or if prices are rising so that storage seems a sensible policy, and this displeasure may, in turn, increase the chances of expropriation.

9 THE DESIRABILITY OF NATURAL RESOURCE DEPLETION

JOHN A. KAY and JAMES A. MIRRLEES

Advice to the reader

This paper was written for a conference on natural resources, and we were asked to talk about the *Club of Rome* model, which we had been examining. Having formed a poor opinion of that model, we decided to devote only an initial section to it, and that is written in a polemical style. Those who have had much to do with the world-dynamics debate will understand why we thought it necessary to express ourselves in terms more vigorous than we would usually think proper. Economists are advised that the real content of the paper is in sections 2 and 3, and accordingly recommended to start reading at section 2.

Section 2 contains some numerical calculations which are intended to shed light on the way in which economies do in fact use exhaustible resources, which we see as a necessary preliminary to any consideration of the extent to which these resources are substitutable for other factors of production. Section 3 discusses the reasons for thinking resource depletion may be taking place at a non-optimal rate, and develops some theoretical arguments which are new and can give some striking indications of the direction and extent of non-optimality. The more technical analysis is contained in an appendix.

The authors would like to acknowledge Alan Chambers's assistance with computing and the compilation of data, and comments by J. Flemming, G. Heal, R. Lecomber and P. Simmons.

1. Resources and world dynamics

We were initially invited to talk to this conference on the resource aspects of the global models developed by J. W.

Forrester, D. L. Meadows, and others,[1] and since there is still some interest in their work the first section of the paper is devoted to it. The topic need not detain us for long. We agree with the opinion of those who are competent to judge, that the models are worthless. The most detailed economic appraisal known to us is that of Nordhaus.[2] While he deals mainly with the original model of Forrester, his strictures apply equally to the Meadows work, which turns out on examination to be no significant advance on Forrester's model.[3] Nordhaus concludes that 'The work marks a significant retrogression in scientific technique, treatment of data, and humility', while two control engineers[4] have concluded that

> World Dynamics is essentially trivial. It may be worse. Whether civilization is restrained or not, one supposes that there will always be gullible people. If education, science and technology should serve the purpose of gulling them, it is shameful.

Even the team at the Sussex Science Policy Research Unit, though disposed to see some value in the kind of modelling done by Meadows and his group, gave a 'largely negative . . . judgement', tempered by the kindly suggestion that *The Limits to Growth* was 'a stimulus for an extremely fundamental debate'.[5] When research is congratulated on the importance of its subject, beware!

Nevertheless, we make only modest apologies for devoting yet more space to these models. Many people are reluctant to accept that a product so superbly marketed can be totally without merit; and the work continues to receive the acclaim of those too credulous or too busy to subject it to critical scrutiny. A journalist, Antony Lewis, has proclaimed *The Limits to Growth* as 'likely to be one of the most significant documents of our age', and a former U.S. cabinet member, Elliot Richardson, has called it 'too thorough, too thoughtful, too significant, to ignore'. Economists are not, after all, very good at predicting the balance of payments, while the successes of physics are all around us. It is, therefore, understandable, if unfortunate, that scientists give more credence to engineers who claim to be able to predict the future of the world economy than we would to economists who claimed to be able to land men on the moon.

In consequence, much work is in progress developing the Forrester–Meadows models, or conducted in similar style. We understand that a group of scientists in the Department of the Environment are engaged in a project of this kind, which is presumably intended to influence British government policy. Other groups at Sussex, in Argentina, Japan, Switzerland and the United States are engaged in similar exercises. We ought, therefore, to look closely at the resource sector of the Meadows model. We will not learn much from it about resources: but we may learn something about models.

In order to understand the Meadows model, we have simplified the equations of *World III* (a somewhat revised version of the model on which *The Limits to Growth* was based), by translating them out of the Dynamo compiler language in which they are formulated, using continuous time and conventional notation, and eliminating redundant variables. In the case of the resources sector of the model, the procedure yields three equations:

$$\dot{r} = -Nf(Y/N) \tag{1}$$

$$Y = \tfrac{1}{3}K\{1 - g(r)\} \tag{2}$$

$$\dot{K} = sY - \delta K \tag{3}$$

where r is the stock of resources remaining; N is the population; Y is the industrial output (gross); K is the capital stock; and f and g are numerically specified functions, as are the parameters s (savings ratio) and δ (depreciation).[6]

This is more or less a Harrod–Domar growth model with a resource constraint. One might object to the assumption that *gross* saving will be a fixed proportion of *gross* income, but since the capital–output ratio has been assumed constant it makes little difference in the model as it stands. The empirical inadequacy of a model with a constant capital–output ratio is well known to economists, and presumably obvious to most other people. We return to the assumptions about resources.

The resource constraint is peculiar in form. As r falls – resource shortage increases – an increasing *fraction* of capital has to be devoted to resource extraction. It would be more reasonable to assume an increasing absolute amount (related also to the volume of resources being extracted). We can easily derive a function for the cost of resource extraction from the model, by dividing the loss of industrial output because of resource-exploitation costs, by the volume of resources being extracted:

$$\text{Extraction costs per unit} = \frac{Kg(r)}{Nf[K\{1 - g(r)\}/(3N)]}.$$

It is plausible that the cost of resource extraction should depend on the volume of resources remaining; it is less plausible that the costs should depend on K and N in this particular way. But consider the quantitative dependence of extraction costs on r. If we set K and N equal to their initial values, we find that the cost of resource extraction rises twenty times by the time 90 per cent of known reserves are exhausted. That is hard to believe, and it is a good deal greater than is suggested even by the extrapolations presented by the Meadows team. Possibly their formulation in fractional terms misled them.

Since the relationship between resource exhaustion and extraction costs is crucial in inducing the 'crises' of *World III*, it is interesting to examine the empirical evidence used in support of it. This evidence is cited in the technical report. There is a relationship derived by Naill (a member of the Meadows team) and reproduced from that report, in Figure 9.1. The crosses apparently represent observations, and the

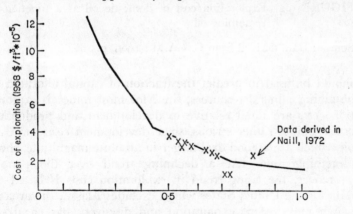

FIGURE 9.1.   Cost of exploration for U.S. natural gas versus fraction of unproven reserves remaining

Source: Data derived in Naill, 1972, from cost and discovery data in A.P.I., 1967, and A.G.A., 1944–63.

curve shown has been fitted to them. Comment would be superfluous. Another source of data – on the costs of oil exploration in the United States – is at first sight more convincing. This is shown in Figure 9.2. The data has been computed on a set of rather speculative assumptions described in the *World III* technical report.

It is a little surprising to find that data on exploration costs

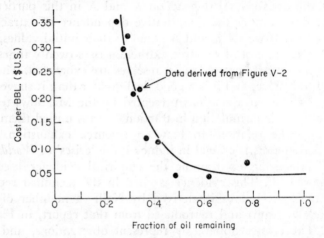

FIGURE 9.2   Exploration cost of domestic oil as a function of remaining oil

Source: Data derived from C.R.A.M., 1969, p. 186.

should be used to predict the fraction of capital allocated to obtaining mineral resources, since for most minerals exploration costs are small relative to development and production costs. This is rather serious, since development costs for U.S. oil, which are a good deal larger in absolute magnitude, show something more like a declining trend over the period. Moreover, the rising trend in exploration costs is based on data for the United States which excludes Alaska, the area in which most recent exploration and discovery has occurred. The authors of *The Limits to Growth* were presumably unaware of the research which has been undertaken on finding and development costs by M. A. Adelman[7] which does not support the relationship they used.

The final source of evidence for the *The Limits to Growth*

relationship is taken from a diagram prepared by Barnett and Morse,[8] and reproduced in the technical report (Figure 9.3). This diagram appears in a chapter entitled 'Ambiguous Indicators of Resource Scarcity'; and is presented in the context of a discussion which concludes 'the extractive labour and the extractive capital percentages are not significant as indicators of increasing scarcity'. The work of Barnett and Morse represents the best empirical study of the relationship sought by

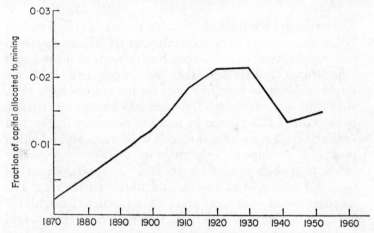

FIGURE 9.3   Fraction of capital allocated to obtaining mineral resources, United States, 1870–1950

Source: Data derived from H. J. Barnett and C. Morse, *Scarcity and Growth* (Johns Hopkins Press, Baltimore, 1963), p. 220.

the Meadows team known to us. In other parts of the book, they set up and test the 'strong hypothesis' that economic scarcity of natural resources, as measured by the trend of real cost of extractive output, will increase over time in a growing economy; and the 'weak hypothesis', that the unit cost of extractive output rises relative to that of non-extractive output. They find that in the case of minerals, empirical evidence from the United States contradicts both hypotheses.

We would not wish to argue that, because increasing scarcity has not manifested itself in the past, it will not do so in the future. As Adelman puts it, 'The history of every mineral industry is a constant struggle between increasing costs . . . and the growth of knowledge',[9] and we would not speculate on how that struggle will develop. What we do wish to argue is the more limited and more serious charge that there is no valid empirical basis provided for the relationship used in *World III*, and that the attempt to give one rests on a selective use of evidence.

The other important empirical input to the model is the quantity of available resources. This is set at 250 times current consumption. The explanation of this choice is given as follows:

> Theoretically, the level of available nonrenewable resources NR should reflect a crustal quantity, or the absolute geological availability of the resources. Such a large number might reflect the optimistic belief that 'free' energy will enable the world economy to satisfy its resource needs from basic rock. However, such an assumption must also include an estimate of the cost of this process in terms of necessary labour and capital, or the amount of unusable solid waste and pollution produced. A more realistic range for the aggregate reserve index is probably between 50 and 500 years, based on available estimates of proven and unproven reserves. The current model uses 250 years as an order-of-magnitude estimate of the 1970 aggregate reserve life index of world resources.[10]

This vagueness is understandable, but it is not very impressive as empirical substantiation.

The behaviour of the model is obvious. Combining equations (2) and (3) yields

$$\dot{K} = (\tfrac{1}{3}s - \delta)K - \tfrac{1}{3}sKg(r).$$

Since $s > 3\delta$, and $g(r)$ is initially small, $\dot{K} > 0$, so that K and Y increase. This implies that $\dot{r}$ is positive and increasing, and as a result $g(r)$ rises, reducing the growth rate and then the absolute level of Y. In due course, this leads to $\dot{K} < 0$, so that finally output declines both on account of decreasing K and on account of increasing $g(r)$. The solution is easily quantified too. If in the next seventy-five years population were to grow by 2 per cent per annum on average, and output per head had not by the end of the period fallen again to below its present level, a simple calculation shows that K will be declining at the end of the seventy-five years. A more careful calculation would show that it will then be falling quite rapidly, and Υ will be falling very rapidly. With a 1 per cent population growth rate, the same can be said with seventy-five years replaced by 100 years. It is easy to see, therefore, that 'catastrophe within 100 years" is implied by the model, provided population projections are at all realistic. This only takes a few minutes to check. The extensive computer calculations reported in *The Limits to Growth* and *World III* can hardly be said to give the conclusions greater weight.

Having found just what substance there is in the technical report, which is a revised version of the unpublished basis for *The Limits to Growth*, it is as well to recall the claims made by the authors of that work:

> Ours is a formal, written model of the world. It constitutes a preliminary attempt to improve our mental models of long-term, global problems by combining the large amount of information that is already in human minds with the new information-processing tools that mankind's increasing knowledge has produced – the scientific method, systems analysis, and the modern computer. . . . We believe that it is the most useful model now available for dealing with problems far out in the space–time graph. To our knowledge it is the only formal model in existence that is truly global in scope, that has a time horizon longer than thirty years, and that includes important variables such as population, food production and pollution, not as independent entities, but as dynamically interacting elements, as they are in the real world. . . . We feel that the advantages listed above make this model unique among all mathematical and mental world models available to us today.[11]

The sponsors of the project further asserted that 'the report presents in straightforward form the alternatives confronting not one nation or people but all nations and all peoples, thereby compelling a reader to raise his sights to the dimensions of the world problematique'.

Yet, on examination, we find that the most important parts of the model are naïve in conception, amateurish in construction, and make negligible – and warped – use of empirical data. The verdict of Graham and Herrick, which we cited above – 'essentially trivival' – is precisely right. The notion that this model might seriously be used for forecasting long-term trends in resource utilisation is absurd. (We should add that the resources sector of the Meadows model is not the worst part: the pollution sector is even slighter; the agricultural sector so complex that we have been unable to make serious assessment of its realism; the 'capital', i.e. production, sector is the worst of all.[12])

As an exercise in this kind of model building, we have explored the effect on the Meadows model of making the minimum modifications required to give it some plausibility. We wanted to modify the production function so as to allow for the possibility of economy in resource use. We therefore chose a C.E.S. production function in resources and capital, which allows us, by choice of the elasticity of substitution to take different views on the extent to which capital may be substituted for resources. We altered the savings assumption slightly, so that net investment was set proportional to net output. Finally, we imposed increasing economy in resource use by setting the price of the resource to rise at a constant annual rate with producers equating the price of the resource with its marginal product. The model is thus:

$$Y^{\alpha} = aK^{\alpha} + br^{\alpha}, \tag{4}$$

$$\dot{K} = sY, \tag{5}$$

$$\frac{\mathrm{d}}{\mathrm{d}t}\left(\frac{\partial Y}{\partial r}\right) = c\,\frac{\partial Y}{\partial r}. \tag{6}$$

We further took $s = 0.11$, $a = 3^{-\alpha}$, b $= 0.02$, $K_0 = 3$ and $r_0 = 1$, values which seem fairly plausible and similar to those implied by the *The Limits to Growth* model. We computed the behaviour of the model for a number of different values of a. An interesting problem arose on a number of computer runs. If the elasticity of substitution between capital and resources is less than one $(\alpha < 0)$, then the C.E.S. assumption implies that resources are essential, in the sense that production without net resource use is impossible. It is also true that $\partial Y/\partial r$, the marginal product of the resource, is bounded above. Suppose the output of our economy were metal pans. Then it is impossible to produce a pan without using *some* metal; and, while one can make thinner and thinner pans, there is a limit to this process also. Thus it eventually becomes impossible to effect the economies in resource use which our model demands. We have, therefore, assumed, following the spirit of *The Limits to Growth*, that our economy is such that when resource economy conflicts too much with growth it is resource economy which is abandoned. We told our computer not to allow the growth rate to fall below 2 per cent per annum: if this were going to happen, it was instructed to abandon economy and use whatever resources were necessary to allow growth at 2 per cent to continue.

By choosing different values of c and a within the range which we thought to be plausible, we obtained a wide range of different scenarios. We could come near to the *The Limits of Growth* model by assuming very low possibilities of substitution and slight incentives to resource economy, such as $a = -10$ and $c = 0.01$. On these assumptions, output grows over the next 250 years by a factor of 8677. This miracle of compound interest is accompanied by a 7000-fold growth in resource use, and requires a total resource input equal to around 200,000 times current annual consumption. Perhaps that is too much. Let us impose resource economy by making the resource price rise at 10 per cent per annum. Then output in the year 2223 will be a relatively manageable 236 times its present level. This involves a cumulative resource use of 8000 years' current consumption.

These figures, though high, do not sound so ridiculous. What would happen if the possibilities for substitution were greater? $a = -1$ means that the elasticity of substitution between the factors is $1/2$. A 1 per cent annual rise in resource prices now means that output will grow 6205 times over 250 years, resource use 1814 times, and total resource use is 62,000 times the present level. But a faster rise in resource prices now involves a substantial substitution of capital for resources. With a 10 per cent rate of increase, growth is clipped back to a factor of 218. But this is accompanied by a less than tenfold growth in resource use, which is made possible by an initial supply of resources only 500 times current use. If the elasticity of substitution is higher still, the problem of resources becomes negligible. With $a = 0.1$, so that the elasticity of substitution is slightly greater than one, a 3 per cent rise in resource prices would allow output to grow 40,000 times with an eightfold growth in resource use.

No doubt most people find these figures quite absurd. How can output possible grow by a factor of 200, far less 40,000? Yet they should not dismiss such numbers too readily. It is almost certainly a conservative estimate that the output of the British economy has grown by 500 times in the past 250 years. It is fair to ask what such a statement actually means: nevertheless, this is what the 2–3 per cent growth rate which the economy has actually experienced over the period implies. For the United States, where population has grown a thousand-fold as well, the figure of 40,000 is probably on the low side. The resources required for this growth have been found. True, there have been worries from time to time:

> By the sixteenth century, the enclosures and the demands of industry for fuel had brought about a shortage of timber trees that seemed likely to hamper shipbuilding and so to threaten national security. Among the causes of this dearth, the voracity of the ironworks was regarded as the chief, and it was urged that the industry should be closely regulated, if not entirely suppressed. . . . When a commission was appointed to enquire into the ironworks of the Weald, it was asserted that the shortage of wood was so great that soon Calais, Boulogne, Rye, Hastings, Dover, and other towns on both sides of the Channel would be without fuel, and that the fishermen would not be able to dry their clothes or warm their bodies when they came in from the sea.[13]

The models may demonstrate that many things can happen; but we do not intend that they should be taken very seriously. From what we know of the economic system, and the availability of resources, we believe they are more plausible than the models of the Meadows team. But as forecasts of the future, these models are as bad as theirs. No rational person could possibly believe that any such model will tell him what output will be in the year 2223. Do they serve any other purpose? It is hard to think of one. They do show that the future is very uncertain; and that the extent to which economic growth is constrained by resource shortages depends on the availability of resources and the ease with which other factors can be substituted for them. They alert us to what all this might mean quantitatively: but, in fact, we did not need computer simulations to tell us. At most, the models demonstrate that anyone who predicts the future for 150 years and claims that 'the basic behaviour modes we have already observed in this model appear to be so fundamental and general that we do not expect our broad conclusions to be substantially altered' is mistaken. We should not need a computer to tell us that either.

Should one conclude that modelling in the social sciences is a waste of time? We think, on the contrary, that mathematical models are an indispensable tool for the economist. But what is wrong with the Forrester–Meadows work is not just that it is badly done. Like alchemists and astrologers, they set themselves the wrong task, developing useless models for illegitimate ends. No doubt we can expect the next few years to produce the world-dynamic equivalent of alchemists who are careful to emphasise that they have not produced gold yet and astrologers who claim to do no more than delineate the outlines of character: such work, more restrained and careful, will have as little value as that of Forrester and Meadows, though its adverse consequences will probably be less severe. There are numerous reasons why we should not aim at vast, complicated, global, simulation models. Perhaps the most important one in the case of exhaustible resources is that forecasting models whose time horizon extends beyond a decade or so are worthless. If one can abandon the naïve view that science is quantitative forecasting, one can think of using models in a flexible, piecemeal way to get insight into relatively limited, but specific, aspects of social systems. To this end, it is often a help to formulate questions of policy, and then to concentrate on what seem to be essentials. It appears that a model that is 'global' in scope is a nuisance, rather than an advantage: the need for computer simulation, which arises only for a model too complex to be understood, should be regarded provisionally as a sign of an ill-formulated model. In later sections we indicate how models might be applied to resources with better effect.

2. Where do resources go?

In our view, some knowledge of where non-renewable resources do in fact go is an essential preliminary to any serious discussion of resource depletion. Naïve assumptions of linear relationships between resource use and output, or about the inexorability of exponential growth of all economic time series, serve only to disguise the wide diversity of actual experience. Over the two decades from 1950 to 1969, British industrial production grew by around 80 per cent and G.D.P. by about 70 per cent. Iron and steel production grew roughly in step, at about the lower of these figures. Aluminium usage almost doubled, while copper consumption increased by around 30 per cent. Our consumption of zinc and lead rose only slightly, while tin consumption fell. Phosphates were used less, but potash more.

We have constructed an index of aggregate use of non-renewable resources. This index is based on ten materials – iron, copper, aluminium, lead, zinc, tin, nickel, magnesium, phosphate and potash. We weighted quantity relatives by estimated values of resources used derived from consumption data and world prices of the materials involved. We also derived a 'total' resource index by adding in three 'power' resources – coal, oil and natural gas – on similar principles. Table 9.1 sets out these indices for the United Kingdom, the United States and Germany. This shows that aggregate resource use has indeed increased with output and industrial production, though rather more slowly than either in two of the three countries. In Germany the reverse is true for the period as a whole, but the base of 1950 is in this case low and somewhat unrepresentative, and since, say, 1955 the pattern conforms to that observed in the other two. This is, of course, in the context of a much more rapid rate of growth. The apparent year-to-year fluctuations should not be taken too seriously, since our 'consumption' series normally reflect deliveries rather than actual consumption. Stock building by consumers, therefore, appears as a change in use.

Table 9.2 presents calculations of a similar nature in a cross-section comparison of resource use in ten different countries in 1969. This demonstrates substantial variations in *per capita* consumption of particular resources; and smaller but still significant variations in total use measured either per head or per dollar of output. The United States appears at the top of the list for *per capita* usage, but near to the bottom in terms of the resource intensity of its output (Table 9.3). This latter competition is comfortably won by Japan. These differences may be exaggerated, since the conversion of these 1969 outputs at the then prevailing exchange rates may be thought to underestimate the value of Japanese output relative

TABLE 9.1   Resource use, 1950–69

Year	United Kingdom				United States				Germany			
	Non power	Total	Ind. prodn	G.D.P.	Non power	Total	Ind. prodn	G.D.P.	Non power	Total	Ind. prodn	G.D.P.
1950	100	100	100	100	100	100	100	100	100	100	100	100
1951	102	103	106	103	104	104	109	108	108	112	119	110
1952	102	103	102	103	99	103	113	111	129	127	128	120
1953	97	101	107	108	116	112	124	116	134	131	138	130
1954	110	110	115	112	98	102	115	114	162	149	157	140
1955	120	117	122	116	120	117	131	123	201	178	183	156
1956	119	118	122	118	120	120	135	125	204	184	196	167
1957	121	118	123	120	118	120	136	127	210	188	206	176
1958	119	118	122	120	102	109	125	126	212	188	213	182
1959	119	119	130	125	114	117	143	134	239	209	230	195
1960	134	131	139	131	111	117	148	137	283	243	257	229
1961	128	128	139	136	114	119	148	140	282	247	273	242
1962	124	128	141	137	122	125	160	149	277	248	285	252
1963	130	134	146	142	136	135	169	155	276	254	294	261
1964	149	147	158	150	154	146	179	163	329	295	317	278
1965	150	149	163	154	165	154	194	174	322	295	335	294
1966	143	144	166	157	177	163	212	185	300	279	340	302
1967	134	138	166	161	166	161	214	190	293	275	335	301
1968	141	145	176	166	159	161	224	199	351	338	273	323
1969	144	149	182	167	165	167	234	205	406	382	423	348

Sources: Annual Abstract of Statistics, Metallgesellschaft – *Metal Statistics*; U.S. Department of Interior – *Minerals Yearbook*; Iron and Steel Board – *Iron and Steel Annual Statistics*; National Accounts of O.E.C.D. Countries; *U.N. Annual Bulleting of Statistics*.

TABLE 9.2   Resource consumption *per capita*, U.K. = 100 (1969)

	Iron	Copper	Aluminium	Lead	Zinc
United States	156	105	261	84	117
United Kingdom	100	100	100	100	100
Germany	143	111	151	104	126
France	103	87	104	80	91
Italy	82	59	69	55	60
Netherlands	91	41	59	76	51
Sweden	164	123	145	138	91
Denmark	103	14	20	81	47
Canada	115	148	150	64	106
Japan	139	96	115	38	113

	Tin	Nickel	Magnesium	Phosphates	Potash
United States	81	108	299	252	197
United Kingdom	100	100	100	100	100
Germany	67	103	608	168	197
France	60	108	74	388	276
Italy	36	52	37	109	38
Netherlands	107	8	22	99	111
Sweden	14	344	62	214	180
Denmark	52	3	—	311	423
Canada	67	107	100	222	125
Japan	72	113	55	84	78

Sources: O.E.C.D., *Statistics of Energy*; British Steel Corporation, *Statistical Handbook*; *Metal Statistics*; National Accounts of O.E.C.D. Countries; *U.N. Annual Bulletin of Statistics*.

TABLE 9.3   Non-power resource consumption*

	Resources per capita	G.D.P. per capita	Resources per $ of G.D.P.
United States	158	238	66
United Kingdom	100	100	100
Germany	134	137	98
France	100	133	75
Italy	74	79	94
Netherlands	77	112	69
Sweden	156	181	86
Denmark	77	146	53
Canada	121	169	72
Japan	125	84	149

* Estimated by authors.

to that of the United States: but this factor is unlikely to be sufficient to account for a difference of almost 100 per cent.

Perhaps the most interesting feature of these calculations is that the differences they reveal are likely to be less surprising to the layman than to the economist. The tourist knows that Holland and Denmark are largely agricultural, that Italy is backward, and has heard that Japan is one extensive assembly line. The economist, on the other hand, knows that the differences between developed countries in the fraction of output accounted for by manufacturing industry are very small; that Italy, Holland and Denmark are by no means the least industrialised among them; and that Japan still has a very extensive agricultural sector.

This suggests that resource use may be largely attributable to a small number of conspicuous industries. We have attempted to ascertain which products are the principal users of particular resources. The main problem here is that the main user of aluminium, say, is the aluminium fabrication industry. It is therefore necessary to trace resources through successive processes until they reach the product in which they are finally incorporated; and conversely to hold the car industry responsible for all the steel in cars whether they are used directly in body pressing or indirectly in manufacturing the headlamps. Input–output analysis allows this in cases where there is a well-identified resource extraction or processing sector. The U.K. matrices are insufficiently disaggregated for this to be attempted, but in the U.S. tables we could identify eight suitably defined sectors, which enable us to make estimates of the ultimate disposition of resources for aluminium, chemical and fertiliser minerals, coal, copper, lead, petroleum and natural gas, steel and zinc.

The results of this are reproduced in Table 9.4, which lists the industries which are principal users of each of these resources. It may require emphasis that all of these are final uses. This means, for example, that the item 'fertilisers' includes only fertilisers sold directly to consumers; fertilisers sold to producers are attributed to the product whose manufacture they assist. Similarly, the refined petroleum products which it is not surprising to discover are the principal users of the outputs of petroleum refineries comprise, in the main, petrol and domestic fuel oil; the oil which heats a food factory appears under food manufacture. It is not possible to pursue the logic of this approach as far as would be ideal because capital goods represent a final use in empirical input–output tables. Refrigeration equipment, therefore, appears as such, and is not and cannot be allocated to whatever it refrigerates.

The pattern which emerges most clearly from this data is that the construction and motor vehicle industries are much the most voracious users of resources. Together they absorb 50 per cent of steel output, 45 per cent of zinc, about 40 per cent of

TABLE 9.4   Principal uses of resources (% of total resource use attributable to direct or indirect use by these industries)

Aluminium

Construction	26·9
Motor vehicles	11·2
Industrial machinery	7·5
Aircraft	6·1
Food manufacture	5·1
Ordnance and accessories	4·8
Other transport equipment	4·6
Communication equipment	2·8
Wholesale and retail trade	2·0
Refrigeration equipment	0·9
Metal household furniture	0·8
Total of these	72·6

Chemical and fertiliser minerals

Food manufacture	14·9
Construction	13·5
Industrial chemicals	10·0
Wholesale and retail trade	3·2
Motor vehicles	3·1
Clothing	2·9
Fertilisers	2·7
Cleaning preparations	2·3
Petroleum refining	1·9
Industrial machinery	1·7
Drugs	1·0
Cigarettes, cigars, etc.	0·9
Total of these	58·0

Coal

Electric utilities	17·4
Construction	14·2
Motor vehicles	6·5
Food manufacture	5·7
Wholesale and retail trade	4·9
Industrial machinery	3·8
Clothing	1·4
Petroleum refining	0·9
Industrial chemicals	0·8
Hospitals	0·7
Total of these	56·2

Copper

Construction	29·5
Industrial machinery	9·0
Motor vehicles	8·2
Communication equipment	3·9
Electrical apparatus	3·1
Aircraft	3·0
Ordnance and accessories	2·1
Refrigeration machinery	1·7
Food manufacture	1·5
Wholesale and retail trade	1·5
Pipes, valves and fittings	0·9
Shipbuilding and repairs	0·8
Total of these	65·2

Lead		Petroleum and natural gas	
Construction	17·6	Refined petroleum products	43·5
Storage batteries	15·1	Construction	9·7
Motor vehicles	11·0	Gas utilities	9·1
Industrial machinery	9·5	Wholesale and retail trade	6·6
Food manufacture	4·8	Food manufacture	6·1
Ordnance and accessories	4·5	Motor vehicles	2·1
Industrial chemicals	4·3	Industrial machinery	2·0
Aircraft	3·9	Toilet preparations	1·7
Wholesale and retail trade	3·3	Electric utilities	1·3
Communication equipment	2·3	Industrial chemicals	1·0
Jewellery	1·5	Air transport	0·9
Clothing	1·3	Clothing	0·8
Petroleum refining	1·2	Motor freight transport	0·8
Shipbuilding and repairs	1·2	Passenger transport	0·7
		Repair services (non-auto)	0·7
Total of these	81·2		
		Total of these	87·1

Steel		Zinc	
Construction	30·0	Construction	25·6
Motor vehicles	19·6	Motor vehicles	19·5
Industrial machinery	10·7	Industrial machinery	10·2
Food manufacture	5·6	Aircraft	4·1
Other transport equipment	4·0	Domestic appliances	3·8
Domestic appliances	2·3	Ordnance and accessories	2·4
Aircraft	2·2	Wholesale and retail trade	2·3
Wholesale and retail trade	1·6	Storage batteries	1·9
Fabricated plate works	1·3	Industrial chemicals	1·7
Shipbuilding and repair	1·0	Miscellaneous hardware	1·2
Communication equipment	0·9		
Total of these	79·3	Total of these	72·7

lead, 38 per cent each of copper and aluminium. By contrast, a number of apparently important uses are quantitatively rather small. Thus the main oil-using products are things which burn it rather than things made from it, and cars use much more aluminium than aircraft. (Aircraft use rather a lot of lead too. This may be a mistake. If a lot of lead is used in making the kinds of things which are used in making aircraft, our approach will suggest that aircraft are relatively lead intensive, even if special things for aircraft are relatively lead free. Our conclusions are vulnerable to errors of this kind.)

In Table 9.5 we consider which are the most resource-

TABLE 9.5   Resource-intensive industries (% of total value of product accounted for by direct and indirect use of the resource)

Aluminium

Metal foil	28·4
Electrical industrial goods	7·0
Sheet metal work	6·3
Tanks and components	5·7
Trucks and trailers	4·9
Trailer coaches	4·1

Chemical and fertiliser minerals

Fertilisers	11·6
Industrial chemicals	3·4
Agricultural chemicals	2·7
Plastics	1·5
Misc. chemical products	1·0
Paints	0·9

Coal

Federal electric utilities	17·6
State and local utilities	6·9
Metal barrels, drums, pails	1·5
Fabricated plate works	1·3
Railroad and street cars	1·3
Sheet metal work	1·2

Copper

Small arms and ammunition	7·7
Pipes, valves and fittings	6·5
Transformers	3·7
Motors and generators	3·3
Welding apparatus	2·8
Switchgear	2·4

Lead

Storage batteries	24·5
Small arms and ammunition	8·4
Paints	1·4
Printing trade machinery	1·2
Metal foil	1·1
Industrial chemicals	1·1

Petroleum and natural gas

Refined petroleum products	53·0
Gas utilities	27·8
Industrial chemicals	6·2
Air transport	5·2
Agricultural chemicals	5·0
Paints	4·2

Steel

Fabricated plate works	39·8
Railroad and street cars	35·7
Sheet metal work	34·1
Safes and vaults	34·0
Metal stampings	29·8
Fabricated metal goods	25·9

Zinc

Miscellaneous hardware	2·6
Storage batteries	2·2
Small arms and ammunition	1·0
Household laundry equipment	0·7
Commercial laundry equipment	0·6
Electric housewares	0·5

intensive products; those products in which the proportion of the total value of output accounted for by direct and indirect use of the resource is greatest. Such a list tends, of course, to be dominated by intermediate goods. Steel tubes are particularly dependent on steel. We have, therefore, excluded all products for which more than 95 per cent of total domestic sales are made to other producers. The six products which then remain at the top of the list are given in the table. These are the goods on which resource scarcities would exert the greatest pressure; here the incentives for both producers and consumers to find substitutes would be greatest.

These figures are presented in an endeavour to increase the information available to those discussing resource depletion rather than in support of any particular line of argument. But we suggest that anyone who examines them is likely to obtain a sense of perspective which some apocalyptic writing on the subject appears to lack. When we know that lead mostly goes into car batteries, we realise that if we want to conserve lead it is a good deal easier and more effective to design a car that does not need a lead–acid accumulator than to halt economic growth.

The diversity of experience, both by country and by resource, also suggests that a rather micro-economic approach to the economic theory of exhaustible resources may be the most useful. In the remaining sections of the paper, we pursue an analysis on these lines, using a simple model as our point of reference, but trying not to let it completely dominate the discussion.

3. Some economics of resource depletion

The chief question at issue is, we think, whether there is, in the world economic system as it works now, a significant bias towards using resources too rapidly. This question leads on to others about the quantitative extent of any bias, and the measures that might be adopted by nations, independently or in consort, to counteract the bias. One should also consider whether there may be other undesirable aspects of the current system, but we shall concentrate on the simple issue of bias. If we are to discuss it, we must have a model of the system as it works now, and there is no question that prices play an important role in that system.

The basic economic principles of exhaustible resources, and the way in which the price system may be thought to deal with them, was worked out many years ago by Hotelling.[14] More recently, many economists have looked at the issues in more detail, using the techniques of control theory, particularly Heal and Dasgupta, Koopmans, Stiglitz, and Dixit.[15] We shall say what we can without going into the more difficult control theory problems.

Consider the owner of a stock of resources, of total amount R, and suppose that he believes the price for this resource at time t will be p_t. He has to incur exploitation costs $c(x, t)$ at time t if he is then extracting resources at the rate x. Assuming that he wants to maximise the discounted sum of his profits, his rate of interest being i, he will relate the marginal cost of extraction at t to the price at t by the equation

$$p_t = c_x(x_t, t) + Q e^{it}. \tag{7}$$

The first term on the right is the marginal cost of extracting the resource. The second term is the imputed cost of drawing on his stock of the resource: this cost obviously rises at a rate equal to the rate of interest because he has the option (at the margin) of lending at interest i instead of keeping the resource in stock. Q is, then, defined as the value, to the owner, of a unit of the resource (not yet extracted) at time o. Its level is such that he plans to just exhaust his stock. (One modification is required in equation (7): if p_t is too low, the owner will not plan to extract any of the resource at t, and it is permissible in that case that $p_t \leqslant Q e^{it}$. For example, he may plan to exhaust his stock at some date T, because after that the term $Q e^{it}$ is so large that it exceeds the difference between the price obtainable and the marginal cost of extraction.) Equation (7) by no means captures all the important aspects of resource exploitation: in general, extraction costs depend upon the stock remaining, for example. This extension is discussed in the technical appendix. But the form of the relationship is quite general, and the case described is sufficiently rich for us to hang a number of arguments upon it.

Notice that p_t is the price the owner expects to get for his resource: since future markets do not exist for any substantial time ahead, we should not think of the p_t as market-clearing prices in the future. For example, if purchasers of the resource are also price-takers, and if short-run equilibrium is reached fairly rapidly, the actual price – let us denote it by P_t – will be a determinate function of the amount of the resource offered for sale.

$$P_t = f(\Sigma x_t, t), \tag{8}$$

where Σx_t means the total offered for sale by all owners of this particular resource and p_t is the resource-owner's estimate of P_t. Presumably p_t will depend upon the behaviour of P_τ at times τ in the past, and also on other evidence of future demand and supply of the resource.

One circumstance in which resource owners might be expected to predict prices rather well is when Q is, for most of them, very small, and the market is, therefore, pretty much like a rather competitive market for a non-exhaustible commodity. This is a more likely case than one might have thought: it can arise, roughly speaking, when current consumption of the resource is small relative to total stocks of the resource. A numerical example will bring this out. Let c_x be a constant, taken to be 1 for convenience, and suppose the demand schedule is constant, with price elasticity ϵ: $f(x) = x^{-1/\epsilon}$. Assuming that price expectations are correct, we may as well pretend there is only one resource owner, with quantity R. Then

$$x_t = [1+Qe^{it}]^{-\epsilon} \tag{9}$$

and Q is determined so that $\int x_t dt = R$. Thus:

if $\epsilon = 1$

$$R = \int_0^\infty \frac{dt}{1+Qe^{it}}$$

$$= \frac{1}{i}\log\frac{1+Q}{Q}$$

so that $Q = 1/(e^{iR}-1)$

if $\epsilon = \frac{1}{2}$

$$R = \int_0^\infty \frac{dt}{\sqrt{(1+Qe^{it})}}$$

$$= \frac{2}{i}\log\frac{1+\sqrt{(1+Q)}}{\sqrt{Q}}$$

so that $Q = 4e^{iR}/(e^{iR}-1)^2$

Using these formulae we obtain the following table:

	Q	
iR	$\epsilon = 1$	$\epsilon = \frac{1}{2}$
1	0·58	3·68
2	0·16	0·72
4	0·02	0·08
6	0·00	0·01

Thus, when iR is greater than 6, Q is less than 1 per cent of the marginal cost of extraction, and may as well be neglected for

F

practical purposes. The rate at which the resource is depleted is pretty much what it would be if there were no property rights in the resource. If, to take a figure not quite at random, $R = 250$ (i.e. resource stocks are 250 times current consumption of the resource), and the (real) interest rate is 5 per cent, $iR = 12 \cdot 5$: in that case, it will be 130 years before iR falls as low as 6. The equilibrium price will remain close to the marginal extraction cost until remaining stocks are less than forty times current annual consumption.

The results of this calculation would not be quite so striking if we allowed for increasing demand; but then, for many resources, 250 years' stock is a very low figure to assume, and unity a low estimate for the long-run price elasticity. The point we want to make is simply that when extraction (and transportation, etc.) costs are borne in mind there is no reason to expect resource prices to be more uncertain than other prices.

This is important, because if prices are correctly predicted we may conclude that resources are being exploited at an optimal rate. The structure of this argument is familiar to economists, but we give a brief outline of it here.

Resource conservation is an investment in the future. It requires us to give up present consumption for the sake of future benefits. In this it resembles other forms of investment which are undertaken in the economy: in education or in plant and machinery. Now efficiency requires that the returns on all these forms of investment should be the same. Otherwise we could increase consumption both now and in the future by expanding one type of investment and contracting the others. A competitive firm will be led to make exactly the same sort of calculation. It will compare the returns from resource conservation and other investment opportunities, and adjust the volume of each it undertakes so that the returns from each are the same. If not, it could increase its profits by devoting more of its funds to the higher yielding investment. Thus the calculation which a firm will make in deciding how rapidly to exploit exhaustible resources will be the same as the one society would make if it were choosing an optimal depletion rate on the firm's behalf.

Of course, this argument when carefully specified depends on a number of strong and implausible assumptions. But it is useful to describe the assumptions under which actual and optimal depletion rates would be the same, since this provides a basis for assessing the ways in which actual and optimal depletion rates will in reality diverge. We must now consider a number of possible reasons for such bias.

(i) *Neglect of future generations*

It is sometimes suggested that leaving resource exploitation to the mercies of the market neglects the interests of our children and grandchildren, or of countries that have not yet become industrialised. But this is a mistake. If prices are correctly predicted, the demands of our children, grandchildren, etc., are being taken into account by resource owners, who are saving up resources to sell to them when the time comes. True there may be a general bias in the economy to consume now and leave too little to our children or our future selves. If so it would be reflected in high rates of interest, which will lead to somewhat more rapid depletion of resources.

Many conservationists might take the view that this did describe their position: that the rate of interest was too high as a result of society's 'defective telescopic faculty' (as Pigou described it). But if this is so, it implies that we are undertaking too little investment of all kinds. And this, in turn, carries the implication that the present rate of economic growth is too low, and that we should increase the investment ratio in an attempt to raise it. It is our impression that rather few of those who worry about excessively rapid resource depletion would accept that conclusion: but, if not, they must find some other basis for their intuition. Similarly, we think that the use of natural resources now to benefit Englishmen instead of in a hundred years' time to benefit Indians is of a piece with the other ways in which all factors of production are unequally applied to the good of Englishmen and Indians, and believe that restraint in using resources would actually be a very expensive way of shifting the balance.

(ii) *Incorrect price predictions*

There is no guarantee that resource owners will correctly predict resource prices. If owners are on average over-estimating future prices p_t (as compared to the equilibrium prices P_t), they will supply less than the equilibrium amount now, while planning to supply more in the future. This will raise prices currently. So long as price anticipations are governed by past as well as present prices in a positive way – and the assumption of interpolative expectations in the long run is reasonable – higher current prices will mean that a slower rate of increase of prices in the long run is expected. Then supplies will increase somewhat, bringing current prices closer to equilibrium prices: demand responses tend to bring about a rate of increase of the market price which is less than the rate of increase of the equilibrium price, which is itself less than the long-run rate of price increase expected by resource owners. This gap between experience and expectation should narrow in time, bringing supplies and prices closer to their equilibrium levels. This heuristic argument, which suggests that the system has stabilising tendencies which could be accelerated by speculation, demand and resource–stock forecasting, etc., is, being non-mathematical, inconclusive.

In fact, we seem to observe that the price of resources which are very far from exhaustion are often much higher than the marginal cost of extraction and transportation. At least, recent substantial rises in raw material prices were apparently not related to cost increases. Since the extent to which resource owners want to deliver currently depends on their price expectations, and these cannot be very firmly based, there is scope for very great divergence of actual prices from equilibrium prices. If our initial argument suggests there are forces for convergence towards equilibrium, it does not suggest that the adjustment of actual towards equilibrium prices would be particularly rapid. For example, it is surely possible for over-supply to persist for many years before the drying up of major sources gives prices the upward push needed to bring about revision of expectations.

The question that has to be considered is whether there is any reason to expect a particular bias, either upwards or downwards, in the formation of expectations. While no very general answer seems possible, our basic equation (7) does provide an important pointer. As we have seen, the second term, Qe^{it}, will not be important when the total stock of the resource is still large: that is to say, the equilibrium price will not be much greater than the marginal cost of extraction. It does not seem likely that an actual price *below* the extraction cost could persist for long. Therefore, if there is a bias, it must be in the upward direction, keeping the price higher than it should be, and thus bringing about under-exploitation of the resource.

We can see this by returning to equation (9), and asking what would happen if resource owners believed the resource would be worthless in future, so that they dumped it on the market until price fell to the level of extraction costs. In that case, price would remain constant at 1, so that over the next 150 years total resource use would be 150 times current consumption. If they had anticipated the whole spectrum of future prices correctly, so that the optimum path was followed, cumulative resource use over this period would be 149·87 times current consumption at $\epsilon = 1$, and 149·73 times current consumption at $\epsilon = \frac{1}{2}$. In other words, if there is more than 100 years' supply of the resource remaining, the maximum extent of possible bias towards over-depletion is negligible.

At a later stage, however, one might expect a tendency for the price to be too. For when the term Qe^{it} becomes important, the equilibrium price, having previously been constant or perhaps falling, should begin to rise, and the rise would accelerate until the price is eventually growing at a rate approaching i (if the resource has not already ceased to be used). It is plausible that people will tend to underestimate distant prices if in fact the rate of price rise is going to accelerate. In that case, there will be a bias towards over-exploitation, which might be significant in the period when the second term in equation (7) begins to be significant. Probably this argument does not deserve too much weight, since as a matter of fact expectations of the kind we are discussing tend to be revised discontinuously, and there may well be over-reaction when it is realised that resource–rent elements in costs are beginning to be important. On balance, we think that incorrect price expectations are more likely to cause under-exploitation of resources than over-exploitation.

(iii) *Risk aversion*

For the sake of clarity, we have not mentioned explicitly the uncertainty about future prices, resource supplies, etc., which tend to dominate discussions of resource depletion. One effect of this uncertainty is that the resource owner is more uncertain about the price he can expect to obtain for his resource in the future than about the price he can expect to obtain now (periods of unusual current confusion apart). If he is risk-averse, he will tend to discount future prices (as he sees them) somewhat, and deliver more of the resources now than he would have done if he had known for certain that future prices would be what he expects. Since the socially important benefits of the resource will be widely distributed, not being especially large for any one person, it may be argued that the private owner's risk aversion implies an undesirable bias towards present depletion.

For example, if half the profits of the resource owner are paid to government, as a result of taxation, the owner and the government receive the same amounts. The government may have no reason to be risk-averse in regard to what, from its point of view, are small risks; while the owner, if for some reason he has failed to diversify his own portfolio and share the risks of his resource ownership with others, may act in a very risk-averse manner. This argument assumes fixed taxation, and that the income of the resource owner himself is not of significant social value. There are, also, important cases where a country, much of whose national wealth is in a particular natural resource, may be more risk-averse than the owner. Economists have perhaps been too ready to assume that in general, and without regard to the particular ways in which costs and benefits are distributed, privately motivated decisions will be too risk-averse. In the present case, a good deal of work requires to be done – allowing, as John Flemming has been doing, for the effects of risk aversion on exploration as well as on depletion – before one can be sure even of the direction in which uncertainty biases depletion, far less its quantitative importance.

In this connection we note that it may not pay even risk-averse owners to explore for new reserves to the extent that would be socially desirable, because the information about reserves is actually valuable to others besides themselves. As with most production of information there are external economies, and, therefore, there is a presumption that too little is invested in research.

(iv) *Ownership uncertainty*
Another way in which uncertainty is important is when the owner is uncertain about the future security of his rights to

the resource, or the profits from it. If the resource owner believes there is a significant risk that the resource will be taken from him with imperfect compensation – say by government expropriation – he has an incentive to deplete his stocks sooner rather than later. Oddly enough, private owners appear to have better prospects of compensation than public owners: a deposed Sheikh has no further rights to the oil still in the ground, nor can a government defeated at the polls expect to gain credit or patronage from as yet unexploited reserves. But, although political instability could in this way lead to over-exploitation, the case of oil suggests that transfer of ownership to the resource's own nation can be expected to eliminate any bias to exploit the resource too rapidly.

(v) *Monopoly*

Many resource owners appear to earn very considerable profits even when the world stock of the resource is many hundred times current consumption. Our earlier analysis suggests that this is strong evidence of monopoly, which may, of course, be exercised by implicit collusion, or by local government taxes.

Ignoring uncertainty for the moment, a profit-maximising monopolist would wish to choose his rates of sale x_t so that

$$f(x_t) + x_t f'(x_t) = c_x(x_t) + Q'e^{it}, \qquad (10)$$

Q' being at such a level that $\int_0^\infty x_t dt = R$. Initially, when $Q'e^{it}$ is small, x_t will, of course, be smaller under monopoly. More generally, we can show that when f and c are independent of t, and the elasticity of deman is constant, x_t is smaller at any given stock of resource than it would be if there were no monopoly. This is proved in section 3 of the technical appendix. When the elasticity of demand is not constant, one can construct counter-examples, but under-depletion may be regarded as the general rule. Thus under monoply, probably, in cases where a natural resource has, or a group of resources subject to explicit or implicit collusion have, a rather inelastic demand, there is a strong bias towards under-exploitation of the resource, as compared at any rate to the competitive outcome.

(vi) *The distribution of benefits*

In a competitive economy without government intervention, part of the benefits from the resource accrues to the owner;

in monetary terms, using our previous notation, the present value is QR. It seems that in the case of most natural resources, this gain goes either to relatively few very rich individuals, or to governments. If we are talking about possible economic policy, it would be very odd to regard the gains accruing to a rich oil-well owner in the same way as gains accruing to an average user of petrol or heating oil. The natural approximation is to regard the gains to a private owner as having no social value. Gains to government revenue might be regarded as having a high or low value depending upon the nation or government in question: how should one regard Malaysia, Chile and the United States from this point of view? But take the case where the resource is privately owned within our country. Then the government should be advised to tax away the whole of the QR that accrues to the owner. In practical terms this means imposing a tax on purchases of the resource which is, at time t, just equal to Qe^{-it}. If the government does that, the rate of production and consumption of the resource will be just the same as before intervention, but the rents accrue to government, not to the owner of the resource. The peculiarity of the tax is that it rises quite rapidly towards the end of the life of the resource.

In fact, since exploitation costs are different for different resource owners, taxation of resource rents faces the same practical difficulties as taxation of land rents. Instead the government might use a profit tax, taking almost all the profits accruing to the resource owner after payment of extraction costs. The interesting point is that the rate of depletion should not be affected by the government intervention. We may put the conclusion this way: if we attach no weight to rents accruing to resource owners, it will be possible to increase welfare by altering depletion rates in either direction; but the tax which leads to the greatest increase in welfare will leave depletion rates unchanged. In this sense, the chief income-distributional argument leads to no presumption of bias.

In the common situation where the resource is subject to some degree of monopoly, and the profits accrue abroad so that profit taxation is not a practical possibility, buyers can only get together and threaten to cut demand, for example by taxation, and they are very likely to have to carry out the threat. In this sense, one might want to see a further reduction in the rate of resource depletion, even though it is already less than optimal, when regarded from a different point of view. But, just as in the competitive case, it is possible that the taxation measures of buyers will not, if properly judged, change rates of depletion, but will simply transfer some of the profits (those arising from ownership of the resource rather than the opportunity to restrict supply) to the buyers' governments.

(vii) *Taxation*

Tax treatment of resource extractive industries is typically rather complicated, but its effect on the rate of resource depletion may be substantial. The simplest case is that in which resource owners are subject to a profits tax on receipts less operating expenditures like other producers. In that case the tax will not affect the rate of depletion if it is expected to be applied at a constant rate over time. But a profits tax will, of course, reduce the rate of return a firm obtains from its other investments, and hence lead it to invest too much in conservation relative to other forms of productive investment. Since rates of profits tax are usually high, this effect may be substantial.

The tax, while not affecting the time profile of receipts, will reduce its size, and this will have a disincentive effect on exploration and development expenditure. Thus the existence of a profits tax may lead to a strong bias towards insufficiently rapid resource depletion: less of the resource will be discovered, less of what is discovered will be developed, and what is developed will be produced too slowly. The complexities of actual tax structure, which involve special tax treatment of development expenditures and of resource related profits, and divergences from our simplified profits tax on other activities (such as free depreciation) will modify and may mitigate this general bias.

We should note also that the governments of producing or consuming countries often impose revenue-raising taxes on the use of exhaustible resources. The effect of this is essentially equivalent to increasing the degree of monopoly in resource extraction, and as we argue above this will tend to lead to insufficiently rapid depletion.

4. Economic policy

The most important point in the previous section, which is demonstrated more generally in the technical appendix, is that the price of a resource ought to be little more than the marginal cost of extracting and transporting it, unless the resource is rather close to exhaustion. Thus the analysis of economists who have concentrated on the case of zero extraction costs, though technically important, is quantitatively misleading.[16] We can best summarise the significance of our proposition, and the rest of our arguments, by outlining the policies that appear to be implied by them.

(*a*) The general trend of the argument is that resource depletion often takes place too slowly because of monopoly power exerted by resource owners. Because of demand inelasticity it is quite likely that the losses arising from monopoly are very large, although it must be remembered that they are sustained chiefly by the industrialised countries, and those who make considerable use of resource-intensive products. The usual measures against monopoly, including negotiation with the governments of countries within which the monopoly profits accrue, are presumably desirable.

(*b*) In many cases it is desirable to impose taxes on exhaustible resources, not because they are being depleted too rapidly, but as a means of taxing pure profits generated by the resource. These policies, if properly carried out, would not change the rates of depletion.

(*c*) Since most of the value of resource stocks is in the last few decades of their life, these taxes on resource use do not become significant until only a few decades of resource life remain (at then current rates of depletion). There is no particular argument in favour of taxing the use of natural resources as such when hundreds of years of reserves exist. (This is not to say there may not be other reasons for imposing commodity taxes on sales of exhaustible resources and commodities made from them, reasons of the same kind which lead one to favour taxes on jewellery, cars and cigarettes.)

(*d*) If monopoly power is expected to grow, or taxation is expected to become more difficult (for example, because of its magnitude) there may be a case for government stockpiling of exhaustible resources; but we have not yet explored this possibility.

(*e*) Since there may be reasons for inadequate amounts to be spent on research into resources reserves (or methods of exploiting them), there is a case for governmental and inter-governmental subsidy of surveys and research in this area.

(*f*) Since it is difficult for participants in resource markets to predict resource prices correctly, governments and inter-governmental agencies can contribute to optimal resource use by gathering the information – about existing proved and probable reserves, demand, including substitution possibilities, development of substitute sources, etc. – and developing econometric models to predict resource prices.

Our analysis may have seemed sketchy to those who are prepared to be impressed by the vast apparatus deployed by devotees of world dynamics, and unaware of the iceberg of economic analysis which lies behind the kind of work we have done. We are uncomfortably aware that to many scientists such argument will look rather casual, and yet will actually be incomprehensible. We would challenge defenders of the large simulation and forecasting models to consider whether they really do understand the arguments we have put forward, and how the work of the modellers has been or could be an answer to them. For ourselves, we find no reason to prefer the kind of work done by the global dynamicists to the more staid analysis undertaken by economists. We confess to having provided no forecasts of the very long-run effects of natural resource depletion. Such forecasts would have very little basis, and, therefore, would be subject to enormous errors. They are neither a necessary nor a sufficient basis for policy recommend-ations. An approach that begins from policy questions shows what kind of data and evidence is most needed, and where further research is likely to be most fruitful.

Economists are well aware that the world's store of ex-haustible resources is limited. But in the light of the arguments presented here, we wish to suggest that there is a real danger that the world's resources are being used too slowly. No doubt some materials are being used prodigally: but in general we believe that the interests of future generations will be better served if we leave them production equipment rather than minerals in the ground. In the currently topical case of oil, the arguments that the world is using too little rather than too much seem irresistible.

Technical appendix

(1) It will be useful to derive the theories of optimal and equilibrium depletion of a resource, for the case where future costs and prices are known with certainty. We consider optimality first.

A rather general way of formulating the problem is to assume that the society wishes to maximise total utility, summed over time, where utility at any time depends both upon the rate of use of the resource x and the total stock remaining R:

$$\max W = \int v(x_t, R_t, t)\,\mathrm{d}t \qquad (11)$$

The case of a fixed stock, the extraction costs of which are independent of the amount remaining, is a limiting, but unrealistic, case of equation (11).* A special case is where utility is a function of consumption $u(z_t)$ where

$$z_t = f(k_t, x_t, t) - \dot{k}_t - c(x_t, R_t)$$

in which k is the capital, f is the output, and c is the cost of extracting the resource. Capital accumulation is chosen optimally, k_t is a fixed function of t, and the maximand can be written in the form of equation (11). More generally, it is natural to write equation (11) in the form

$$\max W = \int v(x_t, c(x_t, R_t), t)\,\mathrm{d}t \qquad (12)$$

(with $v_x > 0$, $v_c < 0$, $c_x > 0$, $c_R < 0$, $c_{RR} > 0$), and to note that c being measured in terms of a conventional numéraire (the consumption good in the special case just mentioned)

$$i_t = -\frac{\mathrm{d}v_c}{\mathrm{d}t}\frac{1}{v_c} \qquad (13)$$

is the rate of interest, which will be the rate of time preference or social discount rate in the optimum.

Turning to the maximisation of equation (12), we could simply apply Euler's equation (since $x = -\dot{R}$), but we prefer to use the integral for R

* The limiting case has $v_R = 0$ for $R > 0$, $v = -\infty$ for $R < 0$.

$$R_t = R_0 - \int_0^t x_\tau \mathrm{d}\tau \tag{14}$$

and deduce that a variation of the depletion rates gives

$$W = \int_0^\infty \left\{ (v_x + v_c c_x)\,\delta x_t - v_c c_R \int_0^t \delta x_\tau \mathrm{d}\tau \right\} \mathrm{d}t$$

$$= \int_0^\infty \left\{ v_x + v_c c_x - \int_t^\infty v_c c_R \mathrm{d}\tau \right\} \delta x_t \mathrm{d}t \tag{15}$$

Thus at the optimum, since $\delta W \leqslant 0$ for any feasible variation

$$v_x + v_c c_x \leqslant \int_t^\infty v_c c_R \mathrm{d}\tau \tag{16}$$

with equality if $x_t > 0$. Using equation (13), we can write this as

$$\frac{v_x}{-v_c} = c_x - \int_t^\infty \exp\left(-\int_t^\tau i_\theta \mathrm{d}\theta\right) c_R \mathrm{d}\tau \tag{17}$$

so long as the optimal $x_t > 0$. When the left-hand side is smaller than the right, x_t must be zero. (Recollect that $v_c < 0$.)

The term on the left-hand side of equation (17) is the marginal rate of substitution between use of the resource at t and the numéraire at t; c_x is marginal cost; and the integral is the generalisation to the present problem of the term Qe^{it} that appeared in the text. Consumption of the resource will fall to zero when equation (17) is satisfied for $x = 0$. In general, this might happen more than once, depending on how v depends on t. For simplicity, let us concentrate on the case where once x falls to zero, the resource is never used again. Exploitation of the resource stops when

$$\frac{v_x(0,c(0,R),t)}{-v_c(0,c(0,R),t)} = c_x(0,R) - c_R(0,R)\int_t^\infty \exp\left(-\int_t^\tau i_\theta \mathrm{d}\theta\right) \mathrm{d}\tau$$

$$= c_x(0,R) - c_R(0,R)\,1/i \tag{18}$$

in the case of a constant rate of interest i. At this point, one would expect $-c_R(\mathrm{o},R)$ to be large, and the marginal rate of substitution of the resource for the numéraire would greatly exceed the marginal cost. But consider the situation when stocks are still considerable – or, to be more precise, when $-c_R$ is small. If $-c_R$ will be small for a period sufficiently long for $\exp\left(-\int_t^s i_\theta \mathrm{d}\theta\right)$ to have become small, the integral in equation (17) will be small, and the exhaustibility of the resource is, therefore, approximately irrelevant until significantly large $-c_R$ is in sight. This is the general proposition illustrated for the limiting case by the examples in the text.

It should be noted that there are now resources for which $-c_R$ is already quite significant and likely to become large. In such cases, we have from equation (17) an approximate condition for optimality

$$\frac{v_x}{-v_c} = c_x + \frac{-c_R}{i} \tag{19}$$

where $-c_R$ is an average value of the effect of resource depletion on costs in the medium future, and i is a long-term rate of interest. Perhaps one can get the best impression of the last term in equation (19) if one writes it in the form

$$\frac{c}{iR} \cdot \frac{-Rc_R}{c} = \frac{\text{annual extraction costs}}{\text{imported interest on resource stock}} \tag{20}$$

$$\times \text{elasticity of costs with respect to resource stock}$$

2. Turning to equilibrium, it is not necessary for us to rework the analysis, but only to reinterpret what has already been done. In competitive equilibrium, producers are supposed to maximise total discounted profits at given prices. Thus the owner of a resource will want to maximise

$$\int_0^\infty \exp\left(-\int_0^t i_\theta \mathrm{d}\theta\right)\{p_t x_t - c(x_t,R_t)\}\mathrm{d}t \tag{21}$$

which is an expression of the same mathematical form as equation (12); i_t is now interpreted as the market interest rate, and p_t is the price obtainable for the resource at t. Notice that the analogue of equation (13) holds. Applying our previous analysis, we have as our condition for equilibrium

$$p_t = c_x - \int\limits_t^\infty \exp\left(-\int\limits_t^\tau i\theta\mathrm{d}_\theta\right) c_R \mathrm{d}t \qquad (22)$$

which is effectively the same relationship as equation (17).

In fact – and this is no more than basic welfare economics tells us – the equilibrium will be the optimum if actual prices p_t are equal to the social marginal rates of substitution $v_x/(-v_c)$, and market interest rates are equal to social rates of time preference.

(3) Next we look at the case of a monopolistic resource owner who manipulates prices for his own long-run advantage. The general case appears to be somewhat complicated. We restrict ourselves here to the special case mentioned in the text where there is a time-independent demand function

$$p_t = f(x_t), \qquad f' < 0 \qquad (23)$$

and the monopolist takes it that his marginal revenue is a constant fraction λ (< 1) of the price. (He would be right if f were a constant elasticity function.) Furthermore, there is a constant rate of interest, and the stock of resource is assumed limited although extraction costs are independent of R. Thus equilibrium is given by

$$\left.\begin{array}{l} \lambda f(x_t) = c_x(x_t) + Q\mathrm{e}^{it} \quad (\text{for } x_t > 0) \\[2mm] \displaystyle\int_0^\infty x_t \mathrm{d}t = R_0 \end{array}\right\} \qquad (24)$$

We can use these equations to obtain a relationship determining x_0 as a function of R_0

$$iR_0 = i\int_0^\infty x_t \mathrm{d}t = \int x_t \mathrm{d}[\log\{\lambda f(x_t) - c_x(x_t)\}]$$

$$\qquad\qquad (25)$$

$$= -x_0 \log\left(\lambda f(x_0) - c_x(x_0)\right) + \int_0^{x_0} \log\{\lambda f(x) - c_x(x)\}\mathrm{d}x$$

on integrating by parts, and assuming that x_t becomes, or tends to, zero eventually.

Equation (25) shows us how x_0 depends on λ for given R_0. Differentiating we obtain

$$x_0 \frac{\lambda f'(x_0) - c_{xx}(x_0)}{\lambda f(x_0) - c_x(x_0)} \frac{\partial x_0}{\partial \lambda} = - \int_0^{x_0} \left\{ \frac{f(x)}{\lambda f(x) - c_x(x)} - \frac{f(x_0)}{\lambda f(x_0) - c_x(x_0)} \right\} dx$$

With our assumptions that $f' < 0$ and $c_{xx} > 0$, the coefficient of $\partial x_0 / \partial \lambda$ is positive, and $f/(\lambda f - c_x) = (\lambda - c_x/f)^{-1}$ is an increasing function of x, so that the integral on the right is negative. Thus

$$\partial x_0 / \partial \lambda > 0 \qquad (26)$$

This means that *an increase in the degree of monopoly*, i.e. a reduction in λ, *reduces x_0, the rate of resource depletion*.

Note particularly that this means monopoly reduces the rate of resource depletion, given the level of resources. It does not mean that the monopolist will plan a future rate of sale that is always less than would have been planned by a competitive industry. But our proposition is the interesting one, since it says what reduced monopoly power, or reduced taxation, should bring about, whenever it should be achieved.

10 COMMENTS ON THE PAPERS BY BUTLIN, HEAL, KAY AND MIRRLEES

PETER SIMMONS

The preceding three papers have indicated that, with a rather loose use of words, the present use of natural resources involves at least two types of externality:

(*a*) dynamic externalities associated with the effect that current extraction of the resource has on future opportunities; and

(*b*) static externalities arising from the common property nature of several natural resources, e.g. a single oil well with competitive drilling for oil.

Kay and Mirrlees concentrate largely on the former and assume sole ownership of the natural resource; Heal's paper is partly purely behavioural, but in so far as it considers the economic policy implications of market mechanisms in natural resources it also largely assumes sole ownership; much of the early fishing literature considered the common property externality almost exclusively but the later fishing literature, as Butlin shows, has attempted to include both sources of externality.

I would like to start by commenting on the papers by Kay and Mirrlees, and Heal. It is clear that both of these papers go a long way towards providing a framework within which one can consider whether market behaviour will be intertemporally efficient and optimal in the case of non-renewable natural resources, but since, to some extent, the papers emphasise different forces at work in the situation and so arrive at rather different conclusions, it appears to be fairly clear that economic theory alone cannot determine whether resources are being over-depleted or not in the situation we face. Empirical investigation is necessary.

Kay and Mirrlees use market-behaviour rules to indicate whether the economy is pursuing an intertemporally optimal path. Such a path must, of course, satisfy two conditions. Firstly, for intertemporal efficiency the own rate of return on any asset in the economy must be equal to that on any other asset. Secondly, the common level of the rate of return should be set at a level which is optimal given whatever criterion of intertemporal optimality is being adopted. Perfectly competitive markets in equilibrium under conditions of certainty will guarantee the first condition. Thus Kay and Mirrlees's efficiency condition – their equation (7) – guarantees that the rate of capital gains on the resource is equal to the market interest rate. There are then at least three potential sources of difficulty. Firstly, as Kay and Mirrlees point out, there may be a divergence between market and social rates of time preference. Secondly, as Heal has investigated, there may be no competitive equilibrium because of the role of uncertainty over the future and because of the absence of future markets. Thirdly, elements of monopoly in the pattern of resource ownership may prevent the establishment of a competitive equilibrium. If the social rate of interest is below the market rate then, as Kay and Mirrlees state, there will in general be under-investment in every asset including resources. However, the effect on different assets will not be uniform but will depend on the levels of the elasticity of demand. In particular, if two asset prices are both rising at a rate faster than that which is socially optimal and both have constant elasticity demand functions, then the asset with the more inelastic demand will experience the greater deviation of its rate of accumulation from the optimal level. To assess the significance of this, we will, of course, have to know the pattern of demand elasticities for different assets.

In the case of monopoly Kay and Mirrlees conclude that it is likely that many resources are being over-conserved. Their analysis rests on the assumptions of constant elasticity demand functions, time-independent demands and costs, resource stock independent costs and conditions of certainty. As they state, if these assumptions are relaxed then examples in which monopoly does not restrict resource output relative to competition can be constructed. The question then becomes whether the features of any 'counter-examples' to their results are likely to hold in reality or not. While this is largely an empirical question some discussion at the level of 'casual empiricism' is possible. In the context of natural resource problems, where the behaviour of the functions involved as the quantity of resources tends towards zero is often of importance, the assumption of a constant elasticity demand function is questionable. For several resources it is difficult to believe that at sufficiently high but finite prices there will not be adequate large-scale substitution to drive the demand to zero. The precise properties of functions at extreme values of their arguments are not very amenable to empirical test since, for most resources, no observations at extreme values exist. Similarly, for many resources, growth in population and incomes in a manner which is largely independent of the particular resource market being investigated is likely to lead to outward shifts of the demand function over time. If there is a class of variable elasticity demand functions with which monopoly will not lead to a restriction of output and with no other bery bizarre properties, then surely the general conclusion must be that the effects of monopoly on resource depletion rates are indeterminate. For example, relaxing only the constant elasticity assumption consider the case where the elasticity of demand increases linearly with $x\{f(x) = e^{-\alpha x}\}$, where marginal revenue is restricted to be positive, and marginal extraction costs are taken to be constant at unity. Applying the arguments of Kay and Mirrlees shows that $dx_0/d\alpha > 0$ so that, since the ratio of marginal to average revenue is $(1 - \alpha x)$, an increase in the 'degree of monopoly' α raises x_0. The simultaneous effect of monopoly and uncertainty is also important since this state is presumably the most accurate characterisation of most resource markets. It may well be that there is less uncertainty over future expectations under monopoly than under competition since it may be easier to predict the market demand curve than the future equilibrium market price under competition. Due to the size and typical diversification of resource monopolists it may also be that uncertainty in any particular market is met with a lower degree of risk aversion by the monoplist than by the competitive resource holder.

With regard to uncertainty it is perhaps worth remarking that the over-all effect of uncertainty which arises due to the effect of the future on current decisions in resource problems is again indeterminate. Thus Heal has shown that sufficient risk aversion on the part of competitive holders of a known resource stock leads to over-depletion of resources. However, one might expect risk-averse consumption good producers to stockpile supplies of resource inputs so that part of the over-extraction of a resource stock on this account may not be met by over-depletion of the stock. It is worth noticing that investment in stocks of many energy resources may well be less risky than investment in many types of more highly specific capital goods since energy resources are typically of use in a large variety of industries and countries. If this is so then risk-averse investor behaviour should lead to either a divergence between the rates of return on energy resources and more specific capital assets, or else to a relatively smaller under-conservation of energy resources than under-investment in capital goods. This may be one reason for the observation that prices of Middle-Eastern oil over the period 1954–70 tended to fall rather than rise at a rate equal to some suitable rate of interest.

Part of Heal's paper is purely behavioural in that he wishes to examine the depletion rates of particular resources that will occur under plausible adjustment mechanisms for price and quantity in disequilibrium situations. Both dynamic systems take no explicit account of any resource constraint that there may be in the following sense.

In the simplest model of adjustment, if the stationary point is attained and if there is a resource constraint of the form $\int_0^\infty S(t)\mathrm{d}t = R$ then the stationary point is not sustainable. Similarly, any path moving towards the stationary point will cease to be attainable once the resource has been depleted. This may occur in finite time in general.

A similar point applies to the more complex models: since the resource stock does not enter into expectations in a way which ensures that expected prices tend to infinity to choke off demand, given the forms of demand function assumed, then the market may plan to use more, less or exactly the resource stock available over time. This means that if Heal's models accurately portray the dynamics of particular resource markets then we cannot rule out unforeseen extinction of the supply of some resources.

Heal's first and second dynamic models are both disequilibrium models of a competitive resource market without a futures market in that resource. In these models there is disequilibrium both because markets do not clear and because expectations over resource prices are incorrect. The instability of the results mean that if equilibrating forces are not rapid and if price predictions are difficult to make then we should expect oscillatory behaviour in the resource markets. Since, in a sense there is so much disequilibrium in these models, the adjustment rules proposed are a little difficult to interpret, particularly for supplies. Consider a special case in which markets always clear with price adjusting instantaneously. At each instant of time current price $p(t)$ is known but future prices $E(\tau)$ $(\tau > t)$ have to be estimated on the basis of past prices, and supplies are determined by resource holders' profit-maximising decisions given their price expectations. At any time t, suppliers know the past history of prices from which they form expectations of future prices and hence profit-maximising planned supplies. They supply the planned amount of resources at the present time which by the market clearing condition determines the price of the next instant. Hence at the next instant the history of prices is updated and so price expectations and supply plans are revised. It follows that, over time, supplies will change according to the effect on planned current supply of a revision of expectations multiplied by the revision of expectations with adjustment for the fact that the level of the stock has changed. In mathematical terms, planned supplies at any time t satisfy

$$p(t) = C_s\{s(t)\} + Q(t)$$
$$E(\tau) = C_s\{S(\tau)\} + Q(t)e^{r(\tau - t)}, \qquad \tau > t$$

where $Q(t)$ measures the user cost at stock level $R(t)$ with given interest rate r and price expectations. $Q(t)$ rises if future expected prices are revised upwards at a given time t and rises if the remaining stock falls. If $f(s_t)$ is the market demand at time t (assuming for simplicity a sole seller) then, since at each instant of time actual supplies are determined by the current market equilibrium condition over time, supplies adjust according to

$$f'(S_t)\dot{S}_t = C_{ss}\dot{S}_t + \frac{\partial Q}{\partial E}\dot{E} + \frac{\partial Q}{\partial R}\dot{R}$$

which leads to

$$\dot{S}(t) = \frac{\partial Q/\partial E}{f'(S_t) - C_{ss}(S_t)}\dot{E} - \frac{(\partial Q_t/\partial R_t)S}{f'(S_t) - C_{ss}(S_t)}$$

Hence, if we use Heal's equation for $\dot{E}$ then

$$\dot{S}(t) = \beta_1(p - E) + \beta_2 S$$

where β_1 and β_2 in general are functions of $E(t)$, $R(t)$ and $S(t)$. Thus Heal's equation for supply adjustment can be interpreted as coming from profit-maximising behaviour if we are prepared to postulate that $\beta_2 = 0$. This corresponds to the assumption that the effect of resource depletion in raising prices and reducing supplies over time is currently foreseen. Of course, Heal's models are more complicated than this in that they also allow for market disequilibrium.

Heal's third model appears to be particularly rich in interpretation. The incomplete arbitrage could arise from varying risk premiums on different assets or from adjustment and transaction costs of various kinds including elements of monopolistic barriers to entry in resource markets. The resource market alone could be competitive or monopolistic depending on the levels of resource price and supply. Since the instability of various types of disequilibrium path reappear in this model one might expect this to be reflected in actual market behaviour because of the fairly wide class of cases to which this model can be assumed to pertain.

Heal wishes to apply his model to the Saudi Arabian and Kuwaiti markets for oil. One could imagine two types of application: the econometric estimation of a discrete time form of Heal's adjustment mechanism and the numerical integration of Heal's differential equations for the initial conditions of the start of his sample period and for a variety of parameter values. As a very rough check on the types of parameter values implied by Heal's model I have taken a crude discrete approximation of his model, eliminated the expected price and estimated the two equations. The discrete form of the model is

$$p_{t+1} - p_t = a\left(\frac{A}{Pt} - S_t\right) + \epsilon_{3t}$$

$$E_t = a_3\rho(1+\rho)^{-t}\sum_{\tau=0}^{t}(1+\rho)^\tau p_\tau + a_2(1+\rho)^{-t}\sum_{\tau=0}^{t}(1+\rho)^\tau S_\tau + \epsilon_{1t}$$

$$S_{t+1} - S_t = a_4(p_t - E_t) + \epsilon_{2t}$$

$$E(E_{it}) = 0, \qquad i = 1, 2, 3$$

$$E(\epsilon_{it}\epsilon_{js}) = 0, \qquad t \neq s, \qquad i,j = 1, 2, 3$$

$$E(E_{it}^2) = \sigma_i^2$$

If we assume that the adjustment equations are correctly specified then it is reasonable to assume zero autocorrelation of errors in each equation and zero cross autocorrelation of errors on different equations.

Eliminating E_t from the supply equation yields estimating equations:

$$P_t - P_{t-1} = a_1\{A/P_{t-1} - S_{t-1}\} + \epsilon_{3t}$$

$$S_t - S_{t-1} = (1 + \rho)^{-1}(S_{t-1} - S_{t-2})$$
$$+ a_4(1 - a_3\rho)p_{t-1}$$
$$- a_4(1 + \rho)^{-1}p_{t-2} - a_4a_2S_{t-1} + u_t$$

where

$$u_t = \epsilon_{2t-1} - \epsilon_{2t-2}(1 + \rho)^{-1} - a_4\epsilon_{1t-1} + a_4(1 + \rho)^{-1}\epsilon_{1t-2}$$

Hence the supply equation includes lagged endogenous variables and a moving average error; ordinary least squares estimates would be biased and inconsistent. On the other hand, ordinary least squares estimates of the price equation are likely to be fairly satisfactory under the stochastic specification adopted. For the Saudi Arabian oil market with prices expressed in \$1958 and quantity data for 1955–73 from the *U.N. Monthly Bulletin*, the price equation has been estimated by O.L.S. and the supply equation by iterative generalised least squares using the decomposition of the variance matrix proposed by Peserans.

$$p_t - p_{t-1} = -\frac{173746 \cdot 0}{p_{t-1}} + 0 \cdot 001297\, S_{t-1}$$
$$(69355 \cdot 0)\ (0 \cdot 0005)$$

$R^2 0 \cdot 237$ D.W. $1 \cdot 8026$ $\epsilon_t = 0 \cdot 0774$ ϵ_{t-1}

$$p_t - p_{t-1} = -\frac{52688 \cdot 4}{p_{t-1}} - 0 \cdot 000373\, S_{t-1} + 568341 \cdot 0\left(\frac{D_{t-1}}{p_{t-1}}\right)$$
$$(71842 \cdot 0)\ (0 \cdot 0007) \qquad\qquad (147848 \cdot 0)$$

$$- 0 \cdot 001035\ (D_{t-1}S_{t-1})$$
$$(0 \cdot 001)$$

$R^2 0 \cdot 767$ D.W. $1 \cdot 4$ $\epsilon_t = 0 \cdot 29$ ϵ_{t-1}

$$S_t - S_{t-1} = 1 \cdot 338(S_{t-1} - S_{t-2}) - 217 \cdot 099\, p_{t-1} + 163 \cdot 921\, p_{t-2}$$
$$\quad (0 \cdot 1262) \qquad\qquad (12914 \cdot 9) \qquad (12463 \cdot 3)$$

$$\quad - 0 \cdot 0000\, S_{t-1}$$
$$\quad (0 \cdot 0000)$$

$R^2 0 \cdot 949 \quad$ D.W. $3 \cdot 038 \quad \epsilon_t = -0 \cdot 535 \quad \epsilon_{t-1}$

Figures in parentheses are standard errors. D is a dummy variable allowing the estimated parameters to shift from 1970 onwards. The rather strange sign pattern of coefficients may partly be due to the rather crude discrete approximation taken. With these results, predicted prices do fall until 1970 and then rise.

An alternative approach is to use plausible parameter values of the correct sign and numerically integrate Heal's system over the sample period. In this case a scaling parameter A has been selected to be of the same order of magnitude as S. For $\rho = 0 \cdot 5$, $0 \cdot 1$, $0 \cdot 01$ and $a_3 = 0 \cdot 5$; $a_2 = 0 \cdot 0001$, $0 \cdot 01$, $0 \cdot 001$; and $a_1 = 0 \cdot 001$ or $0 \cdot 01$ it appears to be difficult to find initial values of E which ensure that quantities rise over the sample period. The typical case appears to be that actual and expected prices first fall and then rise over the sample period, but that, in general, quantities either fall continuously or initially rise and then fall. The integration method used was a fourth order predictor corrector which experience has shown to be fairly satisfactory.

The problem of applying the third model of Heal is very interesting since, while this model can be analytically integrated, it does not appear to be a simple matter to eliminate the unobservable expected prices. Eliminating supplies the model can be written as

$$\dot{E}/E = \left(\gamma - \frac{\beta}{\eta} \right) a_r + \left\{ a \left(\frac{\beta}{\eta} - \gamma \right) - \beta \right\} E$$

or equivalently as $\dot{E} = a\, r\, E + bE^2$. This implies that

$$E(t) = \frac{A\, a\, r\, e^{art}}{(1 - bAe^{art})}$$

on the assumption that r is constant where A is an initial condition on E.

Substituting this equation back into the differential equation for $S(t)$ and integrating yields

$$\dot{S}/S = \frac{ar - e^{art}c}{1 - de^{art}}$$

where $c = a(rbA + arA)$; $d = bA$;

$$S(t) = Be^{art}(1 - de^{art})\frac{a(c-d)}{ad}$$

in which $\quad c = ar\left[\left\{a\left(\frac{\beta}{\eta} - \gamma\right) - \beta\right\}A^2 + \left(\gamma - \frac{\beta}{\eta}\right)aA\right]$

$$d = A\left\{a\left(\frac{\beta}{\eta} - \gamma\right) - \beta\right\}$$

$$a = a\left(\gamma - \frac{\beta}{\eta}\right)$$

$$b = a\left(\frac{\beta}{\eta} - \gamma\right) - \beta$$

and β provides an initial condition for supplies. The problems of attempting to 'estimate' the parameters and initial conditions of this equation appear to be formidable. The coefficients c, d, a, b, a, A, and B are all independent so that in principle some idea of the degree to which such an equation fits the data could be gathered by assuming prior values for d and a, and a constant interest rate and estimating the equation by O.L.S.

A fundamental parameter of both the papers by Kay and Mirrlees and Heal is the elasticity of demand for resources. The quantitative significance of their results depend on its value. Thus there is a considerable need to estimate this elasticity, which, in turn, has clear implications for the kind of data required: not only quantity but also price data are necessary. Since the demand for resource inputs is largely a derived demand it is clear that the elasticity of demand depends on the elasticity of substitution between resources and other inputs into production, and the prices of all inputs and, in general, on the level of output. Relatively little work seems to have been done at a disaggregated level on the elasticity with respect to natural resources. However, the work of Nordhaus and Tobin indicates that it may be greater than unity, thus implying a relatively elastic resource demand function in the aggregate.

Apart from these detailed comments, it is worth making the

rather general point that, with the presence of natural resources and a form of production which may or may not severely curtail present and future consumption possibilities, economists might do worse than consider models yielding the optimal allocations of resources (natural and man-made) to invest directed towards either altering our technological dependence on natural resources or to augmenting the stock of natural resources. It is clear that any such model should take account account of the uncertainty which is intrinsic to much research and development activity and should also focus on those aspects of natural resource scarcity most crucial to the possibilities for future consumption. However, we can abstract from the uncertainty to indulge in some simple exercises which indicate the crucial characteristics of such a model in which resources are devoted to attempting to augment the outstanding stock of natural resources. Thus suppose that there is a single consumable output produced from capital and resources and that increments to the stock of resources may be 'produced' via exploration and innovation under conditions of certainty from capital and resources. The physical production processes are thus governed by the equations

$$c(t) + \dot{K}_1(t) + \dot{K}_2(t) = F\{K_1(t), R_1(t)\}$$

$$\dot{X} = GK_2(t), \qquad R_2(t) - R_1(t) - R_2(t)$$

$$X(0) = \overline{X}, \qquad X(t) \geqslant 0$$

where $C(t)$ is consumption; $K_i(t)$, $R_i(t)$ are capital stock and resource utilisation devoted to sector i (1 for consumption; 2 for resource production) and $X(t)$ is the stock of resources remaining at t. What sort of restrictions might one impose on $G(.)$? As a first approximation it would seem reasonable to take G to be strictly concave with non-negative marginal products. It is more questionable as to whether $G(.)$ should be taken to be bounded above; given the high level of aggregation of models of this kind it is sensible to think of X as measuring the outstanding available stock of all non-renewable natural resources expressed in some energy unit such as Btu. The function $G(.)$ then reflects both increases in the supply of existing resources and innovations in the discovery of new non-renewable resources. Again as a first approximation it might be reasonable to take $G(.)$ to be unbounded but with marginal products which tend to zero, as the input quantities tend to infinity.

Whether the possibility of technical progress will offset the constraint on future consumption possibilities imposed by scarce natural resources is obviously a fairly complex question which depends both on the degree of returns to scale of $F(.)$ and $G(.)$ and on the substitution possibilities between capital and resources. To ensure that there is a problem to investigate, it is sensible to assume $F\{K_1(t),0\} = 0$. If $G(.)$ is homogeneous of degree one then if it is possible to have proportionally growing $K_2(t)$ with positive consumption then from any initial position with $\dot{X}(0) \geqslant 0$, we can preserve $\dot{X}(t) \geqslant 0$ with proportional growth in R_1, R_2 and K_2 and with $C(t) > 0$ indefinitely. On the other hand, the finiteness of the earth suggests that constant returns to scale of $G(.)$ are very unlikely.

Similarly, if $G(.)$ does not exhibit constant returns to scale and for all $K_2(t)$

$$\lim_{R_2(t)\to 0} \frac{\partial G(K_2 R_2)}{\partial R_2} < 1$$

then eventually the economy must run out of resources. This is analogous to the system failing to be productive in the production of natural resources. Hence a necessary condition for technical progress to be adequate in offsetting Malthusian conditions is that for some $K_2(t)$, $R_2(t)$,

$$\frac{\partial G(K_2 R_2)}{\partial R_2} > 1$$

Beyond these rather vague statements, it is worth briefly looking at a definite case in order primarily to get more precise answers about the rate at which the economy should allocate resources to the research and development sector. In this context the Cobb–Douglas case is of some interest partly because it satisfies many of the desirable properties outlined above; partly because quite a lot is already known about properties of optimal resource depletion and accumulation paths in economics without an explicit research and development factor.

For illustrative purposes we may take as a criterion of optimality

$$\int_0^T \frac{1}{1-v} C(t)^{1-v} \mathrm{d}t, \qquad v > 0$$

where $C(t)$ is consumption of period t and $[0,T]$ is the planning horizon. We are thus involved in the problem

$$\max \int_0^T \frac{1}{1-v} C(t)^{1-v} dt$$

subject to

$$C(t) + \dot{K}_1(t) + \dot{K}_2(t) = K_1(t)^\alpha R_1(t)^{1-\alpha}$$

$$\dot{X}(t) = R_2(t)^\gamma K_2(t)^\beta - R_1(t) - R_2(t); \quad \gamma + \beta < 1; \quad \gamma > 0; \quad \gamma > 0$$

$$X(0) = \overline{X} \quad X(t) \geqslant 0 \quad X(T) = 0$$

The variables of choice are $C(t)$, $R_1(t)$, $R_2(t)$ and the allocation of investment to investment in each of the two sectors, and there are also implicitly non-negativity constraints $R_1(t) \geqslant 0$, $R_2(t) \geqslant 0$. Let $\lambda(t)$ be the investment ratio

$$\lambda(t) = \frac{\dot{K}_1(t)}{\dot{K}_2(t)}$$

Then we can write the output balance equation as

$$\dot{K}_2(t) = \frac{1}{1+\lambda(t)} [F\{K_1(t), R_1(t)\} - C]$$

$$\dot{K}_1(t) = \frac{\lambda(t)}{1+\lambda(t)} [F\{K_1(t)_1 R_1(t)\} - C]$$

Applying standard methods we can define

$$H = u(c) + p_1(t) \frac{\lambda(t)}{1+\lambda(t)} \{F(K_1, R_1) - C\} + \frac{p_2(t)}{1+\lambda(t)} \{F(K_1, R_1) - C\}$$

$$+ p_3[G\{K_2(t), R_2(t)\} - R_1(t) - R_2(t)] + \mu(t)X(t)$$

$$+ \delta_1 R_1(t) + \delta_2 R_2(t)$$

Then the following necessary conditions must be satisfied by an optimal time path of investment and resource depletion:

$$u'(c) = p_1 = p_2 \tag{1}$$

$$p_1 F_R = p_3 - \delta_1 \tag{2}$$

$$p_3(G_R - 1 - \delta_2) = 0 \tag{3}$$

$$\delta_1 R_1 = 0 \tag{4}$$

$$\delta_2 R_2 = 0 \tag{5}$$

$$\mu X = 0 \tag{6}$$

$$\dot{p}_1 = -p_1 F_K \tag{7}$$

$$\dot{p}_2 = -p_3 G_K \tag{8}$$

$$\dot{p}_3 = -\mu \tag{9}$$

at all times t, together with the feasibility conditions. These conditions do, of course, have a natural economic interpretation. The shadow prices of investment in each sector must be equal and both equal to the foregone marginal utility of consumption. The rate of capital gains on investment in the consumption sector must be equal to the marginal product of capital in that sector; while in cases in which $R_1 > 0$ the rate of capital gains on investment in the resource producing sector must be equal to the indirect marginal product of capital in that sector in terms of consumption ($\dot{p}_2 = p_2 F_R G_K$). Moreover if $R_2, R_1 > 0$ then

$$\frac{G_K}{G_R} = \frac{F_K}{F_R} \tag{10}$$

so that the allocation of inputs between sectors is efficient. If also in some interval $X(t) > 0$ to yield $\dot{p}_3 = 0$ and $R_1 > 0$ then

$$\frac{\dot{F}_R}{F_R} = F_K \tag{11}$$

so that the rate of return on resource input into the consumption good industry must be equal to the rate of return on holding natural resources in that sector.

Imposing the Cobb–Douglas forms for production and the isoelastic form for welfare we can see that on an optimum path we must have $R_1(t) > 0$ all t since otherwise the equation

$$\frac{\dot{c}}{c} = \frac{1}{v} a K_1{}^{\alpha-1} R_1{}^{1-\alpha} = \frac{1}{v} \beta K_1{}^{\alpha} R_1{}^{-\alpha} \delta K_2{}^{\delta-1} R_2{}^{\gamma} + \delta_1 c^v \delta K_2{}^{\delta-1} R_2{}^{\gamma} \tag{12}$$

cannot hold unless $R_2(t)$ also vanishes which, since $p_3 > 0$ in this case, contradicts the equation

$$\gamma K_2 \delta R_2{}^{\gamma-1} = 1 + \delta_2 \quad \text{for } \delta_2 > 0.$$

Hence $R_1(t) > 0$ at all t on an optimal path. Moreover $p_3 > 0$ and so we also cannot have $R_2(t) = 0$ at any time on an optimal path. Thus on an optimal path $\delta_1 = \delta_2 = 0$.

We can investigate the nature of optimal allocations by first considering phases of the solution with $X(t) > 0$ and, for these phases, modifying the arguments which already exist for slightly simpler resource models. If $X(t) > 0$ then $\mu = -p_3 = 0$. If $k_1 = K_1/R_1$ then equation (11) and constant returns to scale in the consumption good industry implies $\dot{k}_1 = k_1^{\alpha}$ or

$$k_1(t) = \{(1-a)t + k_1(0)^{1-\alpha}\}^{1/(1-\alpha)}.$$

But then we can integrate up the solutions for the other variables using this result. From equations (3) and (12) if $\phi(t) = \{(1-a)t + k_1(0)^{1-\alpha}\}$

$$K_2 = a_0 \phi(t)^{(1-\gamma)/\{(1-\alpha)(1-\delta-\gamma)\}}$$

$$R_2 = a_1 \phi(t)^{\delta/\{(1-\alpha)(1-\delta-\gamma)\}}$$

$$C = A\phi(t)^{\alpha v/(1-\alpha)}$$

$$R_1 = B - Aa_2 \phi(t)^{\{(\alpha v-1)/(1-\alpha)\}+1} \\ - a_3 \phi(t)^{\{1-\gamma-\alpha(1-\delta-\gamma)\}/\{(1-\alpha)(1-\delta-\gamma)\}}$$

$$X = D + a_4 \phi(t)^{\{[\delta/^{\flat}(1-\alpha)(1-\delta-\gamma)]\}+1} \\ - Bt + Aa_5(t)^{\{(\alpha v-1)/(1-\alpha)\}+2} \\ + a_6 \phi(t)^{\{1-\gamma-\alpha(1-\delta-\gamma)\}/\{(1-\alpha)(1-\delta-\gamma)\}}$$

where a_i are positive constants and A, B, D are integration constants which must be chosen to provide initial conditions for c, R_1 and R_2 to ensure that either the relevant fixed endpoint conditions are satisfied or that the appropriate transversality conditions hold at the end of the plan. The initial conditions for K_1, K_2 and X are, of course, historically given.

One deduces from these solutions that all variables except possibly X and R_1 rise monotonically over time. $R_1(t)$ and X may rise or fall depending on the precise parameter values. Moreover K_2/R_2 grows with the sign of $(1-\gamma-\delta) > 0$ while k_1 grows at $1/(1-a)$ so that the relative growth of capital intensity in the two sectors depends only on technological conditions. Generally $K_1 = k_1 R_1$ can also rise or fall over time.

For intervals in which $X(t) = 0$ again $\delta_i = 0$ but $\mu > 0$. In this case it appears to be more difficult analytically to integrate the solution paths, but the qualitative behaviour can be deduced. In this case consumption monotonically increases, the ratio of resource inputs in the two sectors R_1/R_2 is constant and k_1, K_2 and R_1 are not monotonic but typically initially rise and then fall.

11 RESOURCE CONSERVATION AND THE MARKET MECHANISM

IVOR PEARCE

'Then you keep moving round I suppose,' said Alice.
'Exactly so,' said the Hatter: 'as the things get used up.'
'But when you come to the beginning again?' Alice ventured
to ask. 'Suppose we change the subject,' the March Hare
interrupted, yawning. 'I'm getting tired of this . . .'

The Treasury Paper on Economic Growth* is a reasoned and
reasonable document designed perhaps to take some of the
heat out of current debate on the subject of the world's dwindling resources. It may, however, incline the non-specialist
reader towards the acceptance of at least two arguments which
are both false and more than potentially damaging. The first
of these arguments claims that ordinary market forces will
automatically take care of all necessary rationing of scarce
raw material much more effectively than any government
could. The second proclaims that, if problems do arise, we can
always rely upon technological advance to solve them. The
market forces argument goes something like this.

Oil in the ground must always be worth in the future exactly
what would be earned if it were extracted now and sold, the
proceeds being invested at the expected rate of interest until
the future date at which it is intended to extract it. If, therefore,
the present price at which rights to extract oil from the ground
are exchanged is p_0 then the price p_t at which they will be
exchanged at the future time t is given by $p_0(1+r)^t$ where r is
the rate of interest. This must be true for all time t for if any

* This paper was originally prepared as a comment on White
Paper No. 2 on *Economic Growth* published by the Australian
Treasury Department, Canberra.

owner expected that at any time t from zero to infinity the royalty on oil extracted would be greater than $p_0(1+r)^t$ he would earn more than the rate of interest r on his assets by refusing the right to extract oil now, granting it only at time t. Furthermore, the fact that the owner might wish to spend his wealth before time t is irrelevant both to his present rate of earnings and to the decision as to the date of extraction; for there always exists, presumably, someone who would wish to buy an asset at its present value, provided only both buyer and seller share the same views about its future selling price.

It follows that, when a shortage is foreseen at time t so that the expected price p_t rises, it is necessary for p_0 to rise also to maintain the identity $p_t = p_0(1+r)^t$. This discourages current demand reducing the rate of extraction. At the same time the rising current price induces the invention of substitutes well in advance of the time that need becomes desperate. Moreover, since the oil industry almost by definition must know more about the oil industry than anyone else, the market will necessarily do a better job of anticipating the future than could any committee of public servants. Hence, everything should be left to the market.

As a final clincher, we are reminded that not so long ago the same fears now being expressed about oil were then felt about coal, whereas today, following technical advances, it is understood that very large reserves of coal exist relative to usage. The coal problem seems to have disappeared of its own accord. Therefore, by extrapolation we may deduce that the oil problem also will go away if we leave it alone.

We could, of course, attempt to counter this argument from extrapolation by asking anti-conservationists what went wrong with the expectations of the American Indians who sold Manhattan Island to the colonists for a handful of beads; or why the market seems to have failed to protect the bison. We could wish to know why expectation of future scarcity of food did not prevent soil erosion from too intensive farming practices or what happened to the whale industry. Or why, if the market will do the job, has it proved necessary to plunge up to our government ankles into the business of protecting baby seals from fur hunters? But this will not do; for our own examples, as well as those of the Treasury, serve only to illustrate the fact that in the present circumstances extrapolation is an unsatisfactory form of prediction and no substitute for proper enquiry into cause and effect. Indeed, we have already accused the authors of the government paper of unwarranted extrapolation on the subject of technical change. We turn therefore to matters of logic.

Let us assume that the market is in fact working and that our oil reserves are being carefully and efficiently husbanded in accordance with the expectations of an oil industry more knowledgeable than we are or our public servants. The academic theory set out above now enables us to deduce the very knowledge the oil industry has which is denied to us. We can look deeply into its collective mind. Once we know the theory and the expected rate of return we are able to calculate the oil industry's expected future price by the formula $p_t = p_0(1+r)^t$.

At the present time it would be a poor investor who could not, somewhere in the world, get 10 per cent on his money. Let us suppose that this is the expected rate. It now follows that the oil industry must be expecting that in thirty years the royalty on oil extraction will be some sixteen times its present rate. Peering a little further into the future, it must be expecting that in sixty years the charge will be 250 times its present rate and in 130 years more than 65,000 times its present rate.

Of course, it could be argued that 10 per cent is a very high and unrealistic interest rate due largely to current inflation. Let us therefore put the expected rate at a more modest 6 per cent. The expected royalty rate need then be no more than 117 times the current rate after 130 years and requires 250 years to reach 13,000 times the current rate. Perhaps these are the oil companies' expectations! Suppose they are.

Since we have eliminated the effect of inflation we may calculate in figures comparable to today's values the expected price of petrol 250 years from now. Indeed, if royalties currently take up 10 per cent of the selling price of petrol, then \$400+ per gallon is implied. Oil companies must believe now, at this moment, that in 200 years the automobile as we know it will have long since disappeared. And it should be noted that this takes fully into account all known reserves of oil and all expectations of future discoveries which the superior knowledge of dealers in oil enables them to foresee.

Reflect that the grandchildren of persons now living may well

G

have, as part of their immediate family, people who are to live 200 years hence, and consider the nature of the world in which the oil companies can be presumed to expect them to live. Either some technical innovation will have provided them with cheap transport and oil will be required only for some esoteric purpose in the manufacture of some remarkably valuable product or only the very, very rich will have transport at all.

At this point, the reader may well feel that there is something wrong. The expected facts do not seem to accord fully with the notion from which we began, namely that 'oil reserves are being carefully and efficiently husbanded'. Nor does the implicit future seem to be a desirable one. Where does the argument go wrong?

Consider the following imaginary world, Solely to simplify calculations we allow only one product, namely oil. The population is constant over time and consists only of fathers and sons. The expected life span of each person is two time periods only, one period spent as a son and the other as a father, Everyone has exactly the same tastes, that is, derives the same enjoyment from the consumption of oil. It is agreed, therefore, that justice demands that everyone should be treated throughout his life in exactly the same way. We suppose first that this is the world of the Garden of Eden before the fall. Oil is provided from Heaven under the direction of a store-keeper, who offers for sale the same fixed amount in each time period. Only fathers receive incomes. Sons are allowed to borrow from a bank at the rate of interest r on condition they pay back their borrowings when they become fathers.

In this imaginary world each person will arrange his spending so as to maximise his utility according to a function

$$u_t = u_t(x_t, x_{t+1}), \tag{1}$$

where u_t measures the life happiness of an individual born at time t depending on his consumption of oil x_t and x_{t+1} during periods t and $t+1$ respectively. The maximising choice will be subject to a constraint requiring that the value at time t of total expenditure must be equal to the value at time t of total income to be received at time $t+1$. Thus the chosen x_t, x_{t+1} must satisfy

$$p_t x_t + p_{t+1}(1+r)^{-1}x_{t+1} = y_{t+1}(1+r)^{-1} \tag{2}$$

where y_{t+1} is the income given to each father, and p_t and p_{t+1} are the prices paid for oil. The solution to this problem is given by the equation

$$\frac{\partial u_t}{\partial x_t} = p_t \lambda \quad \text{and} \quad \frac{\partial u_t}{\partial x_{t+1}} = p_{t+1}(1+r)^{-1}\lambda \qquad (3)$$

where the left-hand sides are marginal utilities with respect to consumption in each time period and λ may be interpreted as the utility of money at time t.

It is clear from equation (3) that sons will wish to consume less oil than fathers unless the future is discounted. The reason for this is that it is cheaper to buy oil as a father because of the need to borrow when a son. However, we suppose that there are always, in the stationary population, just as many sons as fathers and the utility functions (1) are the same for everyone no matter what the date of birth. It follows that each period will see the same total demands made on the celestial storekeeper who offers the same total supply. Furthermore, incomes to each father y are always the same so that $p_t = p_{t+1}$ and so on for ever. Every person receives the same treatment to achieve perfect distribution.

Note at the same time the operation of the banking system: sons borrow; fathers pay back more than they borrow to meet the interest rate. The banks' profits are returning to Heaven, together with the storekeepers' receipts in order to provide fathers' incomes.

After the fall everything is changed. People, having eaten of the Tree of Knowledge, have come to understand that only a limited amount of oil is available for future generations. As a punishment for sin, the whole stock of oil has been handed over to Satan who now makes available for sale only what is profitable. It has been revealed also that the world is to end at time T.

Incomes continue to be received by fathers at the same rate as before the fall, and there is no expectation of change. The bank is bounded by its rules to borrow from or lend to Satan at the rate r just as for individual consumers. Demand schedules for consumers are readily obtained by solving equations (2) and (3). Satan, however, has been denied direct knowledge of these demand equations. The best he can do is to offer for sale or not offer for sale according to whether prices do or do not satisfy the profit maximising condition

$$p_t = p_0(1+r)^t \tag{4}$$

already noted. But, of course, at any time t no market ordinarily exists in which prices $p_{t+1}, p_{t+2} \ldots$ can be observed. Satan, therefore, has opened a market in futures, and stands ready to offer fully enforceable contracts to purchase oil in the future at future prices up to time T satisfying his supply condition (4), at the same time clearing his total stock by the end of the world. The government, concerned with the rights of unborn generations, has appointed a commission to make contracts on their behalf, a simple exercise since it is known that all persons have the same tastes for ever and the commission (though not Satan) knows these tastes.

Consider now the level of oil consumption in the new world. Prices must be rising at the rate r to satisfy equation (4). Hence, for p_{t+1} in the demand equations (3) we may substitute $p_t(1+r)$ so that we have

$$\frac{\partial u_t}{\partial x_t} = \lambda p_t \quad \text{and} \quad \frac{\partial u_t}{\partial x_{t+1}} = \lambda p_t.$$

It follows that each consumer, and the commission buying for those unborn, will choose quantities of oil so that the last unit purchased in each time period gives the same increment of welfare. If the future is not discounted this means the *same* quantity will be purchased by any given consumer both as father and as son. This is different from the world before the fall.

Clearly also we shall have

$$\frac{\partial u_{t+1}}{\partial x_{t+1}} = \lambda p_{t+1},$$

for the consumer born at time $t+1$. The utility of the last £1 worth bought by each consumer is growing over time. If we make the usual assumption this means that the total oil consumed by each person is getting less and less over time. The less oil one has the more satisfaction is gained from an extra unit.

Clearly, Satan has to be selling a steadily diminishing amount in each time period to satisfy both supply and demand conditions. Those born early are able to consume more oil than those born later. Oil is being used up too fast. *Despite the creation, in the present, of a market in which representatives of unborn generations enter with full knowledge, the free competitive market fails to replicate the ideal conditions prevailing before the fall.*

It is instructive to ask why the free market does fail. The reason is in fact easy to see. The free market works when the real cost of producing utility is exactly measured by the price paid by the consumer. After the fall the real cost of making an extra gallon of oil available at time $t + 1$ is simply one gallon of oil given up at some other time. If the relative prices of oil in different time periods are to be proportional to relative costs (i.e. to be a measure of relative costs) then the price of oil must be the *same* in every time period just as it was before the fall. It is not the same, in fact, because Satan is being misled by the existence of an interest rate into believing that to get oil at time $t + 1$ from oil at time t, he must 'pay', not p_t, but $p_t(1 + r)$, that is, what he would have earned (apparently) if he had sold the oil at time t and lent the revenue to the bank. Satan's policy misled society because the act of selling oil and lending the proceeds does not create any more oil. Indeed, if oil is sold at time t and the revenue invested until time $t + 1$ the money then available would buy back only the same quantity of oil given up; for the price will have risen at the rate r. Satan's mistake is that he chooses to maximise money profit, failing to foresee the effect of his own decision on prices. In modern parlance this would be called an *externality*. It is well known by economists that the market fails in the presence of externalities.

All of this raises the question 'was the Garden of Eden really perfect?' Answer, 'no'. The consumer too is fooled by the rate of interest. Indeed, we have cheated a little in suggesting in the previous paragraph that the price of oil *to the consumer* was the same in every period. It is true that the market price remained constant all the time, but since sons were forced to pay a rate of interest as well as the market price, to each individual the money cost appears to fall. This explains why more was purchased by fathers than by sons. Clearly life consumption in the Garden of Eden was the same for each person. It would have been just as easy to abolish money and give every individual his share of oil at birth. The consumer born at time t would then maximise u_t subject to $x_t + x_{t+1} = $ constant giving,

$$\frac{\partial u_t}{\partial x_t} = \frac{\partial u_t}{\partial x_{t+1}},$$

which is different from equation (3). Eden could have been improved. The externality was present also in the consumer's choice.

The reason why life was so much much more difficult after the fall than before was simply that before the fall the time horizon of the individual consumer was so short that the externality could do little damage. Satan's time horizon, however, reached to the end of the world. Enough time was allowed to reveal the ultimate absurdity of exponentially rising prices. The $400 gallon of petrol had to be envisaged.

We now come to something more difficult. Those who defend the market mechanism are really saying that *no matter what the wishes of consumers may be* and *no matter what the conditions of production may be* the process of competition will determine the best use of resources through prices. In other words, the wishes of consumers will make themselves felt whatever these wishes might be. There is no need to plan. The hidden hand of Adam Smith will do all that is necessary.

We have now refuted this claim with a counter-example. Nothing further is necessary to show that planning and controls are called for in general to deal with the problem of scarce resources. On the other hand, we have identified the externality which causes the breakdown as a rate of interest which leads both consumers and producers to believe incorrectly that the act of saving and investment can create oil. Given that, in the real world, saving creates capital which can produce extra goods in general, even though it cannot create scarce resources, which are – by definition – fixed, might it not be pertinent to enquire whether the introduction into the model of productive capital would restore the value of the price mechanism? The answer is 'no'.

In the first place, a rate of interest can exist, as a consequence of risk, with no productive capital. In the second place, even with productive capital, the externality is still present though in more complicated form.

Let us suppose that we have two commodities, oil and goods in general with prices p and q respectively, And let oil be capable of use both as indestructible productive capital and as a consumption good. One unit of oil may then be rented at an annual rent rp and used together with (say) labour to produce goods. The quantity of goods produced annually by the last unit of oil used as capital will be called the marginal physical product (m.p.p.) of oil in goods. Competitition will ensure that the value, q(m.p.p.) of goods produced annually is equal to the rental of the capital used to produce it, i.e.

$$rp = q(\text{m.p.p.}) \quad \text{or} \quad \frac{p}{q} = \frac{\text{m.p.p.}}{r} \tag{5}$$

Equation (5) determines how much oil will be reserved for use as capital. But the presence of other goods for consumption makes no difference whatever to the need to satisfy equations (2), (3) and (4), and by equation (4) the price of oil which must emerge in Satan's market for futures in oil must be growing over time at the rate r. Furthermore, it is easy to introduce assumptions which will ensure that q remains constant over time provided production is constant. It follows the m.p.p./r must be rising over time if the competitive condition (5) is to be satisfied at each time period.

In order to secure a rising m.p.p./r it is necessary either that m.p.p. should rise or r fall. If m.p.p. is to rise, under the usual assumptions the amount of oil to be used as capital should be steadily reduced. This, in turn, will affect the price p of oil in the market. If, on the other hand, r is to fall, this will render incorrect the choice made by both consumers and producers as to their future consumptions and offers for sale. Notice especially that as r becomes small, the rate at which p must rise equally becomes small.

The reader will indeed notice that in allowing Satan to create a future market in oil to settle for all time the price of oil, we leaned over backwards to be fair to the price mechanism. We allowed the oil owner to have a knowledge of the behaviour of markets in the future which even the most knowledgeable oil mogul could never have in the real world, and we have shown that even then expectations as to future events must be falsified. To imagine that operators in the market could foresee also the effect of their behaviour on the rate of interest in the future would completely destroy both the concept of competition and the notion of profit maximisation.

The Garden of Eden fable was introduced to demonstrate

the difficulty in its most obvious form. Equation (5) illustrates its presence still in the more complicated and realistic case. Even more complex cases can easily be devised. Indeed a limited and non-producible natural resource is a little like a stock of capital which can be used up, and it has long been understood by economists and planners that the market is a poor instrument for the determination of the best social-investment policy. The problem of choosing and attaining an optimal investment/resource use plan is highly complex and requires, before we begin, information which no businessman can be expected to have. The interested reader is referred to an extensive and rapidly growing economic literature where as yet no real consensus has been attained.

So far we have established the fact that a competitive market operating under the most favourable conditions is likely to use up limited resources far too quickly, and will discover its mistake only when it is too late to correct it. Reasons will now be given why the rate of usage may be even greater when conditions are less favourable.

Whenever plans are made about the future an element of uncertainty is bound to be involved. Contrast the attitudes of consumers and producers to uncertainty. Consumers fear that some essential or specially useful commodity may be used up so that their children's standard of living might fall catastrophically. Producers may fear this also in their role as consumers, but they fear also some unexpected technological change, which might devalue the scarce resource which they control. If some close substitute were found for oil, carefully husbanded reserves might lose their worth. The risk effect will be to induce oil producers to extract their wealth from the ground earlier than they otherwise might. Nor is it any answer to this argument to point out that consumers also lose if oil is left in the ground to waste simply because the discovery of a substitute was never foreseen. The consumer in such a case loses very little, but the producer loses the greater part of his personal wealth. The social loss is accompanied by a very considerable redistribution of wealth against the owner of the oil royalty. In short, the risk of obsolescence causes the royalty owner to discount the future much more heavily than the consumer.

Mention of 'discounting the future' brings us to another source of misunderstanding. In academic studies of optimal plans for the future, it is commonplace to assume that future consumption is less valuable than present consumption. If this were true, we should, of course, have an excuse for consuming more oil now. It is worth while, therefore, to examine the origin of this peculiar notion.

First, there is the story of the prodigal son. If all of us are prodigal sons, it is claimed, we must enjoy goods consumed today more than goods consumed in the future. But this is nonsense as the Bible story itself illustrates. When the prodigal son had used up all his substance, he bitterly regretted his behaviour and wished he had consumed nothing earlier. Indeed, he discounted the past as heavily as he previously discounted the future. The prodigal son's 'discounting' arose not because his pleasure from late consumption was less, but because he was a careless planner. We do not wish to plan carelessly. Our plan must look as good to us *after* it is executed as it did when it was conceived.

In a more sophisticated version, the prodigal-son theory of discounting is associated with the rate of interest. Attempts are sometimes made to justify the existence of a rate of interest by arguing that the lender gives up more than his principal; he gives up also the extra pleasure he would have got from consuming now instead of later when the loan is repaid. In consequence, the rate of interest must settle at whatever rate lenders discount future consumption: r is a measure of the social discount rate. However, such a 'theory' can have no more validity than the discredited prodigal-son argument on which it rests. The rate of interest exists for reasons quite different from any notion of time discounting.

Finally, it is suggested that we should discount the future because we expect growth or technical advance. Since future generations are likely on this account to be better off than we are, we are relieved from the necessity of making current sacrifice for future gain. The future can be left to take care of itself.

This last argument is thoroughly irresponsible. Not only does it rest entirely upon extrapolation, but the extrapolation itself is inaccurate. There is no evidence whatever from history to support the hypothesis that real wealth will grow forever at 6 per cent per annum, or even 2 per cent, or any other rate needed to justify a positive social discount rate. On the contrary,

G*

one has only to imagine what the world would be like if it sustained a growth rate of 2 per cent for 1000 years to see how ridiculous the belief in a constant growth rate really is. Moreover, even if it were true that we could be sure of sufficient growth in output per head to justify the application of a social discount rate for just the foreseeable future, it is highly unlikely that the current rate of extraction of oil has very much to do with that rate whatever it is. Much more likely is that natural resources are being used up at the present frightening rate, not on the basis of some nice calculation of the 'proper' rate of social time discounting equal to the rate of interest, having in view some certain or near certain technical advance and known reserves, but on the highly irrational conviction that whatever happens, the price of oil (or any other basic resource) will not rise at the rate suggested by the current rate of interest whatever the extraction rate. A theory which says that the market would work if operators in the market knew the facts is not sufficient grounds for arguing that it is all right to leave everything to the market when the facts, in the nature of the case, cannot be known.

On the contrary, if we understood the full potential of the world's fixed natural resources, it is possible to make a case for using up nothing at all of those reserves except in the sense that the used-up item can be recycled. The only reasonable assumption to make is that a very large number of persons indeed are to follow us and that each is entitled to his share of what the world has to offer. Thus, if the quantity of any good occurring in nature is limited and recycling is not possible, then only a minute quantity rightfully belongs to each person to 'use up' – an amount indeed so small that one might as well say nothing should be used up. We might be thought to owe it to future generations not to take out what we cannot put back.

Of course, this is a counsel of perfection. We do not yet understand the full potential of the resources we have, and this is one of the most powerful reasons given by scientists for not using them up. It may be that due to scientific advance our children will live better than we do. It may be, therefore, that some using up of reserves which might properly be thought to be theirs is justified. On the other hand, there is no guarantee of indefinite scientific advance. How certain must we be of the existence of viable substitutes to judge it safe to consume irreplaceable materials? Do we use it up if there is a 0·5 probability of a substitute being found or is the number 0·7 – or is it 1? Who is to decide? Do we not owe it to our successors at least to begin some serious study of the immensely complicated problem of recycling? What does the word really mean? If we use oil to produce a solar energy plant, is the oil recycled? And so on.

Whatever may be the answer to these most difficult questions, one thing is certain. There is nothing in common sense just as there is nothing in economic theory to suggest that a complete or even a partial solution is given by the operation of market forces in a competitive property-owning economy. Nor have we any right to assume that whatever mess we may leave behind, technical advance will enable future generations to clean it up. It is easy to point to many examples of primitive people with an abundance of land who have reduced a region to desert by over-cultivation and misuse and simply moved on. If the people of the whole world reduce the whole world to a desert, there may be no other place to move to.

12 DISCUSSION

DR J. RAVETZ (Council for Science and Society): I fear that we may largely be dividing into economists who are generally not too worried, and non-economists who perhaps are too worried, and it is a little troubling if we do not seem to be able to find a ground where there is a genuinely shared concern or agreement on the order of magnitude of the problems we face.

With that in mind, I find myself even in a delicate situation, because when I look at some of the more perhaps provocative remarks in the paper by Dr Kay and Professor Mirrlees I am not sure whether these are intended with full poker-faced seriousness.

On p. 163 there is an interesting discussion about whether we are neglecting future generations. A number of remarks are made here, with certain qualifications, of which the conclusion seems to be that we do not neglect future generations because, either through correct predictions of prices or, otherwise, something concerning interest rates, we do keep in mind what our grandchildren will want, and if we do not, then that is the way the whole world runs anyway. This I find a rather remarkable expansion of a very traditional principle of political economy – namely, the hidden hand – and the hidden hand not merely gets economic justice at the moment in an imperfectly competitive market but it also assures a more just distribution of resources from now until the end of time.

When Dr Kay remarked that any detailed forecasting is strictly impossible within any reasonable limits, I think it could be argued strongly that no actual model with numerical parameters is sufficiently robust against change in the parameters to enable to give you anything reasonable for a hundred years. However, knowing so little about the future, it is rather breath-taking for one to be so confident that our present mechanisms of the market will ensure justice for all future generations.

DR KAY: It is one of the basic foundations of argument on this topic that resource conservation is simply a form of investment, like any other. If we do not exploit resources now, that is leaving something for the future, in exactly the same way as any other form of investment in the economy which involves giving up something now which will be useful in the future.

If the economy is efficiently organised, so to speak, then the rate of return of all forms of investment in that economy ought to be the same. In an efficiently organised economy the rate of return which we see on productive investment ought to be the same as the rate of return which is earned on resource conservation, and that rate of return is earned as a result of the appreciation which will occur in the price of a resource along the optimal path.

PROFESSOR MIRRLEES: May I make a brief comment which may help to see the sense in which we mean remarks like this seriously. We are not saying that we are sure that everything is all right for future generations. What we are saying is that what is usually taken to be an argument that says we will use resources up for ourselves and neglect future generations actually is not correct. We do not want to make very definite and absolutely certain assertions about this. We can think of lots of cases of fisheries, which is the example being talked about, where we certainly would not want to see this. We think that people probably were using things up and this would be to the disadvantage of future generations and even ourselves, for reasons that we can understand – we see what they are. It is just that when people begin to worry about resources being used up and they will not be there in future, it seems to us that they must think this out carefully and see exactly why the argument mentioned in the paper does not work; that if people in future are going to pay so much for the resources there will not be somebody now who is willing to hold on to the resources with that in mind. You think it absurd that nobody has a view as to what people are willing to pay for resources in 200 years' time, but I am not so sure that that is true.

PROFESSOR GASKIN (University of Aberdeen): There are two comments that I would like to make on the Kay–Mirrlees paper. First of all, I think that Professor Mirrlees's gloss on the paper which he added in discussion is very important, that really the major lesson that one should take from this paper is that there is an intergenerational problem and this has to be considered carefully, in that the general tendency to think that future generations' rights are being sacrificed to the present is not one that is necessarily always borne out historically, that there are certain inbuilt tendencies to deprive the present in the interests of the future. This is very much the case, I think, with capital accumulation in certain countries and in certain parts of the world. We have seen whole generations sacrificed to accumulation when there could have been a much better distribution of consumption and investment in time.

Also we must remember that future generations, so far as the developed countries are concerned, are really going to be better off in many things than we are, and consequently one should always bear this in mind when thinking what we are inflicting on them.

The second point that I have to make is a more critical one, and that is that basically the model depends, as I see it, on the efficiency of a market mechanism, and here I think it places very great weight, as far as their particular result is concerned, in that we may be under-depleting resources at the moment, on the accuracy and the nature of the telescopic function which the paper mentions and rather dismisses, although it often sees the importance of it. But one wonders just how much dependence one can place on the telescopic function at the range beyond, say, about fifty years. It requires rather a dynastic view of one's successors to place much faith in the way in which the market would work here.

But there is another institutional source of bias which works in the opposite way to the result which they obtain and to some of the biases which they mention, and that is that they have rather assumed that you have cases of countries, of sheikhs or governments which control resources and then allow them to be used by, say, multinational companies, and it is these governments or individuals who are making the decision as to whether they will deplete the resources now or deplete them in the future. But many natural resources are actually taken over and owned by the exploiting companies. These companies have a vested interest in their own managerial structure and their own capital structure as it stands in the present. This, I think, will tend to cause them to want to maximise, or to bias them in the direction of maximising, the exploitation of that structure, which necessarily involves the more immediate use of resources.

PROFESSOR MIRRLEES: The evidence suggests to me that if things are working ideally you really only need foresight of the needs of future generations once resources are beginning to get rather scarce – that is in a situation where, if they continue to be used at the current rate, they would only last for another twenty, thirty or forty years. It is true that in those circumstances they ought in many cases to be used for another 2000 or 3000 years at a continually diminishing rate. It does not seem to me to be putting quite so much strain on the foresight of businessmen, traders and so on to consider that in these circumstances they would foresee that prices would be beginning to rise and continue to rise, and that is the thing I want to emphasise most.

S. KATZ (Birmingham): This is a very tentative question along the same lines. I am wondering if it is not possible that there is a sleight of hand involved in the conclusion that Professor Mirrlees and Dr Kay have come to. The sleight of hand that I am trying to feel for is in what I think is probably an identification of the appropriate social discount rate with the social time preference rate of the resource owners and producers. In other words, let us assume, for example, that I am an evaluator looking at the economy and I have a very different time preference rate from those of your resource yielders; then it would mean that, regardless of what conclusions you have come to in terms of the model you have used, I would still conclude that even with the perfectly functioning telescopic faculty of the resource owners and even with a perfectly functioning market mechanism, resources would be used far too quickly.

It seems to me that what you have done up to a point is just a little too much. You have assumed not only that your market mechanism has solved for a correct intertemporal distribution once you have ascertained your optimal intertemporal distribution of income, but you have also assumed that it necessarily solves your intertemporal distribution of income problem as well. It seems to me that this to a great extent explains some of the difficulties that non-economists have had in intuitively accepting some of the conclusions that you have come to.

It seems to me that what you have done in your model is to assume that the rate of time preference in your evaluation function is coincident with the rate of time preference of this perpetual resource owner, because it is only that if that is the case his optimum reaction to price changes in the future will produce an income distribution over time which is optimal.

DR KAY: If your perpetual resource owner is Saudi Arabia, it is clear that there are opportunities for Saudi Arabia to borrow on international capital markets, with the result of bringing whatever time preference rates that Saudi Arabia buys into line with rates of returns available on the international capital markets. Therefore, I would not agree that one should attach much importance to looking explicitly at the attitudes of time preference of the actual resource owner, but it now is an assumption that this market interest rate, whatever it may be, reflects the appropriate time preference rate for purposes of looking after the interests of future generations.

We would certainly agree that there is an assumption there that these two rates are the same. One would hope that it was an explicit assumption, though if it is not sufficiently explicit I would like to make it explicit here and now. The point that we would like to make is that there we see resource conservation as simply one aspect of a problem which is rather familiar to economists in other contexts: do market interest rates reflect social time-preference rates? That is a problem that has no special significance.

PROFESSOR M. KLIMAN (Queen Mary College): On reading environmental economics, and particularly the techniques of *The Limits to Growth*, I get the sense of the discovery on the part of the writers that it was all there already – that is to say, these problems were invented in economics and there is a lot to be done with the provision of the tools as we have used them up to now. This is both good and bad. It is good because a lot of light has been shed on these questions. Obviously it can be bad too because it implies a kind of strait-jacket as well because it may impose structures on the problems that are not necessarily the best to answer questions. It seems to me, for instance, that there are examples of that in the Kay–Mirrlees paper – the idea, for instance, that the capital of natural resources and the processes of using them are the same and that this correspondence has something to offer because we know so much about capital investment. At the same time, there are differences between the use of natural resources and the use of capital. For instance, the concerns of future generations are not being taken account of sufficiently. In the case of capital, it is the concern that we are not investing enough. If we do not invest enough today the future generations themselves can probably remedy that situation fairly easily – that is to say, we know that within a few years you can build up capital stock quite appreciably and perhaps remedy insufficient capital investment; but the counterpart to that is using up too many natural resources now and if there are no renewable natural resources, then that is it: future generations cannot remedy the problem simply by saving something. There are others, too, and it seems to me that those have to be dwelt upon as well as the similarities.

In the case of the idea that the market will take care of future generations because firms will predict prices, obviously the point should be considered, but to me at least it seems to be a point that comes out of the major paradigm of economics (because that is the mental framework that we have in our heads) and not out of an examination as to how resource-owning firms actually behave. So it seems to me that there is a real danger here, particularly if you are deciding what future research should go on, of getting into the strait-jacket of what economics has been up to now.

MR J. BUTTERFIELD (Leeds Polytechnic): No one has mentioned the extremely high external costs of mineral extraction. If we go round our own country I know there are possibilities of reclamation and so on now, but, on the other hand, we possibly defined our term 'resources' rather narrowly. We could possibly dig up half of Arizona and get very minute quantities of metals over the area or use it for some other purpose. It may not be possible to do both things at the same time. I suggest that if we thought of the external costs of mineral extraction in terms of labour, in terms of what it does to the landscape, in terms of what it does for the future uses of that resource, we would possibly be extracting minerals at a much slower rate and we would not be worried so much about physical depletion. We would still have some very difficult decisions to make. I think we face those decisions in this country, where we have a very active and very necessary extraction industry in our National Parks. We have some very awkward balances to make. I think this is recognised both by the extraction industries and the people who are responsible for planning our parks. I think that it is in these kind of choices that economists have a role to play.

NOTES

Chapter 1

1. See K. Boulding, 'The Economics of the Coming Spaceship Earth', in *Environmental Quality in a Growing Economy*, ed. H. Jarrett (Johns Hopkins Press, for Resources for the Future Inc., Baltimore, 1966); R. U. Ayres and A. Kneese, 'Production, Consumption and Externality', *American Economic Review* (June 1969); and A. Kneese, R. U. Ayres and R. C. d'Arge, *Economics and the Environment: A Materials Balance Approach* (Johns Hopkins Press, for Resources for the Future Inc., Baltimore, 1966).

2. D. Meadows *et al.*, *The Limits to Growth* (Earth Island, London, 1972).

3. See, for example, the massive study by the Battelle Memorial Institute for the U.S. Department of Commerce, *A Study to Identify Opportunities for Increased Solid Waste Utilisation* (U.S. Government Printing Office, 1974).

4. I make no apologies for failing to standardise the notation which differs between the Kay–Mirrlees and Heal papers, and the paper by Pearce.

5. See, for example, W. J. Baumol, 'On the Social Rate of Discount', *American Economic Review* (Dec. 1968); and C. A. Nash, 'Future Generations and the Social Rate of Discount', *Environment and Planning*, 5 (1973).

Chapter 2

1. O.E.E.C., *Europe's Growing Needs for Energy – How Can They be Met?* (Paris, 1956).

2. D. L. Meadows *et al.*, *The Limits to Growth* (Earth Island, London, 1972). Some criticisms of *The Limits to Growth* are given in various studies by the University of Sussex Science Policy Research United published in a special issue of *Futures* (Feb 1973) and in book form as *Thinking About the Future* (Sussex University Press, 1973).

3. W. S. Jevons, *The Coal Question* (Macmillan, London, 1865).

4. For an explanation of the materials balance approach see, for example, A. M. Freeman, R. H. Haveman and A. V. Kneese, *The Economics of Environmental Policy* (John Wiley, New York, 1973). An interesting application to depletion of a finite resource stock is in M. Common, and D. W. Pearce, 'Adaptive Mechanisms, Growth

and the Environment: the Case of Natural Resources', *Canadian Journal of Economics*, IV, 3 (Aug 1973).

5. See Colin Robinson, 'The Technology of Forecasting and the Forecasting of Technology', *Surrey Economic Papers*, no. 7 (Mar 1972).

6. If *The Limits to Growth* is the extreme statement about imminent disaster, the other extreme is perhaps W. Beckerman, 'Economists, Scientists and Environmental Catastrophe', *Oxford Economic Papers* (Nov 1972). More balanced views on the 'optimistic' side are W. H. Heller, 'Coming to Terms with Growth and the Environment', in *Energy, Economic Growth and the Environment*, ed. S. H. Schurr (Johns Hopkins Press, for Resources for the Future Inc., Baltimore, 1972), and H. G. Johnson, *Man and His Environment* (British North American Committee, 1973).

7. Earl Cook, 'The Flow of Energy in an Industrial Society', in *Energy and Power* (W. H. Freeman, San Francisco, 1971).

8. By Dr V. E. McKelvey, U.S. Chief Geologist, *Financial Times* (5 Aug 1971).

9. *World Power Conference Survey of Energy Resources* (Central Office of the World Power Conference, 1968). The next Survey is due in 1974.

10. P. Averitt, 'Coal Resources of the United States', *U.S. Geological Survey Bulletin*, 1275 (1969).

11. M. King Hubbert, 'Energy Resources', in *Resources and Man* (W. H. Freeman, San Francisco, 1969); and M. King Hubbert, 'The Energy Resources of the Earth', in *Energy and Power* (W. H. Freeman, San Francisco, 1971). All subsequent references to Hubbert relate to these two articles which cover similar ground.

12. No reason is given for using 50 per cent; although Averitt uses this percentage for recoverable reserves *in the United States* he also points out that the actual recovery rate might be a good deal higher.

13. Estimates of proved oil reserves vary somewhat according to source as there is no precise generally accepted definition of proved reserves. The figures given are from *Oil: World Statistics*, published by the Institute of Petroleum Information Service.

14. *Oil and Gas Journal* (25 Dec 1972).

15. E. N. Tiratsoo, *Natural Gas*, 2nd edn (Scientific Press, London, 1972), p. 364. Tiratsoo's estimates for later years are lower than those in Table 3.

16. *The Limits to Growth*, p. 58.

17. For some higher estimates see T. A. Hendricks, *Resources of Oil, Gas and Natural Gas Liquids in the U.S. and the World* (U.S. Geological Survey Circular, 1965); and L. G. Weeks, *Marine Geology and Petroleum Resources*, World Petroleum Congress (Moscow, 1971) Proceedings 2, pp. 99–106.

18. Barrels of oil are converted to metric tons coal equivalent, using the following factors: 7·3 barrels = 1 metric ton oil; and 1 metric ton oil = 1.5 m.t.c.e.

19. H. R. Warman, 'The Future of Oil', *Geographical Journal* (Sept 1972).

20. Cubic feet of natural gas are converted to metric tons coal equivalent using the following factors: 100 cubic feet = 1 therm; and 230 therms = 1 m.t.c.e.

21. The latest O.E.C.D. *Oil Report* (O.E.C.D., Paris) suggests that ultimate reserves of oil and natural gas might be ten times the present estimate of proved oil and gas reserves, if tar and shale are included. On the O.E.C.D. figures this appears to mean ultimate reserves of $1·8 \times 10^{12}$ m.t.c.e. A report in the *Financial Times* (25 July 1973) said that the Orinoco tar sands in Venezuela contain more than 700×10^9 barrels of crude oil, which is more than the whole of present world proved oil reserves.

22. The fast breeder reactors now under development, such as the 250 MW(e) prototype at Dounreay commissioned in 1973, convert U-238 to plutonium by a 'breeding' process which provides more than enough plutonium to feed the original reactor, so that the surplus can be used as the first fuel charge for another reactor. Because of the high rate of fuel 'burn-up', fuel costs are very low for breeder reactors and, therefore, low grade ores can be used. A good, simple description of how uranium is used in different types of reactors is given in L. Howles, 'Earth's Dwindling Stocks of Fossil Fuel', *New Scientist* (5 Aug 1971). Sir John Hill in 'The Role of Nuclear Energy in the Total Energy Mix', *Atom* (Dec 1972), explains the uranium savings possible with the use of fast reactors. An excellent survey of likely nuclear power developments in the future is given in T. N. Marsham and R. S. Pease, 'Nuclear Power – The Future', *Atom* (Feb 1973).

23. L. W. Boxer, W. Haussermann, J. Cameron and J. T. Roberts, *Uranium Resources, Production and Demand*, Fourth U.N. International Conference on the Peaceful Uses of Atomic Energy, Geneva, September 1971. See also *Uranium – Resources, Production and Demand*, Joint Review by the European Nuclear Energy Agency and the International Atomic Energy Agency, September 1970.

24. *The Energy Crisis*, A Science and Public Affairs book (1972), contains a number of articles on projects for solar energy and other new sources of energy. See also F. Daniels, *Direct Use of the Sun's Energy* (Yale University Press, 1964), especially chapter 3, table 1 which is the basis for the calculations of the magnitude of solar energy.

25. See Marsham and Pease, 'Nuclear Power'.

26. See G. V. Day, 'The Prospects for Synthetic Fuels in the U.K.', *Futures* (Dec 1972), and L. Lessing, 'The Coming Hydrogen

Economy', *Fortune* (Nov 1972). V. Smil, 'Energy and the Environment – A Delphic Forecast', *Long-Range Planning* (Dec 1972) gives the results of a Delphic study which asked for opinions about new energy sources.

27. The best reference sources are J. Darmstadter, *Energy in the World Economy* (Johns Hopkins Press, for Resources for the Future, Inc., Baltimore, 1971); *United Nations Statistics of World Energy* (Series J); and the *United Nations' Statistical Yearbook*.

28. See, for example, the projections quoted in D. J. Ezra, 'Possibilities of a World Energy Crisis', *National Westminster Bank Review* (Nov 1972), which were taken from a two-volume report by the U.S. National Petroleum Council entitled *U.S. Energy Outlook: An Initial Appraisal, 1971–1985*. The N.P.C. report says that it is not making a 'probable forecast' but merely a 'set of projections' based on specified assumptions, one of which appears to be that energy prices will be only moderately higher so that total energy demand will not be significantly affected. The N.P.C. is evidently in the process of making a study of demand and supply elasticities for various types of energy.

29. U.S. Office of Emergency Preparedness, *The Potential for Energy Conservation* (Oct 1972).

30. It has been reported that steel producers in Europe are considering research into integral nuclear steel-making plant in which a high-temperature reactor produces both electricity for steel making and a reducing gas to replace coke in iron manufacture. See the *Financial Times* (7 June 1973).

31. See G. Leach, *The Motor Car and Natural Resources* (O.E.C.D., Paris, 1973).

32. There have recently been suggestions that the rising price of oil will stimulate improvements in aero engine efficiency and before the end of the century bring about substitution of other energy sources such as liquid hydrogen (*Financial Times*, 8 June 1973.)

33. See J. K. Page, *Energy Requirements for Buildings*, a paper read at the 1972 Public Works Congress 16 November 1972. The *Sunday Times* (25 Nov 1973) reported on an experimental heavily insulated house being constructed by the Cambridge architecture department. The house will rely on solar heat, wind-generated electricity and gas from human sewage.

34. K. Boulding, 'The Economics of the Coming Spaceship Earth', in *Environmental Quality in a Growing Economy*, ed. H. Jarrett (Johns Hopkins Press, Baltimore, 1966).

35. For a brief review see Robinson and Crook, 'Is There a World Energy Crisis?', and the references therein.

36. For detailed discussion, see W. H. Matthews (ed.), *Man's Impact on the Climate* (M.I.T. Press, Cambridge, Mass., 1971);

G. J. MacDonald, in *Energy, Economic Growth and the Environment*, ed. Schurr; and A. Lovins, 'Thermal Limits to World Energy Use', *Bulletin of Atomic Scientists* (forthcoming 1974).

37. Some of the environmental problems of nuclear fission and of energy in general are outlined in A. M. Weinberg, and K. P. Hammond, 'Global Effects of Increased Use of Energy', *Bulletin of Atomic Scientists*, vol. 28, no. 3 (Mar 1972). See also International Atomic Agency, *Nuclear Power and the Environment* (1972).

38. J. W. Gofman, 'Is Nuclear Fission Acceptable?', *Futures* vol. 1, no. 3 (Sept 1972). See also articles in the *Sunday Times* – 25 November 1973 by A. Lovins, and 2 December 1973 by Theodore Stern.

39. F. Rouhani, *A History of OPEC* (Praeger, New York, 1971) deals with the development of the organisation up to early 1971.

40. See *Oil – The Present Situation and Future Prospects* (O.E.C.D., 1973).

41. For a fuller explanation see *Oil* (O.E.C.D.), chapter IV; J. E. Akins, 'The Oil Crisis – This time the Wolf is here', *Foreign Affairs* (Apr 1973); and J. Amuzegar, 'The Oil Story: Facts, Fiction and Fair Play', *Foreign Affairs* (July 1973).

42. For example, M. A. Adelman, 'Is the Oil Shortage Real? Oil Companies as OPEC Tax Collectors', *Foreign Policy* (Winter 1972–3) and the same author's 'American Import Policy and the World Oil Market', *Energy Policy*, vol. 1, no. 2 (Sept 1973).

43. See Akins, 'The Oil Crisis'.

44. *Petroleum Press Service* (Dec 1972), pp. 451–3.

45. Some cost estimates for various processes are given in H. C. Hottel and J. B. Howard, *New Energy Technology – Some Facts and Assessments* (M.I.T. Press, Cambridge, Mass., 1971) chapter 3.

46. See 'Future prospects for Energy Supply and Demand', *Atom* (Feb 1973).

Chapter 3

1. Science Policy Research Unit, University of Sussex. The work in question is collected in C. Freeman *et al.*, *Thinking About The Future* (Sussex University Press, 1973).

Chapter 4

1. The time of writing was January 1974 during a U.K. miners' period of industrial action.

2. The figures are taken from table 8 of Professor Robinson's paper and from M. King Hubbert 'Energy Resources', cited in Professor Robinson's paper. King Hubbert sees oil shales as a source of chemical inputs rather than an energy source. The processing of oil shales requires large inputs of water, while the main U.S. deposits lie in arid areas. It has been questioned whether large-scale

exploitation by the technologies on which current costings are based is feasible, for this reason. See S. H. Schurr *et al.*, *Energy in the American Economy: 1850–1975* (Johns Hopkins Press, for Resources for the Future Inc., Baltimore, 1972).

3. Strictly it could be re-created in geological time, but this is scarcely an interesting possibility.

4. In the rather different context of wilderness areas as a (natural resource) recreation facility, the asymmetry has been considered with respect to the implications of technical progress in some of the contributions to J. V. Krutilla (ed.), *National Environments: Studies in Theoretical and Applied Analysis* (Johns Hopkins Press, for Resources for the Future Inc., Baltimore, 1972).

5. A useful reference is G. Leach, 'The Energy Costs of Food Production', in *The Man–Food Equation*, ed. A. Bourne (Academic Press, London, 1973).

6. A. E. Spakowski and L. I. Shure, 'Large Scale Solar Power Generation Cost – A Preliminary Assessment', NASA Report, no. TMX–2520 (Mar 1972). For a similar conclusion see W. R. Cherry, 'The Generation of Pollution Free Electrical Power from Solar Energy', *Transactions of the American Society of Mechanical Engineers* (Apr 1972).

Chapter 6

1. F. M. Bator, 'The Anatomy of Market Failure', *Quarterly Journal of Economics* (Aug 1958).

2. F. W. Bell, 'Technological Externalities and Common-Property Resources: an Empirical Study of the U.S. Northern Lobster Fishery', *Journal of Political Economy*, LXXX, 1 (1972).

3. A. Burd, 'The North Sea Herring Fishery', mimeo (M.A.F.F. Sea Fisheries Laboratory, Lowestoft, 1973).

4. J. A. Butlin, 'Contribution of Economics to Fisheries Management', *Maritime Studies and Management* (forthcoming).

5. S. N. S. Cheung, 'The Structure of a Contract and the Theory of a Non-Exclusive Resource', *Journal of Land Economics*, XIII, 1 (1971).

6. P. Copes, 'The Backward-Bending Supply Curve of the Fishing Industry', *Scottish Journal of Political Economy* (1970).

7. P. Copes, 'Factor Rents, Sole Ownership and the Optimum Level of Fisheries Exploitation', *Manchester School*, XL, 2 (1972).

8. J. A. Crutchfield, 'Common-Property Resources and Factor Allocation', *Canadian Journal of Economics and Political Science* (1956).

9. J. A. Crutchfield, 'Economic Aspects of International Fishing Conventions', in Scott[29].

10. J. A. Crutchfield and G. Pontecorvo, *The Pacific Salmon Industry: A Study in Irrational Conservation* (Johns Hopkins Press, Baltimore, 1969).

11. J. A. Crutchfield and A. Zellner, 'Economic Aspects of the Pacific Halibut Fishery', *Fishery Industrial Research*, I, 1 (1962).

12. Environmental Economics Study Group of the Social Science Research Council: Bibliography Series: 3, *Fisheries Economics* (1973).

13. D. Garrod, 'On the Management of Multiple Resources', presented to F.A.O. Technical Conference on Fisheries Management and Development, Vancouver, February 1973.

14. H. Scott Gordon, 'The Economic Theory of a Common-Property Resource: The Fishery', *Journal of Political Economy*, LXII, 2 (1954).

15. J. R. Gould, 'Extinction of a Fishery by Commercial Exploitation: A Note', *Journal of Political Economy*, LXXX, 5 (1972).

16. L. C. Gray, 'The Economic Possibilities of Conservation', *Quarterly Journal of Economics*, XXVII (1912–13).

17. R. Hanneson, 'Fishery Dynamics: A North Atlantic Cod Fishery', mimeo (University of British Columbia, Department of Economics, June 1973).

18. R. E. Kohn, 'Urban Air Pollution and the von Thünen Rental Gradient', paper presented to U.K. Environmental Economics Study Group (1972).

19. J. R. March and K. P. Russell, 'Externalities, Separability and Resource Allocation', *American Economic Review*, LXIII, 4 (1973).

20. A Marshall, *Principles of Economics*, 8th edn (Macmillan, London, 1970).

21. G. A. Mummay, 'The Coase Theorem: A Re-Examination', *Quarterly Journal of Economics*, LXXXV, 4 (1971).

22. C. G. Plourde, 'A Simple Model of Replenishable Natural Resource Exploitation', *American Economic Review*, XL, 3 (1970).

23. J. P. Quirk and V. L. Smith, 'Dynamic Economic Models of Fishing', in Scott[29].

24. J. Rich, in *O.E.C.D. Symposium on the Economics of Fisheries Management* (Paris, November 1971).

25. M. Robinson, 'Determinants of Demand for Fish and Their Effects upon Resources, presented to F.A.O. Technical Conference on Fishery Management, Vancouver, February 1973.

26. M. Rothschild and J. E. Stiglitz, 'Increasing Risk II: Its Economic Consequences', *Journal of Economic Theory*, III (1971).

27. P. A. Samuelson, 'Spatial Price Equilibrium and Linear Programming', *American Economic Review*, XLII (1952).

28. A. Scott, 'The Fishery: The Objectives of Sole Ownership', *Journal of Political Economy*, LXIII, 2 (1955).

29. A. Scott (ed.), 'Economics of Fisheries Management: A Symposium', H. R. MacMillan Lectures in Fisheries, University of British Columbia, March 1969 (MacMillan Lectures).

30. A. D. Scott and C. Southey, 'The Problem of Achieving Efficient Regulation of a Fishery', in Scott[29].

31. V. L. Smith, 'Minimisation of Economic Rent in Spatial Price Equilibrium', *Review of Economic Studies* (1963).

32. V. L. Smith, 'On Models of Commercial Fishing', *Journal of Political Economy*, LXXVII, 6 (1969).

33. R. G. Thompson, M. D. George, R. J. Callen and L. C. Wolken, 'A Stochastic Investment Model for a Survival Conscious Firm Applied to Shrimp Fishing', *Applied Economics*, V, 2 (1973).

34. R. Turvey, 'Optimisation and Sub-optimisation in Fisheries Regulation', *American Economic Review*, LIV, 2 (1964).

Chapter 8

1. P. S. Dasgupta and G. M. Heal, *Economic Theory and Exhaustible Resources* (to be published by Cambridge University Press).

2. P. S. Dasgupta, 'Some Recent Theoretical Explorations in the Economics of Exhaustible Resources', paper presented to a meeting of the Bavarian Academy of Sciences (1973).

3. J. E. Stiglitz, 'Growth with Exhaustible Resources', *Review of Economic Studies* (1974).

4. P. S. Dasgupta and G. M. Heal, 'The Optimal Depletion of Exhaustible Resources', *Review of Economic Studies* (1974).

5. F. H. Hahn, 'Equilibrium Dynamics with Heterogeneous Capital Goods', *Quarterly Journal of Economics* (1966).

6. G. M. Heal, *The Theory of Economic Planning* (North-Holland, Amsterdam, 1973).

7. G. M. Heal, 'The Depletion of Exhaustible Resources', University of Sussex Economics Seminar Paper Series 73/07. Presented at the 1973 Meeting of the Association of University Teachers of Economics, and to be published in their proceedings.

8. J. Forrester, *World Dynamics* (Wright-Allen Press Inc., Cambridge, Mass., 1971).

9. D. and D. Meadows, *The Limits to Growth* (Earth Island, London, 1972).

Chapter 9

1. J. Forrester, *Wold Dynamics* (Wright-Allen Press, Cambridge, Mass., 1971); D. H. Meadows, D. L. Meadows, J. Randers and W. Behrens III, *The Limits to Growth* (Earth Island, London, 1972); D. L. Meadows and associates, *World III* (to be published 1974). *The Limits to Growth* does not specify the model used, though there are numerous hints. *World III*, most of which we have seen in typescript, is a revised version of the unpublished technical report that explained the model for *The Limits to Growth*. That technical

report formed the basis of the critique done by a team at the Sussex Science Policy Research unit – H. S. D. Cole, C. Freeman, M. Jahoda, K. L. R. Pavitt *et al.*, *Thinking About the Future* (Chatto & Windus, for Sussex University Press, 1973).

2. W. D. Nordhaus, 'World Dynamics: Measurement without Data', *Economic Journal* (Dec 1973), and Cowles Foundation Discussion Paper CF–20510 (1972).

3. The team have looked at much more emprical data than Forrester did, and some parts of the model have been made much more complicated (by disaggregating the population by age groups, for example). However, as we shall substantiate below in the case of one sector, the changes do not lead to sensible models in most cases, and the use made of empirical data is both primitive and, quite often, perverse. The work does seem to exemplify two serious faults in the practice of simulating modelling: the tendency to take any old model that happens to be available as a starting point, and the fallacy that any increase in complexity is an increase in realism.

4. D. Graham and D. C. Herrick, 'World Dynamics', *I.E.E.E. Transactions on Automatic Control* (Aug 1973).

5. D. Graham and D. C. Herrick, 'World Dynamics', p. 13.

6. The numerical specification of the *World III* model is

$$s = 0.33, \qquad \delta = 0.0714, \qquad r(0) = 1,$$

with the functions f and g are given by Figures 9A and B.

7. M. A. Adelman, 'Trends in the Cost of Finding and Developing Oil and Gas Reserves in the United States, 1946–66', in *Essays in Petroleum Economics*, ed. S. Gardner and S. Hanke (Colorado School of Mines, 1967), and *The World Petroleum Market* (Johns Hopkins Press, Baltimore, 1972).

8. H. J. Barnett and C. Morse, *Scarcity and Growth* (Johns Hopkins Press, Baltimore, 1963).

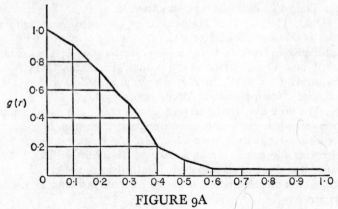

FIGURE 9A

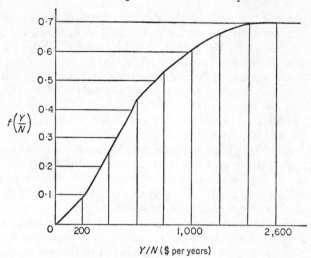

$f\left(\dfrac{Y}{N}\right)$

Y/N ($ per years)

FIGURE 9B

9. Gardner and Hanke, *Essays*, p. 57.

10. *World III*, typescript, pp. v–34.

11. *World III*, pp. 21–2.

12. The equations of the model (which cannot be immediately extracted from *World III*), with discussion of the methodology of modelling, and further comment on some of the assumptions are given in our paper, 'Simulation Modelling for World Problems', mimeo (Nuffield College, 1974).

13. T. S. Ashton, *Iron and Steel in the Industrial Revolution* (Manchester University Press, 1951), p. 9.

14. H. Hotelling, 'The Economics of Exhaustible Resources', *Journal of Political Economy*, XXXIX (1931).

15. The paper by Dixit is as yet unpublished. P. S. Dasgupta and G. Heal, 'The Optimal Depletion of Exhaustible Resources', *Review of Economic Studies* (1974); J. Stiglitz, 'Growth with Exhaustible Resources', *Review of Economic Studies* (1974); T. C. Koopmans, 'Some Observations on "Optimal" Economic Growth and Exhaustible Resources', in *Economic Structure and Development*, ed. H. C. Bos (North-Holland, Amsterdam, 1973).

16. We note also that the case of monopoly gives a misleading impression when extraction costs are ignored, because in that case the constant-elasticity demand function implies that a monopolist depletes at the same rate as a competitive industry. This follows because the effect of monopoly is identical to the effect of a proportional tax on sales, which is simply a profits tax when extraction costs are zero.